Profiles in Canadian Literature 2

edited by Jeffrey M. Heath
Department of English
University of Toronto

Dundurn Press Limited
Toronto and Charlottetown
1980

Design: Ron and Ron Design Photography

Dundurn Press Limited
P.O. Box 245, Station F
Toronto, Canada
M4Y 2L5

Care has been taken to trace the ownership of copyright material used in this text (including the photographs). The editor and publisher will welcome any information enabling them to rectify any reference or credit in subsequent editions.

Dundurn Press wishes to acknowledge the generous assistance of the Canada Council and the Ontario Arts Council.

Canadian Cataloguing in Publication Data
Main entry under title:
Profiles in Canadian literature

Bibliography: p.
ISBN 0-919670-46-6 (v. 1 bound). - ISBN 0-919670-50-4 (v. 2 bound)

1. Canadian literature (English) - History and criticism - Addresses, essays, lectures.* 2. Canadian literature (English) - Bio-bibliography - Addresses, essays, lectures.* 3. Authors, Canadian (English) - Biography - Addresses, essays, lectures.* I. Heath, Jeffrey M., 1943-

PS8071.P76   C810'.9   C81-094164-3
PR9184.6.P76

Table of Contents

Foreword

The growth of the Canadian imagination has long been checked, we are told, by the wintry and confining forces often noted by cultural historians: an awkward geography; an allegedly bland history; a small and indifferent reading public; a colonial frame of mind; proximity to the United States; the moral absolutism and herd behaviour of what Northrop Frye has called the "garrison mentality". These (and other) blighting influences have not disappeared; but as if enforced apprenticeship and borrowed muses brought discipline and through that, freedom, our writers have shed their bonds — often by transforming them into art. Shaped by the land and shaping it in return, Canadian artists have ceased to be exiles in their own country and have begun to feel imaginatively at home. We know the dates of the explorers, the surveyors and the map-makers. If the significant dates of imaginative settlement are the subjects of less universal agreement, we can still say with certainty that our writers are finding a rich summer voice, and that their words, together with an exuberant anthem of critical response, have now combined to create a literary climate barely conceivable only 50 years ago.

That invigorating new climate has generated fresh challenges for the most recent wave of surveyors, the scholars and educators. How, for example, could the mingled currents of creativity and criticism be made available to the large, inquiring new audience of the 1980s? In particular, how could the ever-increasing harvest of information be presented in a manner which would be compact and systematic, detailed yet not too formal — a manner which would combine the virtues of the reference text and interpretive criticism?

The format chosen for the studies which follow provides one solution. In each profile, an essay acquaints the reader with the author's work and supplies insight into themes, techniques and special characteristics; a chronology lists important dates in a convenient form; comments by and about the author provide additional illuminating information and suggest avenues for further investigation; a bibliography of primary works and criticism gives extra documentation. Each profile can be used individually, as a study aid to supplement discussion and to bring forward additional points of view, dates, biographical material and sources for further reading. Alternatively, the entire series of profiles can be read to obtain a sense of the developing styles and preoccupations of Canadian writers from the earliest times to the present day. Except for a few cases, the critical perspective of each study is literary rather than historical or sociological, and each has been written with the needs and abilities of its audience as major concerns.

The writers whose work is discussed in these volumes have not been selected to illustrate a thesis, nor are they linked together according to any over-arching theme, pattern, or influence. They are ordered according to the dates when their work first attracted significant public attention. From Thompson to Laurence, from Haliburton to Nowlan, they come from all periods of Canadian history and represent various regions and aspects of the nation. Many are novelists, others are poets; some are sombre and reflective, while others — defying stereotypical Canadian solemnity — are exuberant and richly humorous. Like the land itself, they are diverse. In drawing these disparate portraits together into book form and in putting a larger frame around them, as it were, I am not attempting to enshrine a pantheon nor am I trying to establish some "great divide" in our literary history through their division into two groups.

While the profiles which appear in these pages belong to very different writers, broad similarities do of course exist for, like David Thompson, the first of them, they are all explorers who investigate what it has meant to live and breathe in "this part of North America"; they all speak with various inflexions of a recognizably Canadian idiom. Nevertheless, questions of a wide cultural and thematic nature exceed the scope of this mosaic, which has been designed only to bring together, in a useful and colourful album, a series of introductions to a selection of Canadian writers. Companion volumes will be added later to this on-going series to correct the imbalances and omissions which, I am well aware, are present here.

The contributors to these volumes are all actively interested in Canadian literature as instructors, researchers and editors, and they too represent many regions of the country. I am indebted to them all for the patience, co-operation and hard work which has made this collection possible.

Jeffrey M. Heath
Department of English
Victoria College
University of Toronto.

The Editor

Jeffrey M. Heath is Associate Professor of English at Victoria College, University of Toronto, where his teaching and research interests include twentieth-century Canadian, British and American literature. He is the author of articles and reviews, and of a forthcoming book on Evelyn Waugh.

Robertson Davies 15
by
Judith Skelton Grant

Courtesy: Paterson.

Distinguished at every stage of his career, Robertson Davies has, satisfyingly, produced his best work last. Beginning with signal contributions to Canadian drama and an outstanding editorship of the *Peterborough Examiner,* he has risen to new heights with his six novels and particularly with the three published most recently. These books — *Fifth Business, The Manticore,* and *World of Wonders* — have attracted a wide audience, for in them Davies has created vivid and distinctive central characters whose eccentric interests have both popular appeal and philosophic undercurrent.

Plays

From the outset of his career Davies' activities commanded attention. His childhood love of theatre, augmented by the practical experience of acting in and directing amateur productions and by scholarly research, bore fruit in his excellent Oxford thesis, published as *Shakespeare's Boy Actors* in 1939. Soon after he began to write plays. Created by a lover of wit and word-play, of song and dance, of theatrical effect, Davies' plays are exuberant and often eccentric. Though uneven, they are never dull. The fourteen published plays fall into three groups: those completed by 1950; those prepared for performance at the Crest Theatre in Toronto from 1954-58; and those produced in the seventies, only one of which has been published. These three spurts of composition and production are reflected in mood and technique.

Included in the first group are *King Phoenix* (written in 1948 and published in *Hunting Stuart and Other Plays* in 1972), the one-act plays in *Eros at Breakfast and Other Plays* (1949), *Fortune, My Foe* (1949), and *At My Heart's Core* (1950). These plays earned Davies a permanent place in the history of Canadian drama because they appeared just as interest in theatre revived after the war and because they caught the mood of the period. Each of them sets out the characteristic postures and attitudes of a small group of characters; then a crisis which is usually associated with the arts causes self-examination and perhaps new orientation. The endings of the plays are either pessimistic or only hesitantly optimistic.

Overlaid, the best of the one-act plays, is typical. When Pop, a retired Ontario farmer, receives a windfall, he dreams of a fling in New York. Dressed elegantly he would dine well, attend the opera, and cap his evening with a night-club strip-tease. His daughter bids, how-

1

ever, to spend the money on a vision of solidity and dignity: a large family plot and tastefully expensive tombstone. The daughter wins because, as Pop says: "There's a special kind o' power that comes from the belief that you're right. Whether you really are right or not doesn't matter: it's the belief that counts." Such blinkered righteousness, Davies' *bête noire* in many of these plays, is given thoughtful examination in several of Davies' novels.

The three plays prepared for the Crest Theatre - *A Jig for the Gypsy* (1954), *Hunting Stuart* (written in 1955), and *General Confession* (written in 1958 but published with *Hunting Stuart* in *Hunting Stuart and Other Plays* in 1972) — are more optimistic. In *Overlaid*, the exponent of life and art is temporarily defeated. In the Crest plays, art, magic, imagination, and love triumph.

Question Time (1975), the sole recent published play, is distinguished by imaginative staging and dialogue. Though uneven in effect and too short for full exploration of its ideas and themes, its simultaneous staging of real and imaginary events, its use of a double for the central character (a technique discussed at length in *World of Wonders*), and its inventive handling of dialogue reveal that drama continues to stimulate Davies' imagination. Nonetheless, the plays of the seventies, like those of the fifties, have been less conspicuous than his earlier work. They have had to compete with a vigorously expanding indigenous drama and they have been overshadowed by the success of his novels.

Journalism

As book review editor of *Saturday Night* from 1940 to 1942 and from 1953 to 1959, editorial writer and later editor of the *Peterborough Examiner* from 1942 to 1962, columnist for the *Toronto Daily Star* from 1959 to 1962, and author of several hundred articles in a wide range of popular and scholarly publications, Davies has been staggeringly prolific. From the beginning this outflow has been distinguished from run-of-the-mill journalism by Davies' powerful personality. In his columns and articles he presents himself as a man amusingly and enthusiastically learned about subjects as diverse as ghost stories, music, circuses, religion, hand-writing, psychology, book-collecting, drama, and saints. And he does know an astonishing amount about all these subjects. The gusto Davies brings to this writing, coupled with his insight and expertise, made the *Examiner* one of the most frequently quoted newspapers in Canada and won for his journalism more than ephemeral interest.

Some of the witty and irascible comment on the passing scene published in the *Examiner* under the pseudonym Samuel Marchbanks was gathered in *The Diary of Samuel Marchbanks* (1947), *The Table Talk of Samuel Marchbanks* (1949), and *Marchbanks' Almanack* (1967). The *Diary* and *Table Talk* were revised for paperback editions during the sixties and all three will soon be reissued again.

A few of the *Saturday Night* review articles appeared in *A Voice from the Attic* (1960), but not many. Instead of simply reprinting earlier articles, Davies seized the opportunity to broaden and deepen an argument present in much of his journalism, namely that the number of intelligent, literate, general readers in Canada must be increased if culture is to flourish and life to be more civilized.

On the other hand, *The Enthusiasms of Robertson Davies* (1979) provides a good sampling of Davies' journalism, drawing primarily on *Saturday Night* articles and *Toronto Daily Star* columns, but including a sprinkling of earlier and later material as well. It offers examples of three of Davies' journalistic preoccupations. The profiles in the "Characters" section reveal his life-long delight in eccentric and unusual people; the reviews in "Books" include typically lively estimates of books both current and classic; the self-revelations in "Robertson Davies" provide glimpses of the most beguiling character in the collection.

Soon to be published is a selection of Davies' observations on Canadian writing and theatre over the past 40 years. This is interesting for several reasons. He had the critical acumen to pinpoint the books which have since become accepted as classics and he charted changes in the state of Canadian literature in overview articles written every two or three years from 1950 on. With regard to theatre he labelled and discussed the problems of establishing vital theatre in Canada and provided a vivid record of the revival of Little Theatre in the late forties and of the first fourteen years of the Stratford Festival. In this volume he is thus astute critic and historian.

Novels

Even in the first flush of success with his plays, Davies thought about writing fiction. In 1947 he told Graham McInnes that if he failed to get his plays produced in England by the time he was forty, he would "turn to novels". And he did. Not long after, he wrote his first trilogy: *Tempest-Tost* (1951), *Leaven of Malice* (1954) and *A Mixture of Frailties* (1958). Focussed successively on a Little Theatre production of *The Tempest*, on editorial problems in a small-town newspaper, and on the training of a singer, these books are in the mode of the satiric romance. Davies' long experience as critic, dramatist, and journalist gave them an astonishingly impressive finish. His dialogue rooted in comedy of manners is lively; his plots are tight and workmanlike.

But these surface strengths cause problems. The plot of *Tempest-Tost* permits significant development for only one of the half dozen characters Davies brings convincingly to life. The frame devices of the first two novels, though interesting and lively, jar, because they differ in subject or tone from the middle parts of the books. And there are technical problems with the omniscient narrator. But Davies learned and developed as he moved from book to book. The third in the series, *A Mixture of Frailties,* is a very fine novel indeed. Here Davies holds satire to a minimum, provides a rich and satisfying frame, keeps his narrative stance consistent, focusses attention on one developing central character, and tackles his theme, the value of culture, seriously and openly.

A decade then passed before Davies tackled fiction again. The three volumes of the Deptford trilogy — *Fifth Business, The Manticore,* and *World of Wonders* — did not appear until 1970, 1972, and 1975, but they were well worth waiting for. Davies had avoided first-person narration in his early novels because he felt uncomfortable with the self-revelation and direct communication he associated with the technique. Now he used it masterfully. The intertwined stories of Dunstan Ramsay, Boy Staunton, and Magnus Eisengrim are told by three sharply defined and convincing first-person narrators who compel the reader's interest in the story that begins when the stone-laden snowball thrown at Dunstan by Boy hits Mrs. Dempster and causes the premature birth of Magnus.

Davies centres each story in a different kind of knowledge. In *Fifth Business* the consequences of the snowball lead Dunstan to saints and myth; in *The Manticore* they lead David Staunton (Boy's son) into Jungian analysis; in *World of Wonders* they lead Magnus to magic and stagecraft. These provide the thematic core of each book; but only in *Fifth Business,* the master work in the trilogy, does Davies create an organic whole from his disparate materials. All the lore on saints and myth is firmly connected to the central character, reflecting his interests, showing how he thinks, influencing his life, and playing a part in his interpretation of events. That this is not the case in *The Manticore* is partly intentional. David Staunton has held his life together by banishing some things from consciousness, acting in stereotyped patterns, and blunting his feelings with alcohol. When his father's suicide shatters his customary defences he needs outside help if he is to find a meaningful pattern in his life, and he finds this help at the Jungian Institute. There is thus an initial inevitable division between the narrated life and the Jungian theory supplied by his analyst. We should, however, experience David's life gradually assuming new form as he assimilates Jung's ideas. This happens only partially, and both the

life and the ideas lose depth in consequence. *World of Wonders* likewise falls short of the standard set by *Fifth Business* and again the problem centres in Davies' handling of data which occupies long stretches of the book. There is no question that all the material on the sideshow and on the acting troupe is linked to the central character, but pages flow by that have little to do with the shaping of Magnus' character. The information seems simply to have taken over as Davies documents life in a small-time carnival and in an old-fashioned touring company early this century.

Though lesser achievements than *Fifth Business, The Manticore* and *World of Wonders* are intriguing and challenging works. With *Fifth Business* they contain the self-revelation that Davies had earlier avoided. What is revealed is not autobiography but philosophy. The ideas that over-arch the Deptford trilogy are of two kinds: the speculations about myth and psychology pertain to natural philosophy; those on saints and magic, good and evil, God and the Devil to moral philosophy. With the first Davies feels sure of his ground as he follows in the footsteps of such trail blazers as Sir James Frazer, Freud, and Jung; with the second he is tentative and exploratory.

Courtesy: Paterson.

Let us begin with his natural philosophy. In the first and third volumes, perceptive characters find in myth a tool for understanding character and for anticipating patterns of human behaviour. (See, for example, Dunstan's references to the tale of Gyges and King Candaules in *Fifth Business*.) In the middle volume, David's Jungian analyst explains why myth lays bare the basic patterns of character and action as she tells David how he could dream of a manticore, a mythic creature unknown to him:

> People very often dream of things they don't know. They dream of minotaurs without ever having heard of a minotaur. Thoroughly respectable women who have never heard of Pasiphaë dream that they are a queen who is enjoying sexual congress with a bull. It is because great myths are not invented stories but objectivizations of images and situations that lie very deep in the human spirit; a poet may make a great embodiment of a myth, but it is the mass of humanity that knows the myth to be a spiritual truth, and that is why they cherish his poem.

Thus, plumbing the psyche's depths and exploring myth are similar activities. Both bring self-knowledge, self-control, and release new energies.

Characters' differing attitudes to myth and the unconscious affect the nature of reality in each book. In *Fifth Business*, Dunstan presents everyday reality; myth interprets but does not transform his world. In *The Manticore*, David finds his dreams presenting glimpses of a myth-like psychic life, hitherto unimagined. In *World of Wonders*, Magnus' daily life in Wanless's World of Wonders, in the travelling troupe, and in the gothic household at Sorgenfrei, is mythic. The heroic world that Liesl challenges David to find in the depths of his unconscious at the end of *The Manticore* is the place where Magnus lives, for he has the "Magian World View" where the archetype of the Magus and the myth of Merlin are one and the same, and exist in broad daylight.

About the relation of God and the Devil to the natural world, Davies is exploratory and tentative. In *Fifth Business*, he creates a character convinced of the saintliness of Mary Dempster (Magnus' mother) and of her three interventions into the natural order. He makes Dunstan curious about saints and belief, about magic and evil, but though Dunstan has a fruitful encounter with his personal devil, he reaches no conclusions. In *The Manticore*, absolute moral questions are largely held in abeyance while Davies explores the psyche, but we are reminded of their presence by Knopwood and his powerful exit line: "God is not dead. And I can assure you God is not mocked." In *World of Wonders*, Magnus' audience probes the nature of evil and good and speculates about the Devil and God. Dunstan moves beyond his earlier limited statement that one can say with certainty only that faith is a psychological reality. Now, with several other characters, he believes that God and the Devil exist, and that

both interfere in people's lives. They feel that man may choose whether to obey the dictates of God or of the Devil and that choices are weighed, then condemned or rewarded, by what Magnus calls the "Great Justice".

If we take the moralists of *World of Wonders* seriously, the Devil may well have intervened, as Boy Staunton threw the stone-laden snowball and Dunstan ducked it. Their moral culpability is no less because the Devil initiated the action since both heeded his prompting. The train of cause and effect which affects the lives of Dunstan, Boy, Boy's family, and the Dempsters arrives at dramatically different destinations, however. For in Davies' world, individuals continue to make meaningful choices, though in the continuing presence of Good and Evil.

Dunstan immediately sees his deed as evil and atones in long years of service to Mary Dempster. His choices lead him to experience manifestations of God and to spend his life contemplating evidences of the Divine on earth. Boy pretends that his evil action did not happen. Ignoring the darker side of his nature all his life, he fails to grow to moral maturity and never understands other human beings. Finding less and less meaning in life, he takes the revelation of his childhood ill-doing as an appropriate moment to end his life. So covert is his evil, that it is not until one sees his effect on his wife (who commits suicide) and his son (who becomes an alcoholic, incapable of relating sexually to any woman) that his full maleficence is grasped. Magnus, innocent victim of the initiating act, a man who for much of his life does not act but agrees to suffer first evil and then good, is an intriguing mixture. Where Dunstan moves toward God, and Boy toward the Devil, Magnus experiences both. He seems to represent psychic wholeness, and the possibility of a rich middle ground where man, conscious of the vigour and omnipresence of the forces of good and evil, lives an heroic life.

And is the "wholeness" which seems to be Davies' ideal, a balancing of opposites? I think not. Rather it seems to be what Padré Blazon has in mind in *Fifth Business* in saying that meeting the Devil is educational and what David's analyst means in *The Manticore* when she urges the value of reclaiming, examining and getting to know one's Shadow (the dark side of the self). For not everything that has been labelled Evil proves to be so, nor all that has been repressed ought to remain so. And the genuinely evil and justifiably banished are weaker if faced and understood. The heroic middle is ultimately achieved, then, by Liesl, Magnus, Dunstan, and probably David.

Speeches

As the Master of Massey College and an eminent novelist known for his pithy pronouncements, Davies is a much sought-after speaker. The diversity of his public presentations is immediately evident in the collection *One Half of Robertson Davies* (1977). Though many of the selections are slight, the five lectures constituting the heart of the volume are meaty reading. "Jung and the Theatre" approaches the Jungian material in *The Manticore* from a different angle; the four lectures called "Masks of Satan" tackle good and evil, broadening the ideas in the Deptford novels. Here Davies talks illuminatingly about poetic justice (Magnus' Great Justice?). He declares that the greatest art is created by those who believe in the existence of Good and Evil, in God and the Devil. He talks of the necessity of opposites. Indeed, he talks with a vigour that prompts one to wonder whether the novel he has just completed draws on the riches of Jungian psychology and speculates further about the impact of God and the Devil on human life.

Chronology

1913   William Robertson Davies born August 28.

1913-28   Lived in Thamesville, Renfrew, and then Kingston. In each of these Ontario towns his father, William Rupert Davies, owned and edited a local newspaper.

1928-38   Attended Upper Canada College in Toronto; Queen's University, Kingston; and Balliol College, Oxford, earning his B. Litt with a dissertation on "Shakespeare's Boy Actors". He was active in the dramatic societies of all three institutions.

1938-39   Acted in the play *Traitor's Gate* and then joined the Old Vic Company as an actor of minor parts, writer, and teacher of the history of drama.

1940-42   Married Brenda Mathews who had been a stage manager with the Old Vic. He then returned to Canada where in November he became literary editor of *Saturday Night*, writing lead book review articles for "The Bookshelf" and contributing many other articles, primarily on ballet, music, and theatre, until February 1942.

1942   Moved to Peterborough, Ontario as editorial writer on the *Peterborough Examiner*. To the *Examiner* he gave much of his energy for the next 20 years, becoming editor and publisher of the paper in 1946. He sold the *Examiner* in 1968.

1943   Created a crusty character called Samuel Marchbanks whose diary and, later on, journal and correspondence appeared in a regular Saturday column until 1953. Selections from these columns were the basis for the three Marchbanks books (1947, 1949, 1967). "'Marchbanks'' was also the pseudonym Davies used for his regular columns of comment and book reviews in the *Examiner* and the *Kingston Whig-Standard* through the 1940s.

1947-53   Active in the Little Theatre movement both directing and writing plays which received many productions.

1951   Published the first of the Salterton novels, *Tempest-Tost*. The other two, *Leaven of Malice* and *A Mixture of Frailties*, appeared in 1954 and 1958.

1952   Wrote *A Masque of Aesop* for Upper Canada College.

1953   Became literary editor of *Saturday Night* writing lead book review articles for the "Books" section until 1959. Elected to the Board of Governors of the Stratford Shakespeare Festival, a position he held until 1971. With Tyrone Guthrie he documented the theatre's activities in its initial years in three books: *Renown at Stratford* (1953), *Twice Have the Trumpets Sounded* (1954), and *Thrice the Brinded Cat Hath Mew'd* (1955). He also reviewed each season's productions until 1967, contributed many short articles to the Festival's Souvenir Programs, and several times addressed its annual seminar.

1954-58   Wrote three plays for the Crest Theatre in Toronto: *A Jig for the Gypsy* in 1954, *Hunting Stuart* in 1955, and *General Confession* in 1958. Only the first two were produced.

1959   Began his "A Writer's Diary" column in January in the *Toronto Daily Star*. It appeared weekly until June 1962. In 1959 he prepared a dramatized version of his novel *Leaven of Malice*, called "Love and Libel", which was produced the following year under the direction of Tyrone Guthrie.

1962   Wrote *A Masque of Mr Punch* for Upper Canada College.

1963   Moved to Massey College at the University of Toronto as Master. His professional energies were now focussed on the college and in his teaching. He retires as Master in 1981.

1966	With four other authors contributed one act to a five-act Centennial play.
1967	Elected a fellow of the Royal Society of Canada.
1970	Published *Fifth Business,* the first novel in the Deptford trilogy. *The Manticore* and *World of Wonders,* the other two volumes, appeared in 1972 and 1975.
1973	Renewed interest in Davies' plays resulted in a spate of productions of earlier plays and in the writing and production of new plays. A TV drama, "Brothers in the Black Art" was aired on the CBC in February 1974, *Question Time* acted at the St. Lawrence Centre in 1975, and "Pontiac and the Green Man" produced at the MacMillan Theatre, University of Toronto, in 1977.
1977	Published *One Half of Robertson Davies,* a collection of pieces originally read aloud.
1980-81	Completed a new novel and published a collection of his observations on theatre and writing in Canada.

Comments
by Robertson Davies

. . . it is not the first duty of a book to be utterly honest; its first duty is to be readable. Bleak, flat-footed honesty, unrelieved by literary device or artistic selection, is characteristic of telephone directories and the inventories of department stores.

> Robertson Davies, "Graphy: Bio- and Autobio-", *Saturday Night* (14 February 1953), p. 30.

In my enthusiasm for a more ornate and varied style of writing than is generally recommended I know that my readers will not suppose that I am praising what Walter Savage Landor called "the hot and uncontrolled harlotry of a flaunting and dishevelled enthusiasm". In writing, as in architecture, ornament is never an end in itself; it is a splendid and sometimes playful exuberance; it is not stuck on for effect, but is indivisible from the whole. To manage it a man must be at the least a fine craftsman.

> Robertson Davies, "Is Plain Style Always Best?" *Toronto Daily Star* (1 August 1950), p. 30.

I think of an author as somebody who goes into the marketplace and puts down his rug and says, "I will tell you a story" and then he passes the hat. And when he's taken up his collection, he tells his story, and just before the dénouement he passes the hat again. If it's worth anything, fine. If not, he ceases to be an author. He does not apply for a Canada Council grant.

> Quoted by Peter C. Newman in "The Master's Voice: The Table Talk of Robertson Davies", *Maclean's* (September 1972), p. 42.

I am very interested in the condition of sainthood. It is just as interesting as evil. What makes a saint? You look at the lives of some of the very great saints and you find that they were fascinating people. Just as fascinating as great criminals or great conquerors. Most saints have been almost unbearable nuisances in life. Some were reformers, some were sages, some were visionaries, but all were intensely alive, and thus a living rebuke to people who were not. So many got martyred because nobody could stand them. Society hates exceptional people because such people make them feel inferior.

> Quoted by Peter C. Newman in "The Master's Voice: The Table Talk of Robertson Davies", *Maclean's* September 1972), p. 43.

My outlook is very much conditioned by the thought of C.G. Jung and my complaint about Christianity is the fact that it does not come to grips with certain basic problems. One is sexuality and the other is evil. Christian teaching on both these points, it seems to me, is inadequate. Christianity's focus is entirely on the achievement of perfection and I don't think that is either a possibility or indeed, perhaps, desirable, because perfection is inhuman.

> "Conversations with Robertson Davies", *Time* (3 November 1975), p. 10.

I've always resented the way critics make your own past pursue you. You get older and you see things in a different way, in a new light. But not a bit of it. The critic is there to tell you it is all one and whatever new thing you do was always there anyway . . . .

> Quoted by John Fraser in "Davies and his Revenge Therapy", *Globe and Mail* (5 March 1977), p. 37.

[My work may be categorized as] comedy, in the broadest sense of the term. But I take it to include a great measure of romance, of pathos, of the rueful awareness that life is short in time and that what we can understand of it is only a trifle of the whole; the extraordinary variety of life inclines it toward the comic rather than the tragic. Tragedies are usually about people with a limited sense of reality who live in closely contained worlds of their own making; they may be great figures because of the vigour of their passions, but they have no power to see themselves objectively. . . . We would not want to be without tragedy, but the greater part of life is lived in the mode of comedy . . .

> "Robertson Davies" in Geraldine Anthony, ed., *Stage Voices: 12 Canadian Playwrights Talk about their Lives and Work* (New York: Doubleday, 1978), p. 74.

Comments
on Robertson Davies

Mr. Davies has been accused of too self-conscious a pursuit of epigram and of writing a prose that is far too polished and sophisticated for a good Canadian. This, surely, is criticism of a peculiarly dispiriting variety. Qualities of mind such as Mr. Davies has are so rare that we should gladly welcome them even when they appear in excess.

> Claude T. Bissell, "Letters in Canada: 1951, Fiction", *University of Toronto Quarterly,* XXI (1952), 266.

He writes dialogue which is pithy and speakable, knows how to plant information deftly and memorably; and has a good feeling for theatrical climax.

> Tyrone Guthrie, "The Small City's Ogre", the *Globe and Mail's Globe Magazine* (5 November 1960), p. 15.

His novels *[Tempest-Tost, Leaven of Malice, A Mixture of Frailties]* study in symbolic fashion a problem that has concerned Canadian writers since Susanna Moodie: the plight of the imagination in this chilly cultural climate. This central theme in his work has generally gone unrecognized because the genre of satirical romance is unfamiliar to Canadians...

> Hugo McPherson, "The Mask of Satire: Character and Symbolic Pattern in Robertson Davies' Fiction", *Canadian Literature,* No. 4 (Spring 1960), p. 18.

Although his earlier work had suggested that Davies was a brilliant but shallow satirist, capable of coruscating caricatures and devastating reduction of Canadian social and literary provincialism— a view reinforced by the publication of *Samuel Marchbanks' Almanack* in 1967— the plays and novels he published in the early 1970s show a much greater depth of psychological understanding.... His style remains urbane, witty, magnificently and elegantly controlled. He uses it not to display a superiority over bourgeois ambitions but to forge his way into myth and magic and discover their significance for everyday life.

> William H. New, "Fiction" in Carl F. Klinck, ed., *Literary History of Canada* (2nd ed.; Toronto: University of Toronto Press, 1976), III, 254-55.

Selected Bibliography
Works by Robertson Davies

(First publication only. Davies' novels and many of his plays and articles have been reprinted in collections and in paperback editions.

Shakespeare's Boy Actors. London: Dent, 1939.

Shakespeare for Young Players: A Junior Course. Illustrated by Grant Macdonald. Toronto: Clarke, Irwin, 1942.

The Diary of Samuel Marchbanks. Decorations by Clair Stewart. Toronto: Clarke, Irwin, 1947.

Eros at Breakfast and Other Plays. Toronto: Clarke, Irwin, 1949.

The Table Talk of Samuel Marchbanks. Decorations by Clair Stewart. Toronto: Clarke, Irwin, 1949.

Fortune, My Foe. [Play] Toronto: Clarke, Irwin, 1949.

At My Heart's Core. [Play] Toronto: Clarke, Irwin, 1950.

Tempest-Tost. [Novel] Toronto: Clarke, Irwin, 1951.

A Masque of Aesop. Decorations by Grant Macdonald. Toronto: Clarke, Irwin, 1952.

Renown at Stratford: A Record of the Stratford Shakespeare Festival in Canada, 1953. With Tyrone Guthrie and Grant Macdonald. Toronto: Clarke, Irwin, 1953.

Leaven of Malice. [Novel] Toronto: Clarke, Irwin, 1954.

Twice Have the Trumpets Sounded: A Record of the Stratford Shakespeare Festival in Canada, 1954. With Tyrone Guthrie and Grant Macdonald. Toronto, Clarke, Irwin, 1954.

A Jig for the Gypsy. [Play] Toronto: Clarke, Irwin, 1954.

"The Double Life of Robertson Davies", by Samuel Marchbanks, *Liberty,* April 1954, pp. 18-19, 53-58.

Thrice the Brinded Cat Hath Mew'd: A Record of the Stratford Shakespeare Festival in Canada, 1955. With Tyrone Guthrie, Boyd Neel, and Tanya Moiseiwitsch. Toronto: Clarke, Irwin, 1955.

A Mixture of Frailties. [Novel] Toronto: Macmillan, 1958.

A Voice from the Attic. [Essays] Toronto: McClelland and Stewart, 1960.

A Masque of Mr Punch. Toronto: Oxford University Press, 1963.

Marchbanks' Almanack. Toronto: McClelland and Stewart, 1967.

Stephen Leacock. Toronto: McClelland and Stewart, 1970.

Fifth Business. [Novel] Toronto: Macmillan of Canada, 1970.

Hunting Stuart and Other Plays. Toronto: New Press, 1972.

The Manticore. [Novel] Toronto: Macmillan of Canada, 1972.

Question Time. [Play] Toronto: Macmillan of Canada, 1975.

World of Wonders. [Novel] Toronto: Macmillan of Canada, 1975.

One Half of Robertson Davies: Provocative Pronouncements on a Wide Range of Topics. [Addresses, Lectures, and Stories] Toronto: Macmillan of Canada, 1977.

"Robertson Davies" in Geraldine Anthony, ed. *Stage Voices: 12 Canadian Playwrights Talk about their Lives and Work.* New York: Doubleday, 1978.

The Enthusiasms of Roberston Davies. [Newspaper Columns and Articles] Edited by Judith Skelton Grant. Toronto: McClelland and Stewart, 1979.

Selected Criticism

Buitenhuis, Elspeth MacGregor. *Robertson Davies.* Toronto: Forum House, 1972.

Callwood, June. "The Beard", *Maclean's,* 15 March 1952, pp. 16-17, 30-33.

Cameron, Donald. "Robertson Davies: The Bizarre and Passionate Life of the Canadian People", *Conversations with Canadian Novelists, Part One.* Toronto: Macmillan of Canada, 1973.

Grant, Judith Skelton. *Roberston Davies.* Toronto: McClelland and Stewart, 1978.

McInnes, Graham. "An Editor from Skunk's Misery Is Winning Fame for Peterborough", *Saturday Night,* 26 April 1947, pp. 14-15.

McPherson, Hugo. "The Mask of Satire: Character and Symbolic Pattern in Robertson Davies' Fiction", *Canadian Literature,* No. 4 (Spring 1960), pp. 18-30.

Morley, Patricia. *Robertson Davies.* Profiles in Canadian Drama Series. Toronto: Gage Educational Publishing, 1977.

Owen, Ivon. "The Salterton Novels", *Tamarack Review,* No. 9 (Autumn 1958), pp. 56-63.

Roper, Gordon. "A Davies Log", *Journal of Canadian Studies,* XII, 1 (February 1977), 4-19 [a bibliography].

——————. "Robertson Davies' *Fifth Business* and 'That Old Fantastical Duke of Dark Corners, C.G. Jung' ", *Journal of Canadian Fiction,* I, 1 (Winter 1972), 33-39.

Steinberg, M.W. "Don Quixote and the Puppets: Theme and Structure in Robertson Davies's Drama", *Canadian Literature,* No. 7 (Winter 1961), pp. 45-53.

A   A Note on the Contributor

Judith Skelton Grant has written a short book on Robertson Davies in McClelland and Stewart's Canadian Writers Series and has edited two collections of his journalism. She is currently teaching Canadian literature at the University of Guelph.

The Enthusiasms of Roberston Davies. [Newspaper Columns and Articles] Edited by Judith Skelton Grant. Toronto: McClelland and Stewart, 1979.

W. O. Mitchell 16

by
Michael Peterman

Courtesy: Norman Chamberlain and the CBC.

One of the most overlooked facts about W.O. Mitchell is that he has been a successful professional writer in Canada for nearly 40 years, virtually as long as Hugh MacLennan and Robertson Davies. But while Mitchell's staying power is as noteworthy as his talents are various, he has received remarkably little critical attention over that long career. As far as I know this is the first time even a pamphlet-length study of his work has been undertaken.

It is appropriate, then, to begin by noting certain factors that underlie the limited rec-ognition W.O. Mitchell has thus far received. One obvious reason is his versatility. As a dramatist, script-writer, journalist, editor, entertainer, *raconteur* and novelist, he has developed his talents with admirable agility and energy. Secondly, there is the distinctive subject matter of his early work, which has led some critics to dismiss him as a specialist on childhood. As the author of the consistently popular *Who Has Seen the Wind* (1947) and the "Jake and the Kid" radio series (some 300 episodes of which were heard across Canada from 1950 to 1958), it is perhaps inevitable that Mitchell's reputation should be associated with children, buoyant spirits, humour, and charming whimsicality. Finally, Mitchell is too conveniently labelled a folksy, broad-humoured Westerner, at his best in capturing the regional flavour of small prairie towns — the local characters, their voices and preoccupations.

Nevertheless, with the appearance of novels like *the Kite* (1962) and *The Vanishing Point* (1973), both of which have western settings but middle-aged protagonists, critical recognition of Mitchell's work has continued to be hesitant.[1] Generally speaking, thematic studies of Canadian literature such as Margaret Atwood's *Survival*, Northrop Frye's *The Bush Garden*, and John Moss's *Patterns of Isolation* have allowed little place for his writing. As recent a study as David Dooley's *Moral Vision in the Canadian Novel* makes no mention of Mitchell's work, despite the fact that "moral vision" must surely be one of Mitchell's central concerns. Thus, for the most part only those interested in Western Canadian fiction—Edward McCourt, Laurence Ricou, Dick Harrison and Ken Mitchell — have paid close attention to Mitchell's achievements as a writer. Though *Who Has Seen the Wind* may be, as Dick Harrison has argued, "the nearest approach we have to a national classic",[2] national recognition of that fact has been slow in appearing.

While it is important to make note of the curious place W.O. Mitchell holds in contemporary Canadian letters, it is, I think equally important to emphasize certain formative aspects of his background. Though he spent his first twelve years on the edge of the Saskatchewan prairie in Weyburn, he was, in his own words, "not a rural person" thereafter. At that point his widowed mother, having discovered that he was suffering from a tubercular wrist, took the advice of a Winnipeg clinic and sought out a warmer climate, first in California and then for Mitchell's last three high school years in St. Petersburg, Florida. His developing imagination was therefore affected not only by the prairie but by the Gulf of Mexico, not only by Saskatchewan folkways and tradition but by American culture – by writers like Emerson, Twain, Steinbeck, and Cather. It was in Florida that he first learned an appreciation of literature, particularly of the oral expression of character through tone, inflection, and dialect. It was there too that he developed a passion for acrobatics and springboard diving, activities which came to serve as metaphors for individual release and freedom in his later writing.

The Depression and drought years of the 1930's were also a vital phase in Mitchell's "training". After two years at the University of Manitoba (when his illness again flared up, forcing him to abandon medicine for liberal arts and philosophy) and a summer in Europe, he spent two years in Seattle writing newspaper advertising copy while acting and writing for a local theatre troupe, the Penthouse Players. As his persistent interest in drama evinces, Mitchell was first of all a playwright and actor, not a writer of fiction.

The latter years of the "dirty thirties" were not less open-ended and formative. Mitchell travelled the continent, sometimes riding the rails, sometimes when opportunity arose, a water-clown in itinerant Red River shows, a salesman, or a hired man. With the war, however, he returned to school completing his B.A. and the Faculty of Education course at the University of Alberta. Here he pursued his interest in Platonism (originally awakened by Rupert Lodge at Manitoba), familiarized himself with the work of child psychologists like Jean Piaget, and came under the influence of Professor F.M. Salter, in whose creative writing class Mitchell wrote "the earlier stages" of Who Has Seen the Wind. It was from Salter that Mitchell learned to respect and value what he calls "the innocence of experience" or "the artist's innocence, a sort of inner balance between spontaneity and discipline which must never tip too far in either direction."[3]

One further aspect of Mitchell's formative experience is worth noting here. Having completed the teacher-education course and having married, he spent two years as a teacher and principal in two small Alberta "Composite Schools", first in Castor and then in New Dayton. Though he left teaching at this point to take up freelance writing and has subsequently taught only for brief periods,[3] teaching — effective, supportive, stimulating teaching — has become one of the most pressing themes in his fiction. The education of the imagination, the awakening of the individual's vital inner resources, is central to W.O. Mitchell's vision, so much so that the reader can often distinguish between the "good" and the "bad" characters in his novels on the basis of whether or not they stimulate or defeat the growth of a boy's imagination or a man's capacity for embracing life. "I like teaching only slightly less than to write," he noted recently; "in both I am concerned with the corruption of the living thing by the patterning and forming mind."[4] The theme amounts to a passion in Mitchell's work, both in his fiction and in the terms he chooses to express his artistic credo. That passion and commitment help to explain as well certain didactic and melodramatic tendencies in his writing, tendencies with which numerous critics have been uncomfortable.

The preservation of "the living thing" is central to Who Has Seen the Wind and Jake and the Kid, which had a sort of simultaneous birth in W.O. Mitchell's imagination. More specifically, the important relationships in Who Has Seen the Wind had their beginnings in the interaction of the kid and Jake Trumper, the hired man. As the kid looks up to the irrepressible Jake, so Brian O'Connal finds a supportive, surrogate father and guide in figures like Ab (a hired man himself), Uncle Sean, Digby, and even Saint Sammy. If the advice received or the example given is in many of these cases unconventional and "maverick", it nonetheless stimulates vision and intuitive understanding in the young boy. Such unconventional guidance, while typically a source of humour for the reader, is Mitchell's vital means of sidestepping the powerful and restrictive moral boxes relished by "the patterned and forming mind[s]" that dominate most prairie towns, the moral boxes of puritanism (or Presbyterianism) respectability, social status, prejudice, and fear. While Jake and the Kid explores this general territory light-heartedly and episodically,[6] Who Has Seen the Wind utilizes its larger structure and more serious mood to dramatize these threats as they exert themselves upon both children and adults in a prairie community.

In reviewing Jake and the Kid in 1961, as generous a reader as Margaret Laurence found herself somewhat uneasy. Though it provided her with "a thrill of recognition", she was only willing to grant the collection the status of "a Canadian classic" if it were judged simply as a book for children. Today, such hesitancy seems unnecessary, a function perhaps of Laurence's nostalgic desire at that time to find in the stories more than was there. While thre is considerable unevenness in *Jake and the Kid*, the best of the stories have an exuberance and well-turned delightfulness that constitute a brilliant achievement in an area in which Mitchell excels–popular, formula humour. Furthermore, from the "war" episodes forward there is a clear sense of an apprentice writer learning his craft and achieving greater control and sophistication in his use of character, dialogue, mood, and situation.

At his best Mitchell effectively uses issues of local importance to unify his stories, but in such a way as to put the preoccupations of the people of Crocus, Saskatchewan in a perspective which is at once amusing, endearing, and of universal application. Such typical prairie concerns as the weather, local pride, and the passion for exaggeration are deftly treated. As Wallace Stegner has noted in *Wolf Willow,* there is a rich folklore of water in prairie experience, a function of Saskatchewan's low annual rainfall and persistent droughts. Mitchell's "The Day Jake Made Her Rain" anticipates Robert Kroetsch's treatment of big-talking in a dry land in *The Words of My Roaring* (1966). In "The Golden Jubilee Citizen", Mitchell presents not only an instance of sensitive, effective teaching on Miss Henchbow's part but uses Jake– here in a more restrained mood– to counter Repeat Golightly's bland chauvinism:

> "Crocus and Saskatchewan has – have had– a colourful past. Colourful."

> "Thunderin' hooves the mighty fur-traders– like of that," Jake said.

> "Wild elements — bred in the blood and bone of Crocus citizenry. Blood and bone."

> "Don't forget the top, Repeat." Jake squinted up at him. "Most of the folks I know — early days — hail from Ontario. They come out for free land or a chance to start out a general store from scratch. They just got Ontario in thair blood an' bone. Kind of thin on the wild elements you was...."[6]

Using comedy for serious purposes — here to reveal both the myopia of local pride and basic truths about prairie settlement and history –is typical of Mitchell's art in the stories. So too in "The Liar Hunter" he offers both a comic anatomy of the westerner's imaginative penchant for telling tall-tales and a thoughtful insight into the sort of "lying" involved. As Mr. Godfrey, the liar-hunter, puts it:

> Rust and dust and hail and sawfly and cutworm and drouth are terrible things, but not half as frightening if they are made ridiculous. If a man can laugh at them he's won half the battle. When he exaggerates things he isn't lying really; it's a defence, the defence of exaggeration. He can either do that or squeal.[7]

Though a comedy in form, *Who Has Seen the Wind* is above all a serious investigation of a young boy's instinctive desire to understand his relationship to the world in which he finds himself. It is a dramatic presentation of the force and potential of "the living thing" within Brian O'Connal as his curiosity and imagination are made to confront the definitive factors of life –morality, the natural cycle, God, other people and various aspects of imposed social order and convention. Above all, however, *Who Has Seen the Wind* is a celebration of life, one that wisely recognizes and challenges the many factors that threaten to diminish or inhibit the growth and capacity of "the living thing" in man.

Who Has Seen the Wind's scope is deliberately narrow. It covers Brian O'Connal's growth only from age four to twelve, and is neatly divided into four sections, each a distinctive two-year phase taking him to a new level of awareness and understanding. With each gain, however, there are corresponding losses. Brian is characterized by Mitchell as a Wordsworthian child who enters the world "Not in entire forgetfulness,/And not in utter nakedness." In his freshness, even as the "Shades of the prison-house begin to close/Upon the growing Boy," he has the inner capacity to perceive "the visionary gleam" and to be "Nature's Priest".[8] Such intuitive reservoirs are his special power in seeking out answers, even at his young age, to the puzzles of human existence that lead older men to philosophy and religion. If Brian is somewhat precocious in his perceptions and development, Mitchell makes his precocity credible by emphasizing the elemental or "skeleton" condition of life on the Saskatchewan prairie, by providing stimulating (if eccentric) guides for him, and, most important, by locating Brian's daily life firmly in the context of the domestic and ordinary. The art of *Who Has Seen the Wind* depends in large part upon Mitchell's ability to make Brian's development at once dramatic and plausible though much that happens around the boy is heightened for comic effect and rendered melodramatic by Mitchell's moral position.

There are three important realities in *Who Has Seen the Wind* — the reality of prairie, of town, and of the assimilated wisdom that balances the best attributes of prairie and town. Prairie reality is natural and universal. Its system is cyclical and ecological; yet, as Brian discovers, there is little in its operations to provide conventional Christian or romantic solace. As a young boy, Brian is drawn instinctively to the prairie and its symbolic residents, the Young Ben and Saint Sammy, who become guides to his understanding, priests to and interpreters of nature's laws. Typically, Brian experiences his most exhilarating moments — what he calls "the feeling"–when he is in the presence of the prairie and the wind. But prairie and wind, he learns, can also be dark, frightening, alienating forces. They have as much to do with life as with death.

Hence, it is part of the novel's design that each of its four sections ends with a death and a funeral of sorts on the prairie. Mitchell as well deliberately emphasizes the mistakes that occasionally occur in the natural process. In no sense does he want Brian's prairie education to be partial or romantic. He must experience "a feeling of nakedness and vulnerability that terrified him" when alone at night on the prairie;[9] he must feel helpless and frustrated before the deformity of a two-headed calf; he must know in various ways the anguish and loss of death; and he must become aware of and accept the presence of larger, inhuman forces at work in the universe: "a still and brooding spirit, a quiescent power unsmiling from everlasting to everlasting to which the coming and passing of the prairie's creatures was but incidental".[10]

Characters who are closely linked with the prairie stimulate Brian's growth. With hair the colour of the prairie, the Young Ben becomes "a personified eternal" and "a sort of incarnate life-urge" in the novel.[11] Years of schooling have proven him unadaptable to the usual social conditions. But if he is "naked of right and wrong", as Digby says, he does manifest a pure, violent passion in reacting against the cruelty of Art's treatment of the gopher and of Miss MacDonald's punishment of Brian. Saint Sammy, whom Ken Mitchell calls "the archetype of the visionary madman",[12] also becomes a guide for Brian. Loving above all his horses and the prairie, Sammy calls down vengeance upon the avaricious Bent Candy, Baptist deacon and land speculator. Sammy's vivid language suggests to Brian "the sound of the wind...singing vibrance in a void, forever and forever wild", an echo of his earlier recognitions of "a quiescent power unsmiling".[13]

The reality of the town is obviously the most negative realm. It is distinguished for Mitchell by a tendency to evade the vital and elemental. Town experience generally involves taking refuge behind masks, rituals, institutions, credoes – symbolically, behind false fronts. More than merely taking refuge, however, its worst members strive to control, manipulate, and judge others. Mrs. Abercrombie and Mr. Powelly are essentially insensitive to others, yet they use their social status and institutional authority to order the lives of others as they see fit. Mitchell soundly criticizes such characters, seeing in their strained puritanism the most dangerous and deadening of human attitudes. That Powelly should offer a sermon on "the Vital Things" or that Mrs. Abercrombie, who inspires prejudice in her own child, should be high-mindedly concerned about the "spiritual life" of the town's children, are examples of their blind hypocrisy and inability to see life positively. The moral impetus of *Who Has Seen the Wind* is so unyielding that the "bad" characters, who constitute but a small number of the town's adults, receive appropriate comeuppances near the novel's end.

A never-complacent intelligence blending insight and thought, the elemental and the rational, characterizes the town characters Mitchell holds up for our admiration. One finds it particularly in the enlightened principalship of Digby, the compassionate teaching of Miss Thompson, and the austere wisdom of Brian's grandmother. Uncle Sean, an avowed maverick, manifests it in his progressive plan for an irrigation system while Brian's desire to become a dirt-doctor similarly blends a passion for the land with a recognition of science's importance. Such assimilated wisdom is the mark of Brian's growth in the novel. If he has lost "the feeling" as he fears, he has moved significantly closer to a state of mind W.O. Mitchell might well call "mature".

Who Has Seen the Wind is a remarkable novel. Though the moral view it creates functions melodramatically and at times simplistically, it achieves an extraordinary power and charm. Its success, I would argue, lies in its focussing so precisely upon Brian's growth; all the events, though often episodic in themselves, serve that purpose, even when those events pertain specifically to the adult world. By juxtaposition and contrast, Mitchell makes even his most colourful and memorable characters—Uncle Sean, the Ben, Sammy, Milt Palmer — serve his central design. The consequence of the young boy's struggle to understand his place and to see the wind is in fact increased by Mitchell's clever integration of various adult perspectives appropriate to Brian's own naive search.

While *The Kite* and *The Vanishing Point* are impressive attempts by Mitchell to shift his attention to the adult world, neither book is finally as successful as *Who Has Seen the Wind*. Both suffer from an insufficient dramatic focus. Neither David Lang nor Carlyle Sinclair fascinates the reader or holds his interest as does Brian O'Connal. The middle-aged, middle-class *malaise* that besets the respective protagonists is not especially absorbing in itself and certainly not vivid enough to carry an entire novel. The real energy of the novels lies elsewhere, in the figure of 111 year-old Daddy Sherry whom Lang, an Alberta-born Toronto journalist, comes West to interview, and in Archie Nicotine, the highly individualized Stony Indian whose cleverness and wisdom for so long befuddle and elude Sinclair, the Paradise Valley Reserve's teacher and agent. What Robert Fulford wrote in reviewing *The Vanishing Point* applies to both novels; each gives "an impression of a novelist who had excellent material but never quite figured out how to use it". The educative relationship between a boy and his older guides is less effective when the boy becomes a middle-aged man as he does in *The Kite* and *The Vanishing Point*.

But if *The Kite*'s weaknesses are numerous

- I would add the sentimental treatment of David Lang's love affair, the digressiveness that results from Daddy's recollected adventures, and the overt didacticism with which the novel concludes - it is, like *Who Has Seen the Wind*, a celebration of life that dramatizes the emotional and personal rejuvenation of Lang through the example of Daddy's maverick vitality. Daddy Sherry is many things in *The Kite* - a living history of the West (having come out from Ontario as a freight-driver and buffalo hunter, and having guarded Louis Riel after Batoche), a shaman figure, a barometer of the essentials, and a poet who "comes to everything as though it were fresh and new".[14] Beside him, David Lang's struggle for self-recognition and imaginative release sadly pales. Daddy's life, governed by his insistence upon living "loose an' soople" and never settling for less, becomes a kind of wonderful tale.[15] Be it goose hunting for Old Croaker or horse ranching with Ramrod or wearing a yachting cap as his house is carried away by flood waters, Daddy's adventures are appropriately matched by the unrestrained exuberance of his language and oaths. As such, David Lang's ordinary and more ponderous search for "the magic release of imagination" seems too often simply to get in the way of the novel's real force.[16]

In *The Vanishing Point*, W.O. Mitchell returned to the material he had begun and abandoned in the early 1950's under the title, "The Alien". But while the earlier work ended in the despair and suicide of the protagonist (and led a dissatisfied Mitchell to withdraw it in mid-publication), *The Vanishing Point* is, like *The Kite*, a novel of achieved release and imaginative insight. Carlyle Sinclair works his way through his present difficulties as White administrator-teacher and his past losses and repressions. Through the cryptic guidance of Archie Nicotine, his love for an Indian girl, Victoria (the name, interestingly, haunts Daddy Sherry as well), the force of Spring, and the power of the Indian dances, Carlyle overcomes his self-restraint and bridges the chasm between the White and Indian worlds, at least on a personal level, thus escaping - in the book's central metaphor - the constipation of his puritan upbringing and inhibited behaviour.

Though overly-didactic in its conclusion, *The Vanishing Point* reveals a more adventurous side to W.O. Mitchell's art. He experiments interestingly with first-person narration, jumbled chronology, and stream-of-consciousness techniques. He expands his range of extraordinary characters and voices to include not only Stony Indians like Archie Nicotine, Norman Catface, and Ezra Powderface, but also a self-deceiving evangelical con-man like Heally Richards. Furthermore, he sensitively undertakes a very difficult subject matter — the kind and quality of life on Indian reservations and the problems of White-Indian relations in Canada. Yet for all its careful attention to the pros and cons of both cultures, *The Vanishing Point* concerns itself with themes consistent in Mitchell's fiction— the struggle to express one's genuine inner feelings, the repressiveness of puritanism, the dangers inherent in wielding authority over others, and the need to recognize human accountability. Of all W.O. Mitchell's major fiction, then, *The Vanishing Point* takes the reader into the most complex moral territory and closest to the anguish, the difficulty, "the terror of being human".[17] And it achieves its insights, without sacrificing the familiar signs of Mitchell's genius: the celebration of "the living thing" in man and the gift for creating superbly comic scenes and vivid, unforgettable characters. *The Vanishing Point* reveals W.O. Mitchell as an artist who continues to grow without sacrificing the essence of his vision.

[1] Mitchell's important play, "Back to Beulah", which was first staged in the mid 1970's but has not yet been published, is further evidence of his venturesomeness as a writer.

[2] Dick Harrison, "Prairie Fiction: Life on the Bibliographical Frontier", in *Papers of the Bibliographical Society of Canada*, XVII (1978), 19.

[3] One important teaching job was his work at the Eden Valley Reserve in the early 1950's. His experiences there are evident both in "The Alien" and *The Vanishing Point*.

[4] W.O. Mitchell, "Debts of Innocence", *Saturday Night* (March 1976), p. 37.

[5] Labelled "A Novel" by its publishers, *Jake and the Kid* is simply a collection of 13 sketches or stories.

[6] W.O. Mitchell, *Jake and the Kid* (Toronto: Macmillan, 1961), p. 175.

[7] *Jake and the Kid*, pp. 100-101.

[8] William Wordsworth, "Ode: Intimations of Immortality from Recollections of Early Childhood". See particularly Stanza 5. Mitchell himself makes specific reference to Wordsworth's poem at a crucial point in the novel.

[9] W.O. Mitchell, *Who Has Seen the Wind* (Toronto: Macmillan, p. 236.

[10] *Who Has Seen the Wind*, p. 128.

[11] William New, *Articulating West* (Toronto: New Press, 1972) pp. 47-8.

[12] Ken Mitchell, "The Universality of W.O. Mitchell's *Who Has Seen the Wind*, *Lakehead University Review* IV (1971), 37.

[13] *Who Has Seen the Wind*, p. 270.

[14] W.O. Mitchell, *The Kite* (Toronto: Macmillan, 1962), p. 136.

[15] *The Kite*, pp. 191, 210.

[16] *The Kite*, p. 57.

[17] W.O. Mitchell, *The Vanishing Point* (Toronto: Macmillan, 1975), p.384.

Chronology

1914   Born in Weyburn, Saskatchewan, a town of some 5000 inhabitants, where he spent his first 12 years.

1921	Mitchell's father, the Weyburn druggist, died suddenly, leaving his wife and four sons to live on the income of his successful business.
1926	Contracted bovine tuberculosis of the wrist from drinking unpasteurized milk.
1927-31	Upon receiving medical advice, his mother took her four sons to Long Beach, California for the first year, then to Florida where the boys attended St. Petersburg High School from 1928-1931. They returned to Canada in the summers.
1931	Entered the University of Manitoba intent upon a career in medicine. Another flare-up of the wrist problem led to his missing valuable laboratory time, as a result of which he switched to an arts course in reading and philosophy under the direction of Rupert Lodge, a noted Platonist.
1933	Summered in France, working as a lifeguard in Biarritz, and travelling.
1934-36	Worked in Seattle in advertising and selling for the *Seattle Times* and was involved in some occasional acting and playwrighting for a local group, the Penthouse Players.
1936-40	A period of odd jobs and travel during the latter years of the Depression.
1940-42	Enrolled at the University of Alberta where he completed his B.A. in 1940-41, took the course at the Faculty of Education, and studied under Professor F.M. Salter in his Creative Writing course. *Who Has Seen the Wind* was written in part under Salter's guidance.
1942	Married Merna Hirtle.
1942-44	Principal in successive years of two rural Alberta Composite schools, first in Castor and then in New Dayton, where he taught a variety of subjects - French, Drama, and Mathematics - in addition to his administrative duties. During these years, his first stories were published in *Maclean's* (the first of the "Jake and the Kid" episodes), the *Canadian Forum*, and the *Atlantic Monthly*.
1944	With his income from writing outgrowing his teaching salary, Mitchell gave up teaching and began freelancing. He bought a home in High River, having been impressed by the town while writing an article about it.
1948-51	Became fiction editor for *Maclean's Magazine* and moved to Toronto. During this period he became increasingly involved in radio, television, and journalistic work, so much so that, to free himself for writing, he returned to High River in 1951.
1950-58	The radio presentation, usually at the rate of 39 episodes a year, of the "Jake and the Kid" series. *The Black Bonspiel of Wullie MacCrimmon* was written in 1950.
1953-54	About one-third of a novel-in-progress, *The Alien,* appeared in serial form in *Maclean's.* This manuscript with which Mitchell was finally unsatisfied later was reworked into the material for *The Vanishing Point.*
1961	*Jake and the Kid* appeared, a selection of 13 stories which formed the basis of a number of the radio scripts. The book earned Mitchell the Stephen Leacock Award for Humour in 1962.
1962	*The Kite* published.
1968-(79)	Moved to Calgary where, for three years, he was one of the University of Calgary's Artists-in-Residence. Subsequently, he has been Writer-in-Residence at the University of Alberta, York University, the University of Toronto, and in 1979-80 at the University of Windsor. Mitchell has also taught Creative Writing for many years at the Banff School of Fine Arts.
1972	Completed the screenplay of *Alien Thunder* but refused to let his name stand in the credits because of changes made by new writers brought in from Hollywood. Awarded the Order of Canada.
1973	*The Vanishing Point* published and a play, *The Devil's Instrument,* was produced by the Ontario Youth Theatre.
1974-75	A play, "Back to Beulah", produced first by Theatre Calgary and then by the Tarragon Theatre in Toronto. Before its initial stage production it was directed for the C.B.C. by Eric Till. Though the play has not yet appeared in print, it won the Chambers award for drama.
1977	*Who Has Seen the Wind,* with illustrations by William Kurulek, reprinted.
1978	A play, "Sacrament", produced for the CBC by Philip Kentley.

Comments
by W.O. Mitchell

Innocence is the best human quality.
"Debts of Innocence", p. 37.

Well, the prairie does create mystics. When I was a kid in Weyburn, ... [very] early you were in touch with the living whole. You walked out onto the prairie, onto great areas of still-untilled land, and with the prairie wool stuff, and I guess that makes mystics, people who, without being aware of it, in some strange way are in tune with wind and grass and sky. Subsequent education, including great interest and study in philosophy and closed systems, never did really make me a rational animal.

Donald Cameron, *Conversations*, p. 61.

I can't go to work on a piece unless I have some essentially human truth that I believe very passionately and that I hope shall transcend time and region.

Patricia Barclay, "Regionalism and the Writer".

...for a long time I thought of myself as a Platonist, with Presbyterian overtones, but at some point in my writing apprenticeship I suddenly realized that it wouldn't do, there could be no closed systems in art. Since it rests upon life, it is made up of contradiction, of dilemma, of not either/or but of both.

Donald Cameron, *Conversations, p. 52.*

For artists, indeed for all humans, living is a matter of balance between the world of the many and the world of the one, the world of the wild horses of passion and appetite, and reason, the caprices of childhood and the discipline of experience. Pulling off the trick of living is one hell of a difficult, acrobatic trick.

"Debts of Innocence", p. 37.

About 17 years ago, I worked on a novel, very close to where I thought it was finished, and then I was unhappy with it. I returned to it several times over a period of about five years, and then about seven years ago I suddenly realized what was wrong. The novel had grown in such a way that it said No to life. It ended in despair, and that was what had crippled it so terribly for me.

Weekend Magazine, Mar. 29, 1975, p.9.

I would say that four-fifths of my writing has been exterior, visual playwrighting rather than prose writing. Most people don't realize this about me. I was an actor before I was a writer, and the first things I wrote were one-act plays.

In conversation with Sid Adilman, *Toronto Daily Star*, Sept. 25, 1976.

The idea of a kite, a lively thing held by a thin thread of life, is comparable to man and his mortality, and [*The Kite*] is a study in mortality, and awareness of the shortness of man's days upon the earth — it's quite a serious novel with a picaresque surface. Any novel will probably involve a search, and a questioning — and in most cases, an answer. When I wrote *Who Has Seen the Wind*, I didn't have an answer. It was just a question, which is a perfectly fine reason for writing a novel. In *The Kite*, there is an answer....

Patricia Barclay, "Regionalism and the Writer".

Comments on W.O. Mitchell

The focus of W.O. Mitchell's fiction is on man as question mark. His pages are filled with mystics, egoists and poets; his best characters, indeed, combine something of the qualities of all three. For Mitchell upright man in the prairie flatness is essentially a thinker. He is forced by the contours of his environment to ponder his own meaning in the universe. Yet his questioning is not exclusively inner-directed. Knowing oneself involves knowing one's world.

Laurence Ricou, *Vertical Man/Horizontal World*, p. 95.

His sensibility enlivens fairly traditional comic forms to a breadth and depth of human comedy never approached by [other contemporary western writers].... More than the other writers of comedy he faces seriously the questions of man's relationship to the prairie... [and] is the only major writer in the period of "prairie realism" to present a reconciliation of the human spirit with the prairie.

Dick Harrison, *Unnamed Country*, p. 172.

The structure of *Who Has Seen the Wind*, in four distinct parts based on Brian at four different ages, is a way of focussing attention on Brian's development and of understanding its nature. In using this definite pattern Mitchell shows a kinship to the psychologist who, although he knows that a child's growth is an uninterrupted continuum, invents "stages" to make comprehension easier.

Laurence Ricou, "Notes on Language and Learning in *Who Has Seen the Wind*", p. 6.

[S]ome critics have accused Mitchell of losing his focus by shifting away from his main character [Brian] to develop the social comedy of the town, but they overlook the fact that there are two protagonists in the action, Brian and Digby the school principal. Mitchell develops a second focus of this sort in most of his fiction; there is not only the Kid, but Jake, and in *The Kite* there are David Lang and Daddy Sherry. It is a method of pinpointing reality by triangulation, the younger and the older consciousness at work on an experience ....

Dick Harrison, *Unnamed Country*, p. 175.

Mitchell's choice of the Indian viewpoint as a possible alternative marks another major development in contemporary prairie fiction.... [Until 1973 we had] felt free to forget the Indian entirely, which may say something about the robustness of our consciences or merely about how thoroughly we have been confined to the perspective of Old Kacky. It has not been until contemporary novelists began breaking out of this perspective that they have discovered the Indian culture —

somewhere near the vanishing point.
Dick Harrison, *Unnamed Country*, p. 199.

Selected Bibliography
Works by W.O. Mitchell

"The Owl and the Bens", in Martha Foley, ed., *The Best American Short Stories, 1946*. Boston: Houghton-Mifflin, 1946.

Who Has Seen the Wind. Toronto: Macmillan, 1947.

Who Has Seen the Wind. Toronto: Macmillan, 1976. [Illustrations, some in colour, by William Kurelek.]

The Alien. Maclean's (Sept. 15, 1953 - Jan. 15, 1954). [A novel published only in part.]

Jake and the Kid. Toronto: Macmillan of Canada, 1961.

The Kite. Toronto: Macmillan of Canada, 1974.

The Black Bonspiel of Wullie MacCrimmon. Chinook Books No. 1. Calgary: Frontiers Unlimited, n.d.

The Devil's Instrument. Toronto: Simon and Pierre, 1973.

The Vanishing Point. Toronto: Macmillan of Canada, 1973.

"Debts of Innocence", *Saturday Night*, XCI (March 1976), 36-37.

"Patterns", in David Carpenter, ed., *Wild Rose Country: Stories from Alberta*. Toronto: Oberon Press, 1977.

"Back to Beulah" [1975; a play as yet unavailable in print but much performed on stage and filmed by the CBC under Eric Till's direction.]

For reasons of space, no attempt has been made to list here W.O. Mitchell's numerous published short stories and articles, many of which have appeared in *Maclean's*. Published excerpts from novels and radio and telescripts (for example, the Foothills Fables series) are also not included. The forthcoming *Annotated Bibliography of Major Canadian Authors*, eds. David and Lecker, will include a section on Mitchell compiled by Sheila Latham.

Selected Criticism

Barclay, Patricia. "Regionalism and the Writer: A Talk with W.O. Mitchell", *Canadian Literature*, No. 14 (Autumn 1962) pp. 53-56.

Bartlett, D.R. "Dumplings and Dignity", *Canadian Literature*, No. 77 (Summer 1978), pp. 73-80. [A study of *The Vanishing Point*.]

Cameron, (Silver) Donald. "W.O. Mitchell: Sea Caves and Creative Partners", *Conversations with Canadian Novelists, Part Two*. Toronto: Macmillan of Canada, 1973.

Cameron, (Silver) Donald. "Merna Mitchell thinks this man is the most endearing, hopeless, fascinating dolt she has ever met", *Weekend Magazine* (Mar. 29, 1975), pp. 7-9.

Carpenter, David C. "Alberta in Fiction", *Journal of Canadian Studies*, X (November 1975), 12-23.

Gross, Konrad. "Looking Back in Anger?: Frederick Niven, W.O. Mitchell, and Robert Kroetsch on the History of the Canadian West", *Journal of Canadian Fiction*, III, 2 (1974), 49-54.

Hornyansky, Michael. "Countries of the Mind", *Tamarack Review*, No. 26 (Winter 1963), pp. 58-68.

Harrison, Dick. *Unnamed Country: The Struggle for a Canadian Prairie Fiction*. Edmonton: University of Alberta Press, 1977, pp. 172-80, 197-99.

Laurence, Margaret. "A Canadian Classic?" *Canadian Literature*, No. 11 (Winter 1962), pp. 68-70. [Review of *Jake and the Kid*.]

Laurence, Margaret. "Holy Terror", *Canadian Literature*, No. 15 (Winter 1963), pp. 76-77. [Review of *The Kite*.]

McCourt, Edward A. *The Canadian West in Fiction* Toronto: Ryerson Press, 1970. [Revised.]

McKay, Catherine. "W.O. Mitchell's *The Kite*: A Study in Immortality", *Journal of Canadian Fiction*, II, 2, (Spring 1973), 43-48.

Mitchell, Ken. "The University of W.O. Mitchell's *Who Has Seen the Wind*", *Lakehead University Review*, IV (1971), 26-40.

New, William. "A Feeling of Completion: Aspects of W.O. Mitchell", *Canadian Literature*, No. 17 (Summer 1963), pp. 22-33. [See also New, William. *Articulating West: Essays on Purpose and Form in Modern Canadian Literature* Toronto: New Press, 1972, pp. 45-59.]

Phelps, Arthur L. "W.O. Mitchell", in *Canadian Writers*. Toronto: McClelland and Stewart, pp. 94-102.

Peterman, Michael A. "The Good Game: The West in W.O. Mitchell's *Who Has Seen the Wind* and Willa Cather's *My Antonià*". [A paper given at the Canadian Association of American Studies' conference in Vancouver (Nov. 1, 1979) and to be published in a special issue of *Mosaic* (1981) entitled "Beyond Nationalism" edited by Evelyn Hinz and Robert Kroetsch.]

Ricou, Laurence. "The Eternal Prairie: The Fiction of W.O. Mitchell", in *Vertical Man/Horizontal World: Man and Landscape in Canadian Prairie Fiction*. Vancouver: University of British Columbia Press, 1973, pp. 95-110.

Ricou, Laurence. "Notes on Language and Learning in *Who Has Seen the Wind*", *Canadian Children's Literature*, No. 10 (1977-1978), pp. 3-17.

Sutherland, Ronald. "Children of the Changing Wind", *Journal of Canadian Studies*, V (November 1970), 3-11.

Tallman, Warren. "Wolf in the Snow", *Canadian Literature*, No. 5 (Summer 1960), pp. 7-20.

A Note on the Contributor

Michael Peterman teaches Canadian and American literature at Trent University, where he is an Associate Professor. He is currently interested in prairie fiction. His other research interests include Edith Wharton, Susanna Moodie and Catherine Parr Traill. He has taught secondary school at Bishop's College School, Lennoxville and at Crescent School, Toronto. He is a member of the Editorial Board of the *Journal of Canadian Studies*.

Ernest Buckler 17

by
John Orange

Courtesy: McClelland & Stewart.

Ernest Buckler was born on July 19, 1908, in Dalhousie West, Nova Scotia, to Appleton Buckler, a farmer of English descent whose ancestors were Loyalists in the Annapolis area as far back as the late eighteenth century. His mother was Mary Swift, and Ernest was the third child, and only son, of a family of five children, though one sister died at the age of four. The tone of Buckler's childhood and early school experiences can be found in his "fictional memoir", *Ox Bells and Fireflies,* and his descriptions of rural family life in all of his works are no doubt based on his own childhood impressions and feelings.

Buckler was such a bright and conscientious student that he completed his senior matricula-

tion just before his thirteenth birthday. Since he was too young to go on to university, he spent the next five years working on the farm and taking summer jobs such as bellboy, waiter, and desk clerk at Kent House (a rather expensive lodge) in Greenwich, Connecticut, in order to save money for his post-secondary school education. He says that his adolescence was very short and that he "turned adult" very early.

He apparently did not read much serious literature at this time though he was very interested in mathematics and philosophy. At seventeen he entered Dalhousie University and pursued those interests so that in 1929 he earned his B.A. with a distinction in mathematics. Hugh MacLennan was attending Dalhousie at the same time, and visitors to the university were, among others, Bliss Carman, Wilson MacDonald, and Charles G.D. Roberts, all well known writers in their day. Buckler developed his interest in literature during these years and in his final year he published an article and six poems in the university newspaper, *The Dalhousie Gazette.*

In 1930 he moved to the University of Toronto to work on a master's degree in Philosophy which he obtained in that year by writing essays on a number of philosophers including Aristotle, Croce, Kant, and Spinoza. Then he gained employment as an actuary for Manufacturers Life Insurance Company in Toronto. He lived alone in a single room for five years and worked up an intense dislike for cities and urban life. While he was in Toronto his father died, and that, coupled with his own ill health, convinced him in 1936 to go back to Dalhousie West to help his mother on the farm. While in Toronto, though, he had managed to publish two short stories in *The Trinity University Review* and that must have encouraged him to write more.

He lived with his mother and sister, Nellie,

and her husband, and in 1937 he noticed an advertisement for a contest in *Coronet* magazine which his sister had picked up when she and her husband were returning from a trip to Montreal. He entered the contest on a whim and his essay was given the one-hundred dollar first prize. In March of 1937 he also began submitting letters to the "Sound and Fury" column of *Esquire Magazine,* commenting on, and criticising, the stories in their fiction section. A number of readers wrote to Arnold Gingrich, the editor, that they enjoyed Buckler's letters even more than the stories by the well-known writers, and Gingrich asked Buckler to contribute manuscripts of his work. The first stories were not published because, in Gingrich's judgment, Buckler's fiction did not "travel well", but eventually *Esquire* published two stories in July and December of 1941. As early as 1939 Buckler published a review of a novel in *The New York Herald Tribune Book Review,* and two years later *Saturday Night* asked Buckler to write for a regular feature in their magazine called "The Back Page". His first article appeared in their April, 1941, number. So Buckler began his career as a short-story writer and as a free-lance journalist, and now and again in his letters he wrote what amounted to reviews and critical commentary on literature. He has sustained each of those interests ever since, but his reputation as a fiction writer has all but totally eclipsed his work as a journalist and literary critic.

If Dalhousie West is like the valley in *The Mountain and The Valley,* then the farm to which Buckler and his mother moved in 1939 is the counterpart of the mountain setting. This farm is located in Centrelea, about three miles southwest of Bridgetown, and Buckler still lives there. While working that soil and helping an ailing aunt and uncle, Buckler took to writing short stories partly to supplement his income and partly to explore his relationship with the region to which he had returned.

His first stories were sentimental, (usually set around Christmas or Easter), conventional, and clearly aimed at the commercial market served by *Saturday Night* and *Collier's* magazines. Even in these early stories, however, one can find patterns which recur throughout the Buckler canon. "Another Christmas", (1941) for example, deals with an artist's feelings of frustration that he cannot make words "tell truly" the feeling he sometimes has that the million separate things in creation are all united and part of each other. He yearns for "a single light" that will suddenly pull all the "broken lines" into a "single image" where "everything was part of the same thing".[1] This early story anticipates not only the ending of *The Mountain and The Valley* where David Canaan feels the same sense of frustration, but also the long dialogues in *The Cruelest Month* on the impotence of words to capture

reality. Buckler time and again comes back to the paradox that the writer expects words to clarify, and to give unity and meaning to experience in some transcendent way, when in fact they seem always to fragment, separate, and focus our attention on individual things both inside and outside of ourselves. In fact this paradox finds its way into Buckler's own writing style which struggles (sometimes painfully) to capture every nuance of texture and feeling in relationships either among people or between people and their surroundings, while at the same time it ironically exposes the idealistic expectations of artists who try to do that very thing. The tension produced by this paradox is not resolved until the writing of *Ox Bells and Fire-flies,* in which Buckler seems to capture perfectly the equations of feeling which link the subjective and the objective worlds. It is clear that Buckler began meditating on the nature and function of art even at the beginning of his writing career. This theme also offered him a way of writing about just what it is to be human, as we shall see later.

Another pattern which becomes characteristic of Buckler's fiction can also be found in "Another Christmas". After Steve, the writer, thinks about what he *cannot* do with words, the story switches to a childhood memory concerning the time he had received a pair of skates for Christmas. He remembers feelings of wholeness and harmony from his rural childhood, and the suggestion is made that art, which attempts to recreate those feelings, can produce only a poor imitation of them. Memory, however, is a crucial instrument for the writer because it winnows out emotionally charged episodes in character's life, as well as significant details associated with those episodes. The imagination then connects remembered feelings and details together, often through the use of figurative language, and the result is usually a structure of illuminated symbols which not only recall the past perfectly, but also give it shape and meaning in the present.

Buckler developed and refined his ideas on the inter-relationship of memory, words, feelings and imagination as they combine in the artistic process when he wrote his best stories for *Maclean's* magazine. "Penny in the Dust" (1948), "The Quarrel" (1949), "The Clumsy One" (1950), and "The Rebellion of Young David" (1951), are each narrated by a character who is recalling an episode from his past in such a way as to locate a central symbol which then illuminates the episode's meaning and recaptures the quality of feeling in some human relationship — often among members of a family. The penny in "Penny in the Dust", to cite only one example, comes to symbolize a feeling of childhood rapture with the land, subsequent feelings of fear and loss, and the ultimate unspoken awe and affection which develops between a father and his son who both realize the fragility of dreams. The tragedy is that they can communicate their knowledge only through the penny which the narrator finds in his father's burial suit. The son buries the penny back in the "dust" with his father as a way of "holding" the feeling it carries above, or outside, the transience of time. Of the later works, *The Mountain and The Valley, Ox Bells and Fireflies,* and the stories in *Nova Scotia: Window on the Sea,* are also given form by the memory of the narrator selecting and arranging items from his past in order to find their symbolic meaning. The earlier short stories were, in a sense, "probes" for the longer works, but that is *not to* say that many of them cannot stand very well on their own.

Buckler wrote many stories in the decade before his first novel, as well as radio plays and articles on a wide variety of topics. In some ways both the published and the unpublished material contain ideas, characters, and episodes which later converge in the three longer works of fiction.[2] There is always, for example, a marked preference for a rural way of life over an urban one and a nostalgia for its loss. Country life is associated with childhood, home, the family, feelings of intimacy with nature (often represented by a brother or father who is inarticulate), and a quality of timelessness. City life is associated with adult experience, education (represented by someone whose thoughts are "word-shaped"), fragmentation, materialism, competition, technology, glib and superficial sophistication. That is not to say that Buckler always makes an easy choice between country and city, because he knows that each way of life brings its own rewards and hardships. Besides the more "pastoral" way of life seems to be disappearing forever. It is not even an option anymore.

It is more important to examine the way that Buckler *uses* his notion of a lost pastoral existence. Very often it is used to signify a character's sense of spiritual alienation — the feeling of belonging nowhere, of being caught between the vanished values of the past and a future which will not provide validity or meaning for his life. Sometimes it signifies a lost opportunity for a communion between a father and his son, or between a husband and wife, or between brothers as in "The First Born Son", "The Wild Goose", and "The Clumsy One". The memory of a precious lost opportunity is linked to feelings of guilt, loneliness and the need to redeem time somehow, if only by suspending memories in the unstable medium of words. Seen in this way characters in rural Nova Scotia come to represent the conflicts experienced by everyone anywhere. Extend the pattern further and Buckler can be seen creating his own local version of the fall of man from the Garden of Eden into the present as we experience it here and now.

Buckler was encouraged by a one-thousand dollar award for "The Quarrel" in 1949 and he continued to write stories for magazines such as *Chatelaine, The Atlantic Advocate, Weekend,* and *The Canadian Home Journal* through the 1950's and into the early 1960's. Two stories, "Anything Can Happen At Christmas" (1957) and "The Dream and the Triumph" (1958), won best short story of the year awards from the University of Western Ontario. Most of these stories, however, are of lesser quality than the 1941 – 1952 group possibly because with the final publication of *The Mountain and The Valley* Buckler was anxious to move into new territory without losing the market he had gained for his fiction. He tried mystery stories, romances, melodramas, and stories with urban settings and characters, all of which are interesting only insofar as they are testing grounds for his second novel.

With the publication of *The Mountain and The Valley* in New York and then in Toronto in 1952, Buckler quickly established his reputation as a serious and gifted novelist. He had worked on the novel for six years and he said that it was a novel which he *had* to write even though at times it was extremely difficult for him to do it.[3] All of the themes he had wrestled with in the short stories come together in this novel about the life and early death of a romantic, separated from everyone and everything he loves because he can find no outlet for his dreams of harmony and unity with his world.

David Canaan is pictured in the prologue at the age of thirty, standing at the kitchen window, staring at the highway, and thinking of the log road which leads to the top of the mountain. Beside him his grandmother, Ellen, is hooking a circular rug out of garments once used by members of the family. Buckler's themes and essential elements of his style are contained in the first few paragraphs. Each detail holds symbolic significance. The window suggests David's separation from the rural world outside. The highway represents his futile attempts to escape to the city. The kitchen is the warm, secure, world of childhood and family which is now gone forever. The log road and the mountain represent David's romantic dreams and his destiny. Ellen is the unselfconscious artist weaving patterns out of the past – possibly the kind of artist David wants to become but cannot.

The novel is a long flashback which groups episodes in David's childhood around central symbols. Buckler narrates the story as though we are observing David from the outside, yet at the same time we are made to feel and think what David felt and thought at various times in his life. Usually episodes are described in the kind of language that David would use if he ever had a chance to write down his memories. This technique allows Buckler to manipulate the reader's sympathies in favour of David, while at the same time it allows for the use of irony from time to time when he wants the reader to stand back and to make judgments about David's overwhelming romanticism. Also this technique permits Buckler to explore relationships between characters, as well as man's relationship to time, memory, the land, "progress", his need for transcendence and the possibilities of art to meet that need.

Even as a child David dreams of finding a perfect moment and then stopping time so that that moment can become a permanent state. He often projects this moment of transcendence and suspended time onto a journey to the top of the mountain. At other times he dreams of becoming the greatest general in the world, then the richest man, the best skater, the greatest actor, the most potent lover, and finally, the finest writer. Usually his aspirations are connected with heights – the mountaintop, the stage during a play, the beam that he climbs in the barn, his attic room. Yet each time he achieves that height, he "falls". He is chided back down to earth when he confuses his dream with reality during a play in which he is a prince. Humiliated, he runs home to hide in the attic. He falls from a beam which he climbed to prove his courage, and he is scarred for life. He dies as a result of his climb up the mountain.

David's romanticism forms part of an intricate network of relationships with other characters. Ellen had an affair with a sailor and his picture in her locket resembles David. The locket is given to David's twin sister, Anna, who "escapes" to the city and marries Toby, David's friend, who becomes a sailor only to die at sea. David's father, Joseph, is killed by a tree he is cutting to make a keel for a magnificent boat. David inherits his weak heart from his mother and he strains it when he ascends the mountain past the fallen keel piece and dreams of becoming the world's best artist.

It is, in fact, David's romanticism which colours his emotional relationships with those around him and which leads finally to his alienation and solitude. He is a tragic figure destined to fail because of the nature of his dreams, his inheritance, the changes taking place in his society, his inability to compromise and to adjust to those changes, and also because of his artist's "secret extra senses".[4] The figure of Herb Hennessey appears in the prologue and at crucial times in the story to indicate the fateful nature of David's tragic destiny.

On the top of the mountain David realizes that his real vocation all along was to be the voice of his people. Once again, however, he goes too far. He decides he can "*become* the thing you told" and find the "single core of meaning" in all things. Buckler gently intrudes to remind us:

"He didn't consider *how* he would find it".[5] So the potential artist is buried in snow after "one final transport of self-deception"[6] and the real artist, Ellen, completes her work of art made from memories by inserting a scarlet rag (David's cloak from the play) and a white centre (her own lace) into the middle of the rug. Buckler's exploration of the limits of his art, time, memory, alienation, all come together in his novel.

Other themes introduced first in the short stories are also present in the novel. The intimate yet inarticulate feelings among family members in the country are beautifully captured. The disintegration of the family, the loss of innocence which was the result of rural isolation, and the disappearance of old rural values are themes found throughout the novel, but nowhere are they rendered so intensely as in a scene where David tries to help his father move a huge rock out of the ground. Scenes in the graveyard, others involving David and his brother, Chris, and one describing the slaughter of a pig, are among the finest in Canadian literature for their rich texture and evocative imagery.

Throughout the 1950's and early 1960's Buckler continued to publish short stories, articles and letters. In 1962 he became a regular book reviewer for *The New York Times Book Review*, and in 1964 he also reviewed books for the weekend "Calendar" section of the *Los Angeles Times*. A Canada Council Arts Scholarship helped him in the writing of his second novel, *The Cruelest Month*, which was published in Canada in 1963. The next year he received a Canada Council Senior Arts Fellowship, and another in 1966 helped in the writing of his third book, *Ox Bells and Fireflies* (1968), which was published simultaneously in New York and Toronto.

The Cruelest Month deals with adult experience rather than childhood and adolescence, and its structure and language are sophisticated and very complex. Buckler collects together five urban characters, each with a difficult personal problem, and he groups them around two country people — Paul, who has a heart problem, and Letty, who is part of the older rural way of life. They all meet at Endlaw (an anagram of Walden), and eventually they wind up talking at length about their troubles: Kate's lost youth (sacrificed nursing her father), Bruce's guilt over the accidental death of his wife and son, Morse's loss of his creative ability, Sheila's loss of love, Rex's loss of innocence. Other themes emerge from the elaborate dialogue: urban wastelands (employing images from T.S. Eliot's *The Waste Land*), death, the inadequacy of words, the destructive side of love, how people fool themselves, uses of memory, possibilities of renewal and redemption, and others.

In this "novel of ideas"[7] Buckler makes enormous demands on his readers. The characters come to life through what they *say* rather than through an action – at least for two-thirds of the novel. There are too many themes, and the interlocking of characters and ideas is extremely complicated, though well crafted. The ambivalence, the layers of irony, the dense (sometimes convoluted) prose, which includes many similes, metaphors and symbols, show Buckler at his best and at his worst so that many readers find the novel too uneven, or perhaps too challenging.

The work which followed, *Ox Bells and Fireflies,* brought Buckler back to his earlier prose style and his early themes. Many critics consider it to be Buckler's real masterpiece. In this "fictional memoir"[8] Buckler creates a narrator, Mark, the artist who is a spokesman for his community. He is no longer alienated, lonely or tortured. He feels at one with his people though everything occurs in "memory time". He takes us from his childhood through his adolescence and adulthood and back to his childhood again. This pattern suggests renewal and a cyclical rhythm to human life. Although the individual chapters include episodes of death, loss, decay and loneliness, the fireflies of freedom atone for the ox bells of sorrow or the crows of death. Time passes in the book, but at the end it has moved no further than the hands of a clock.

The real source of beauty in the book lies in Buckler's superb style. The prose is rich with personification, alliterations, onomatopoeic verbs, similes which set out perfect equations between feelings and objects. There is also Buckler's characteristic celebration of the proliferation of things as well as his fusion of concrete and abstract images: shingles with fatherly knowledge, thistles with wit, hills that feel their own internal rhyme, "bees as intent as theologians" in a crabapple tree that "foams with blossoms".[9] The style gives the prose a metaphysical quality. The feelings expressed are universal, elemental, and consequently they transcend time.

Three books were published in the 1970s. Buckler's text for Hans Weber's photographs in *Nova Scotia: Window on the Sea* is a combination of descriptive essays and short stories. The characteristic intensity of tone, the proliferation of similes and metaphors, his use of contrasts between the particular and the universal, abstract and concrete, are all present in the prose style. What makes this book different from the earlier ones is the way Buckler stretches his prose so far that it overlaps with poetry. Lines break off abruptly, catalogues of images form prose poems, verse rhythms take over the prose, the macrocosm is reflected in the smallest details from local life. As in the other works, the reader is left with the impression that imaginative participation in life's processes, with its consequent sense of wonder and reverence, can lead to feelings of renewal and even of transcendence.

The Rebellion of Young David and Other Stories (1975) is a collection of the best short stories from the 1940-1960 period. Robert Chambers has grouped the stories by themes and for the first time readers can find all the early stories together. The book was generally favorably received.

In 1977 Buckler published a book of humorous essays, poems, and sketches. *Whirligig* surprised some readers but anyone who had followed Buckler's career as a journalist, essayist, and reviewer through the 1950s and 1960s, or who had read his letters to *Esquire* or his essays in *The Globe and Mail* in the 1970s knew what to expect. His love of word play, his earthy humour, his criticisms of pseudo-sophistication are consistent with his other works, but his lighter side and his own personality are more in the foreground in this work. The book won the Stephen Leacock Award for Humour in 1978.

In the last decade Buckler has received a number of awards, honorary degrees, and medals, and he has also gained a great deal of critical attention. Recently critics have noted the ironic elements in his fiction and they are beginning to see him as more than simply a gifted craftsman of regional pastoral idylls. There is a myth at the core of his writing which is inseparable from his prose style and this is the mark of a superior writer. The unpublished manuscripts of stories, radio and television plays, and essays attest that Buckler has not been overly aggressive about publishing his work. However the canon available to us even now is sufficient to make him one of the finest writers of fiction that Canada will ever produce.

[1] Ernest Buckler, "Another Christmas", *Saturday Night,* 57 (December 20, 1941), p. 25. Reprinted in *The Rebellion of Young David and Other Stories,* ed. Robert D. Chambers (Toronto: McClelland and Stewart), pp. 29-34.

[2] For an initial discussion of the growth of the short stories in *The Mountain and The Valley* see: Alan R. Young, "The Genesis of Ernest Buckler's *The Mountain and The Valley*", *Journal of Canadian Fiction,* No. 16 (1976), pp. 89-96.

[3] Ernest Buckler, "My First Novel", in *Ernest Buckler,* ed. Gregory M. Cook (Toronto: McGraw-Hill Ryerson, 1972), p. 22.

[4] Ernest Buckler, *The Mountain and The Valley* (Toronto: McClelland and Stewart, 1961), p. 28.

[5] *Ibid.,* pp. 298-299.

[6] University of Toronto Library, Buckler Manuscript Collection, Letter from Ernest Buckler to Dudley H. Cloud, May 15, 1951.

[7] University of Toronto Library, Buckler Manuscript Collection, Letter from Ernest Buckler to Mr. Ivan Von Auw, March 20, 1961.

[8] In a letter to Miss J. Rogers, June 30, 1967, Buckler called it "a memoir cast in imaginative form; the kind of novelistic non-fiction on which I think Capote is quite wrong in his claim to have registered the first patent". University of Toronto, Library, Buckler Collection.

[9] Ernest Buckler, *Ox Bells and Fireflies* (Toronto: McClelland and Stewart, 1968), p. 26.

Chronology

Comments
by Ernest Buckler

Well, of course, it all boils down to the problem of the isolation of the artist, doesn't it? if I can use so pretentious a word...I think you can find yourself, can find what you have to write about, much better in isolation than you can if you are inside a clique....Not that I classify myself in the same category as people who produce pearls or ambergris, but it is the *sick* whale that produces the ambergris, it is the irritated oyster which produces the pearl....

Donald Cameron, *Conversations With Canadian Novelists*, Vol. I (Toronto: Macmillan of Canada, 1973), 4-5.

On the other hand, I think that if you don't have other things on your mind you can't write. You sit down, it's an absolutely clear day, and you think, Now it's going to come today — and all you get is this blank white sheet, and the blank white sheet is the blank white sheet of the day really. So I've always found that when I was actively farming — you know, had cows to worry about, whether it was their time to be taken to the bull, or whether the peas were lolling in the rows and should be propped up — this I thought at the moment a distraction, but actually I think you write best when you're getting this kind of influx to your consciousness.

Cameron, p. 7.

The greatest novel ever written is a mere phrase, a word, a letter, if you like in the infinite language of human relations....I tried to get my characters straight right at the start [and] then I let them more or less work their own passage....I didn't fret too much about action....I think that insides are far more important...*and* interesting — than outsides. That action...is far less important than its motivation.

Gregory M. Cook, *Ernest Buckler* (Toronto: McGraw-Hill Ryerson, 1972), p. 23.

I find [revision] the most exacting and time-consuming of all. Carefully as I do compose even the first draft, I still feel obliged to weigh and examine each and every sentence again and again, groom it to the best effect I can manage. And even when the book is "all down", basically, each section must then be reassessed *in the light of the whole*. Certain sections must be shifted from one placement to another for better co-ordination. Lopsided emphases must be corrected by lengthening this paragraph, shortening that. Joints must be better articulated, transition seams erased. From time to time, better ways of saying the same thing will suggest themselves and order the recasting of a passage. Later ideas, in the light of the whole, must be inserted; and earlier ones, if suspected of clashing with the whole, must be pondered and, if found guilty, excised or replaced. Characters may need an added development, relationships a further clarification. Etc.

Cook, p. 118.

As for the idea that David's death [in *The Mountain and The Valley*] was an arbitrary device to end the story, it actually happens to be the very first thing I wrote; the foundation of the whole thesis. (Later I split the opening chapter and shifted that part to the epilogue.) It was to be the crowning point of the whole dramatic irony, (and, of course, the most overt piece of symbolism in the book), that he should finally exhaust himself climbing the mountain, and, beset by the ultimate clamour of impressions created by his physical condition and his whole history of divided sensitivities, come, at the moment of his death (prepared for, not only by long accounts of the results of his fall, but by the medical officer's advice to him at the time of his enlistment examination; and, more immediately, by the excitement, the panic, the climbing), achieve one final transport of self-deception; that he would be the greatest writer in the whole world.

Ernest Buckler, Letter to Dudley H. Cloud, May 15, 1951, in the Buckler Manuscript Collection, University of Toronto Library.

Comments on Ernest Buckler

About his sense of place: much has been made of Buckler's rural love of the earth, yet his landscape is a generalized one. We know it's Nova Scotia, but it feels like everywhere. What marks the quality of this writer is not his regionalism or his so-called ruralness, but his fine and deep psychological understanding, and based on that, his consciousness and articulation of human history.

Miriam Waddington, "Ernest's Importance of Being", *Books In Canada*, IV, 7 (July 1975), 7.

I am sure this kind of writing will put many people off....The cries of 'Too much!' will go up but it appeals to me simply because it is defiantly too much. The impossibility of *actually* showing things as they *actually* are is accepted, and full rein is given to any conceit that can help suggest their glittering liquefaction.

Dave Godfrey, "Buckler and Allan", *Tamarack Review*, No. 36 (Summer 1965), p. 83.

Remembering is an intellectual process and Mr. Buckler, like many deep thinkers, is anti-intellectual in the sense that he sees the fundamentals of life as being instinctive, intuitive, beyond reason. Specifically, memory is seen as a function of the active mind and so its recollections are less real than those inexplicable translations by which the present and the past momentarily unite [and result in a transcending of time itself].

Douglas Spettigue, "A Review of *Ox Bells and Fireflies*", *Quarry*, XVIII, 4 (Summer 1969), 53.

To me, Ernest Buckler's *The Mountain and The Valley* is not only the best novel yet written by a Canadian, but one of the great novels of the English language.

In my opinion, Buckler is one of the great masters of the simile. Buckler's most powerful similes not only illustrate the universality of a situation, but also its uniqueness....

Alden Nowlan, "All The Layers of Meaning", in *Ernest Buckler*, p. 116.

Selected Bibliography

Works by Ernest Buckler

Books

The Mountain and The Valley. New York: Henry Holt and Co., 1952 (in Canada: Clarke, Irwin and Co., Toronto.) [Published in paperback, New York: New American Library of World Literature, 1954.] [Published in paperback with an introduction by Claude Bissell. Toronto: McClelland and Stewart, 1961 and 1966.]

The Cruelest Month. Toronto: McClelland and Stewart, 1963. [Published in paperback with an introduction by Alan R. Young. Toronto: McClelland and Stewart, 1977.]

Ox Bells and Fireflies. Drawings by Walter Richards. Toronto: McClelland and Stewart, 1968 (in United States: Knopf, New York). [Published in paperback with an introduction by Alan R. Young. Toronto: McClelland and Stewart, 1974.]

Nova Scotia: Window on the Sea. Photographs by Hans Weber. Toronto: McClelland and Stewart, 1973.

The Rebellion of Young David and Other Stories. Selected and arranged by Robert D. Chambers. Toronto: McClelland and Stewart, 1975.

Whirligig. Introduction by Claude Bissell. Toronto: McClelland and Stewart, 1977.

Selected Short Stories and Articles not included in the Books above

"One Quiet Afternoon", *Esquire*, XIII, 4 (April 1940), 70, 199-201.

"On The Third Day", *Saturday Night*, LVIII, 33 (April 24, 1943), 33.

"David Comes Home", *Collier's*, CXIV (November 4, 1944), 24.

"Yes Joseph, There Was a Woman; She Said Her Name Was Mary", *Saturday Night*, LXI, 14 (December 8, 1945), 48-49.

"Goodbye Prince", *Canadian Home Journal* December, 1954, pp. 6-7, 52-55, 59-60.

"The Line Fence", *Better Farming*, CXXV (February 1955), 32-33.

"The Concerto", *The Atlantic Advocate*, XLVIII, 6 (February 1958), 65-67.

"The Darkest Time", *Canadian Home Journal*, May 1958, pp. 31, 64-66.

"The Accident", *Chatelaine*, XXXIII 5 (May 1960), 38-39, 117-118, 120-122.

"The Doctor and the Patient", *The Atlantic Advocate*, LI, 11 (July 1961), 65-66.

"Nettles Into Orchids", *The Atlantic Advocate*, LI, 12 (August 1961), 79-71.

"Choose Your Partner", *The Atlantic Advocate*, LII, 12 (August 1962), 62-64, 66-67, 69.

"A Little Flag for Mother", *Farm Journal*, LXXXVII (May 1963), 69-70.

"Guilt on the Lily", *The Atlantic Advocate*, LIII, 12 (August 1963), 61-69.

"This Side Paradise, Nova Scotia (Home is Where You Hang Your Heart", edited by Gregory Cook, *Maclean's*, LXXXVI, 9 (September 1973), 40-41.

"Dictionaries of the Blood. Bless You Kate Reid", *The Globe and Mail*, October 23, 1976, p. 6.

"To Sleep Perchance? No, It's Never Lights Out For The True Insomniac", *The Globe and Mail*, July 23, 1977, p. 10.

Selected Criticism

Listed Alphabetically

Barbour, Douglas. "David Canaan: The Failing Heart", *Studies in Canadian Literature*, I, 1 (Winter 1976), 64-75.

Chambers, Robert D. *Sinclair Ross and Ernest Buckler.* Studies in Canadian Literature Series. Toronto: Copp Clark; Montreal: McGill-Queen's University Press, 1975.

Chapman, Marilyn. "The Progress of David's Imagination", *Studies in Canadian Literature*, III, 2 (Summer 1978), 186-198.

Cook, Gregory M. *Ernest Buckler.* Critical Views on Canadian Writers Series No. 7. Toronto: McGraw-Hill Ryerson, 1972.

Dooley, D.J. "Style and Communication in *The Mountain and The Valley*", *Dalhousie Review*, LVII, 4 (Winter 1977), 671-683.

Dyck, Sarah. "In Search of a Poet: Buckler and Pasternak", *Germano-Slavica: A Canadian Journal of Germanic and Slavic Comparative Studies*, II, 5 (Spring 1978), 325-336.

French, William. "Ernest Buckler: A Literary Giant Scorned?", *The Globe and Mail*, June 24, 1972, p. 23.

Kertzer, J.M. "The Poet Recaptured", *Canadian Literature*, No. 65 (Summer 1965), pp. 74-85.

MacDonald, Bruce F. "Word-Shapes, Time and the Theme of Isolation in *The Mountain and the Valley*", *Studies in Canadian Literature.* I, 2 (Summer 1976), 194-209.

Moss, John. *Sex and Violence In The Canadian Novel.* Toronto: McClelland and Stewart, 1977, pp. 90-95.

Noonan, Gerald. "Egoism and Style in *The Mountain and The Valley*", *Atlantic Provinces Literature Colloquium/Colloque Littéraire Des Provinces Atlantique.* In Marco Polo Papers One. Ed. Kenneth MacKinnon. St. John: Atlantic Canada Institute, 1977, pp. 68-78.

Orange, John, "Ernest Buckler, An Annotated Bibliography", in Robert Lecker and Jack David eds., *The Annotated Bibliography of Canada's Major Authors*, Vol. 3, Downsview, Ont.: E.C.W. Press, 1981.

Ricou, Laurence. "David Canaan and Buckler's Style in *The Mountain and The Valley*", *Dalhousie Review*, LVII, 4 (Winter 1977-78), 684-696.

Sarkar, Eilen. "*The Mountain and The Valley:* The Infinite Language of Human Relations", *Revue de l'Universite d'Ottawa*, XLIV, 3 (July - September 1974), 354-361.

Thomas, Clara. "New England Romanticism and Canadian Fiction", *Journal of Canadian Fiction*, II, 4 (Fall 1973), 80-86.

Westwater, Sister A.M. "Teufelsdrockh is Alive and Doing Well in Nova Scotia: Carlylean Strains in *The Mountain and The Valley*", *Dalhousie Review*, LVI, 2 (Summer 1976), 291-298.

Young, Alan R. "The Pastoral Vision of Ernest Buckler in *The Mountain and The Valley*", *Dalhousie Review*, LIII, 2 (Summer 1973), 219-226.

——————. *Ernest Buckler.* Canadian Writers Series No. 15 (NCL). Toronto: McClelland and Stewart, 1976.

——————. "The Genesis of Ernest Buckler's *The Mountain and The Valley*", *Journal of Canadian Fiction*, No. 16 (1976), pp. 89-96.

A Note on the Contributor

John Orange teaches Canadian literature at King's College, University of Western Ontario, and has published articles and reviews on writers such as Morley Callaghan, Ernest Buckler, Hugh Hood, Jack Hodgins and Alice Munro.

Al Purdy

by
Laurie Ricou

Courtesy: Susan Wood.

"But how it relates to hockey — don't ask"
"Homage to Ree — shard"

In a poem called "House Guest" Al Purdy tells us of arguing with Milton Acorn whether "hockey was rather like a good jazz combo/never knowing what came next" (*BA*, 102).[1] Hockey, another friend pronounces grandly in "Homage to Ree—shard", " 'is the game we're made of all our myth/of origins' " (*SD*, 37). Thinking of two of Purdy's favourite games — hockey and poetry — makes a good place to begin for two reasons. First because Purdy, more than any other Canadian poet, finds his subject in the games we're made of and in our myth of origins, appropriately expressed in a hockey player's voice mingling

bravado and an almost inarticulate embarrassment. Second because Purdy's poems are shaped (like jazz, like hockey) by both improvisation and finesse: in Purdy's typical poetic form we never know what will come next. If there were an NHL for Canadian poets, Al Purdy would be some completely unlikely figure, a combination of Bobby Orr and Eddie Shack perhaps. He'd be, modestly, one of the best players on skates, but an entertainer as well, with an unpredictable clear-the-track burst of energy — and a bit of a wobbly knee.

"Hockey Players" (*BA*, 66-8) is Purdy's longest poem on this specially Canadian subject. Its nationalism, verbal extravagance, and ultimate sadness are typical. (Indeed, one distinguishing feature of Purdy's poetry is that his method of crowding in as many rambling thoughts as possible makes so many of his poems seem to be *the* central poem.) The poem begins as if it were catching Purdy in the middle of a thought, or a one-sided conversation: "What they worry about most is injuries." The poem ranges from stockbrokers to the crucifixion, from northern landscapes to the training room, but the focus is on worry and injury — not only physical, but emotional and psychological. Hockey is "roaring feverish speed" and "a rapid pouring/of delight", but when Purdy wonders "how . . . the players feel about it" he finds mostly fear: "worrying wives", an "aching body",

and the self indulgence
of allowing yourself to be a hero and knowing
everything ends in a pot-belly.

"Hockey Players" sprawls over two and a half pages, with lines varying from sixteen syllables to only two. The poem's variety and physical appearance suit the pace of the game: "In the hockey player poem, I wanted a strong contrast between the metrics and prose; and I tried to make several passages about as prosy as possible to contrast with the swift metrical rhythms."[2] Yet, such contrast describes a more general method appropriate to a poetry in which you never know what's coming next.

Courtesy: Susan Wood.

A description of a "breakaway" causes Purdy to break away from his hockey players into religious myth:

> I've seen the aching glory of a resurrection
> in their eyes
> if they score
> but crucifixion's agony to lose
> — the game?

A few lines later "auroras" become "tubercular". If these surprises are calculated, some of the jumbled syntax, particularly describing the flight of the players through the end boards and north across the tundra, seems to catch the poet, as much as the reader, uncertain about what's coming next:

> stopping isn't feasible or possible or lawful
> but we have to and we have to
> laugh because we must and
> stop to look at self and one another but
> our opponent's never geography
> or distance why
> it's men
> — just men?

Certainly the confusion, here, is partly due to Purdy's usual awkwardness with the possible ambiguities of line endings, and to the problems of ignoring punctuation: commas, for example, would show that "opponent's" can only be read as a contraction of "opponent is", and not as possessive. But a player with Purdy's bravado skates right over such difficulties: so many unfinished lines, ending with prepositions and conjunctions, not only leave room for the unpredictable, they express the flow and interruption of the game, and Purdy's view of life as an unending process.

Yet, despite the bluster of his end-to-end rushes, Purdy almost always pauses to ask himself whether he's made the right play. The most memorable example of his self-questioning is his wry admission at the end of "Trees at the Arctic Circle": "I have been stupid in a poem" (*BA*, 43). The two passages from "Hockey Players" which I've just mentioned both end in pauses and question marks. We are turned back by these questions to reconsider the entire argument of the poem: perhaps our opponent is superhuman — fate, or time, or greed, or geography — but then again . . . Similar questioning is provoked by the poem's ending. Purdy likes to end his poems with an after-thought, to suggest that his thinking about a subject goes on, that there is still more to be said. In "Hockey Players" the effect is achieved by a parenthesis:

> (and out in the suburbs
> there's the six-year-old kid
> whose reflexes were all wrong
> who always fell down and hurt himself and cried
> and never learned to skate
> with his friends)

Purdy's constant interest in the outcast and the failure shows in this poignantly sentimental picture. But it also returns us to the worry and injuries at the beginning of the poem. Purdy often writes about the enormous pain of being human, a characteristic which the poet's boisterousness has often caused us to overlook. "The six-year-old kid" reminds us of inexplicable inequalities, and social injustice, but also that all hockey players, who are, after all, "boys playing a boy's game in a permanent childhood", ultimately face the same humiliation and loneliness. Purdy clarifies this discovery in a later piece of journalism based on an interview with Brian Glennie:

> There's a kind of agony in all this that I
> didn't quite expect. . . What it amounts to
> is: men playing a children's game, but
> forced to be adults in their private lives,
> forced to look at themselves squarely as
> human beings, prone to human as well as
> athletic errors.[3]

It startles me, now, to realize that the same agony lies behind and within Purdy's poems.

"Hockey Players" is, as I've said, one of many poems which might be thought to sum up all of Purdy's poetry. But it's only typical if we think of the poetry written since the first version of *Poem for all the Annettes* in 1962. Most of the poetry in the first four books gives no indication of what will come next. Purdy describes almost all of his early work when he writes:

> I wrote such bad poems
> when I was very young
> when I was about fourteen
> and thought poems were "poems"
> instead of what they are.
> ("Jean", *WGW*, 40)

What they are, presumably, are the verbal hockey games and jazz compositions I've been describing. They are not "poems" with a fixed definition, to be set on a shelf and sighed over; therefore,

Purdy dismisses his early poetry in which he worked within set rhyme schemes, with unvarying metres. The early poetry is filled with heavy alliteration, and strained, antiquated diction:

> Oaf, lout and churl, in fief forever
> To barony of yellow hair.
>
> ("Cantos", *ER,* 4-5)

Careful searching can discover in these early poems some glimmer of the Purdy who has had such an influence on Canadian poetry in the last twenty years: the interest in the extinct and the nearly extinct, the bizarre metaphors, the laconic self-burlesque, and the extravagant digression. In occasional poems, there is a hint of his later poetic voice:

> I would like to be a dirty, unkempt, old man,
> Creating a drunken row.
>
> ("Meander", *POS,* 11-12)

But generally, Purdy's early poetry is only interesting for such historic reasons, for its anticipation of the poetry which creates its own row.

That poetry, like "Hockey Players", has a free-wheeling form which sets the imagination winging into fantasy; it speaks with a casual, self-deprecating voice; it re-invents the process of a poet's mind groping from experience to idea to image to meaning. The most obvious indication of process in Purdy's poetry, however, is not the form, but the subject matter. No aspect of Purdy's work has received more attention than his sense of history. He often takes historical events as subject matter: "The Northwest Passage", "William Lyon MacKenzie", or "The Battlefield at Batoche". But every one of these poems moves deliberately into the present, because Purdy is interested not in history as curiosity, but in history as part of our present being. How we live at a given moment in a particular place is affected, often in a clearly identifiable way, with all that has happened in that place for aeons and centuries past:

> Walking sometimes in the streets of the town
> I live in and thinking of all the people who
> lived here once and fill the space I fill —
> if they'd painted white trails on the sidewalk
> everywhere they went, it would be possible
> to see them now.
>
> (*BA,* 82)

This "Method for Calling up Ghosts" is one Purdy uses over and over to establish continuity with the past. So a few horses, "hitched at taverns" in north central B.C., are given dignity and mystery when Purdy uses this method, seeing the trails of extinct breeds — powerful Kiangs, and speedy Onagers — in the pastures outside the town. Seen in this way the horses are no longer obsolete and decrepit: we see the nobility of the past still breathing in them, and we recognize that the evolutionary process that led from "the last Quagga screaming in African highlands" to the Cariboo horses, will in turn give continuing meaning to these horses.

Purdy also knows that the process of historical discovery works in another way, in that the past is always changing according to our changing present perception of it. As he observes in "Elegy for a Grandfather", a poem later incorporated in his most ambitious historical poem, *In Search of Owen Roblin,* "I've somehow become his memory" (*BA,* 55). Purdy is remembering, and altering, what his grandfather, himself, once remembered. This line is a clue to the tricky backward/forward movement (often envisioning the future) in Purdy's poems on history. As he says in a poem I quoted earlier,

> Just because something is gone
> doesn't make it a poem
> but maybe the reason you remember
> does.
>
> ("Jean", *WGW,* p. 41)

Once again, our attention is directed to process (of motive, of thinking, of remembering) rather than to an object. Imagining the overlaid white trails left by the people of the past "exalts me", says Purdy. John Lye nicely sums up this attraction to history when he describes Purdy's humanist view of history as unity and continuum: "This sense of history guarantees that the values of sentiment, care, effort, the struggle for full humanity, are not meaningless."[4]

Courtesy: Susan Wood.

To establish history in the present of his poems, Purdy must visualize in his imagination the places and objects of the past. We are mistaken though, if, misled by Purdy's reputation as a poet of place, we think of him as a poet of precise visual images. In "Hockey Players" there is no exact picture of arena, or game, or player, but a stunning sense of how the players feel about it. It's part of Purdy's wanting to keep the poem and the thinking open to the unpredictable, that he mistrusts definition, and favours more elusive feelings. Purdy's images are like "piece[s] of mosaic" added "to the coloured meaning inside" ("Tourist Itinerary", *BA* 148). That is, they are indeterminate fragments in themselves, which blend together into an emotional impression. For example, in "Tourist Itinerary", which describes the country north of Kirkland Lake, the most specific images, "raspberries are red earrings", belong to a bizarre metaphor which teases the reader with unlikely associations rather than enabling him to "see" the place.

Purdy's various poems on painting, such as "The Cave Painters" (*ER*, 14), or "The Horseman of Agawa" (*BA*, 145-7), suggest an interest in the visual element of poetry. Purdy praises A.Y. Jackson for his ability to show us the place, to paint the details of this "country of the young":

> You have to stoop a little
> bend over and then look up
> — dull orange on a cliff face
> that says iron deposits
> olive leaves of the ground willow
> with grey silver catkins
> minute wild flower beacons
> sea blue as the world's eye.
>
> ("The Country of the Young", *BA*, 48-9)

Jackson is not a model, however, since Purdy seldom bends to look so closely at the landscape, seldom focusses the eye, and says, like Jackson, " 'Look here —' ". Even in poems whose focus is more limited, such as "Detail" (*BA*, 86) and "Arctic Rhododendrons" (*BA*, 41), there is little that is visually specific, despite Purdy's claim, in the first poem, that "they [the apples] were there and that's all." Not so; their shading in the memory is more important than their form and presence. What Purdy does see clearly are the artifacts through which he may call up the past, such as the "carved ivory swans" which provoke his famous "Lament for the Dorsets" (*BA*, 50-51). But for the most part change, and not the relative permanence of exact imagery, is the essential of his poetry:

> People and things, including Purdy's wife, only exist in the flux of association, are registered in the poem as mental events rather than as substantial entities in their own right. Figurative language is used only in representing his own mental life, his response to his subject or occasion.[5]

The usual nature of that response might be summed up in a phrase from the poem "Old Alex": "No — not exactly anyhow" (BA, 21). Continually, he recognizes, and admits openly in poem after poem, that his words are an approximation. He mocks his own role as poet. His language is by turns delicate and reticent, illiterate and extravagant. The poetic voice Purdy consolidated in *Cariboo Horses*, the voice which has shaped his many poetic discoveries since then, has the not-exactly-anyhow tone of a between-periods interview. The voice is identifiable in very different poems. For example, the half-drunken brawler in "At the Quinte Hotel" (*BA*, 18-19) and the lonely lover in "Arctic Rhododendrons" speak a different language in different rhythms. Yet, their shared sensitivity is suggested by their use of the same image: one is "drinking beer with yellow flowers", while the other knows that "flowers were their [the lovers'] conversation". The taste for the extravagance of the "peculiar fight" in the Quinte Hotel is similar to his creation of a "water floorshow" in the Arctic's "outdoor hotel". And one can hear the same self-deprecating, hesitant voice both in the realization that "poems will not really buy beer or flowers/or a goddam thing", and in the "whispering" letter he sends, almost as an afterthought, at the end of "Arctic Rhododendrons".

There are few certainties, and many variables, in Purdy's world. The voice, saying "not exactly, anyhow" in different words, in a scramble of long and short and run-on lines, which trail off into dashes, and ellipses, and groping repetitions, gives continual expression to the flux in which Purdy is caught. "To be a fool", he writes at the end of "Over the Hills in the Rain, My Dear", "is sometimes/my own good luck". Like the Fool, his nonsense, his irreverence, even his repetitions and his silence, are his intelligence and wisdom. The danger in playing the Fool, of course, is that he may, as in the exaggerated gestures of "Home-Made Beer" (*BA*, 71), appear merely silly. The poet who takes such risks will occasionally be wildly inappropriate. But the honour of the Fool is that, even at his silliest, he is self-aware, and because he includes himself in his own analysis of the world, he disarms criticism.

As Eddie Shack did on the ice, Purdy has made fooling possible in Canadian poetry. He's made it possible for a new generation of younger poets (to whom he has been a model, and often a personal friend) to relax in their poems, to make their personal pasts and their doubts part of the subject and method of their poems. Purdy has shown these poets the poetry in their most prosaic experiences, and the life and meaning in their national and personal histories. As he writes in introducing a group of younger poets:

> There is no one thing in the world I think
> more worthwhile than writing good poems
> — which encompasses and includes all the
> other activities of life.[6]

With Purdy's view of the inclusive poem as model, poetry has become since 1965 almost another national game. "Not exactly, anyhow" Purdy would say. And we'd understand. Writing which encompasses and includes all the other activities of life makes poems that never end. Something will change, something unexpected may happen at any moment. The poet may be checked into the boards, or he may wheel and get a breakaway. He may be "skating zig-zag" from audacious metaphor to sudden curse, or he may be pausing to wonder about "the faces after the game of if" ("English Faculty Versus Students Hockey Game", *SD*, 20). In this game Purdy has become a star, while he still longs for a game of shinny on a frozen pond. As he neatly sums himself up in *In Search of Owen Roblin:*

> Now I am extraordinary
> and I want to be like everyone else again.
>
> (*ISOR*, 64)

[1] Abbreviations are identified in the Bibliography. Where possible, I have quoted from the most recent and most comprehensive Purdy collection, *Being Alive* (1978).

[2] Gary Geddes, "A.W. Purdy: An Interview", *Canadian Literature*, No. 41 (Summer 1969), p. 69.

[3] Al Purdy, "Seven League Skates: An Interview with Brian Glennie", *No Other Country* (Toronto: McClelland and Stewart, 1977), p. 104.

[4] John Lye, "The Road to Ameliasburg", *Dalhousie Review* LVII (Summer 1977), 250.

[5] Ants Reigo, "The Purdy Poem", *Canadian Literature*, No. 79 (Winter 1978), p. 129.

[6] Al Purdy, "Introduction", *Storm Warning: The New Canadian Poets* (Toronto: McClelland and Stewart, 1971), p. 23.

Chronology

Born, once upon a time, in a mythological village called Wooler; mythological because the same village could not now be found. Height and weight, tall and heavy, but unlikely to cause a collapse of athletic stadiums. Education from institutions, nil; from approx. 10,000 books, considerably more; from living, a great deal more. Military career, checkered. Religion, show me. Marital status, almost. Disposition, cloudy and variable. Present occupation, scribbling. Hope for the future, to write one novel.

> Purdy's own biographical note, *Emu, Remember!* (1957)

1918   Born Wooler, Ontario, December 30, son of Alfred and Eleanor Louise Purdy, United Empire Loyalist descendants. Public school education: Dufferin Public School, Trenton, Ontario; Albert Collegiate, Belleville, Ontario; Trenton Collegiate Institute.

1937   Rode the freight trains to Vancouver, and, homesick, hopped an east-bound train the day of his arrival.

1941   Married Eurithe Mary Jane, daughter of James Parkhurst, Belleville, Ontario, November 1. One son, Alfred. World War II service in the RCAF. At the time, he

was publishing poems on the poetry page of *The Vancouver Sun.*

1944   Paid to have 500 copies of his first book of poetry, *The Enchanted Echo,* printed for him by Clarke and Stuart, Vancouver. Three hundred and fifty of these are said to have been destroyed by a company warehouse-man.

1944 - Worked in his father-in-law's taxi business,
1950   and as storekeeper for a steel contractor in Belleville.

1950 - Worked, and tried to organize a union,
1954   in a mattress factory, Vancouver Bedding.

1955   His second book, *Pressed on Sand,* published by Ryerson Press. In October, en route to Europe, he first met Irving Layton and Louis Dudek in Montreal.

1956   Moved from Vancouver to Montreal where he wrote plays and other programs for CBC. First met Milton Acorn.

1957   Moved to Roblin Lake and built his own A-frame house.

1959   Returned to Montreal. Worked at Johnston's Mattress Company. With Acorn founded the magazine, *Moment.*

1960   Returned to Roblin Lake. Used his first Canada Council Fellowship to travel to the Cariboo country, British Columbia.

1962   *Poems for All the Annettes,* his fifth book, showed a marked development in form and voice, and established his reputation.

1964   President's Medal, University of Western Ontario, for best poem by a Canadian printed in a Canadian magazine in the previous year.

1965   *The Cariboo Horses.* Governor-General's Award.

1967   *North of Summer,* the book based on Purdy's trip to Baffin Island on his second Canada Council grant. By 1967, Purdy was generally described in terms such as "the most arresting and significant poet writing in Canada" (Louis Dudek).

1968 - Canada Council Fellowship to Greece,
1969   Italy and England.

1971   Travelled to Hiroshima, Japan.

1973   A.J.M. Smith Award. Travelled to South Africa.

1973 - Writer-in-residence, Loyola.
1974

1975   Travelled to Peru. In 1972, Purdy wrote: "Sometimes, it seems I've been wandering most of my life. Come to think of it, maybe wandering is my life" (*NOC* 172).

1975 - Writer-in-residence, University of Mani-
1976   toba.

1977 - Writer-in-residence, University of Western
1978   Ontario.

(Note: Purdy's view of changing history is, unfortunately, reflected in the published details of his biography, most of which are presented in the spirit of the excerpt from *Emu, Re-*

member!, and subject to startling alterations. See for example, the longer biography in *The Poems of Al Purdy* (1976)).

Comments
by Purdy

"Now you take me
I am a sensitive man
and would you believe I write poems?"
       . . . .
"What kinda poems?"
"Flower poems"
       "At the Quinte Hotel", *BA*, p. 19.

There ought to be a quality in a good poet beyond any analysis, the part of his mind that leaps from one point to another, sideways, backwards, ass-over-the-electric-kettle. This quality is not logic, and the result may not be consistent with the rest of the poem when it happens, though it may be.
       "A.W. Purdy: An Interview", Conducted by Gary Geddes, *Canadian Literature*, No. 41 (Summer 1969), p. 69.

My own country seems to me not aggressive, nor in search of war or conquest of any kind. It is exploring the broken calm of its domestic affairs. Slowly it investigates its own somewhat backward technology, and sets up committees on how not to do what for whom. My country is trying to resolve the internal contradictions of the Indian and French-Canadian nations it contains. In rather bewildered and stupid fashion it stared myopically at the United States, unable to assess the danger to the south — a danger that continually changes in economic character, and finally confronts us from within our own borders.
       "Introduction: The Cartography of Myself", *No Other Country* (Toronto: McClelland and Stewart, 1977), p. 18.

I have been stupid in a poem
I will not alter the poem
but let the stupidity remain permanent
as the trees are
in a poem.
       "Trees at the Arctic Circle", *BA*, p. 43.

The open-endedness is both device and philosophy, but it doesn't bar formalism if I feel like it: i.e., I reject nothing.
       "Purdy: Interview", p. 69.

I don't think of fireworks. I think of saying something. The mistake a great many writers make, it seems to me, is that they spend so much time on new things — change everything, innovation, puns, make it new — and they think more of that than what they're saying.
       "Perspective: An Interview with Al Purdy", Conducted by S.G. Buri and Robert Enright, *CV II* II, 1 (January 1976), 53.

Unlike anonymous airline jets that all look the same to me, the Canadian Argus might be said to possess much the same character as that of its fellow countrymen. Slow and reliable, its cruising speed is only 180 to 220 miles an hour, but an Argus can stay in the air more than twenty-four hours if necessary.
       "Argus in Labrador", *No Other Country*, p. 163.

I write poems like spiders spin webs, and perhaps for much the same reason: to support my existence. I talk, I eat, I write poems, I make love — I do all these things self-consciously.
       "Purdy: Interview", p. 66.

my poems you have failed
but when I have recovered from
this treachery to myself
I shall walk among the hills chanting
and celebrate my own failure
transformed to something else
"On Realizing He has Written some Bad Poems",
       BA, p. 189.

Comments
on Purdy

Purdy's head is in the planets a good deal of the time; the stars and moon have a habit of invading his bedroom and participating in his nocturnal activities.
       Tom Marshall, *Harsh and Lovely Land* (Vancouver: University of British Columbia Press, 1979), p. 93.

Eskimos in the flesh Purdy finds alien and difficult to communicate or identify with (except, of course, the carvers whose work is rejected or broken, the old men, and so forth). It is natives who are dead or extinct that really say something to him, give him a meaningful reflection of himself; it is these whose "broken consonants" he can hear.
       Margaret Atwood, *Survival* (Toronto: Anansi, 1972), p. 95.

Purdy's are poems that go round and round, as Gwen MacEwen puts it, and where they stop nobody guesses. The meaning is all in the tone of the talk and the gathering up of the detail, not in the ending, not in a conclusion.
       D.G. Jones, *Butterfly on Rock* (Toronto: University of Toronto Press, 1970), p. 171.

Al Purdy is the world's most Canadian poet.
       George Bowering, *Al Purdy* (Toronto: Copp Clark, 1970), p. 1.

It is the balancing of these opposing forces of romanticism and realism that governs Purdy's development as a poet.
       Peter Stevens, "In the Raw: The poetry

of A.W. Purdy", *Canadian Literature*, No. 28 (Spring 1966), p. 23.

Purdy is an outstanding shaper of the Canadian past. I say more, however: the peculiar virtue of Purdy's evocations of the past lies not in the skill with which he lays bare certain buried contours of the historical experience. His real gift is instead found in the way his sense of the past grants him a series of metaphors for capturing the present.

Dennis Duffy, "In Defence of North America: The Past in the Poetry of Alfred Purdy", *Journal of Canadian Studies* VI, 2 (May 1971), 18.

Despite the vivacity, the bluster, and the ironic mask, Purdy's essential stance is sentimental and conservative.

John Lye, "The Road to Ameliasburg", *Dalhousie Review* LVII (Summer 1977), 242.

Purdy might be described by a superficial reader as a versifying journalist. He goes on a journey and out of its experiences a book of verse emerges . . . . The interval between conception and creation is often surprisingly short; the poems sometimes seem to serve Purdy as a diary might serve another man.

George Woodcock, "Al Purdy", *Supplement to the Oxford Companion to Canadian History and Literature* (Toronto: Oxford, 1973), p. 272.

Many of Purdy's poems are themselves acts of running and dwelling. For three and a half decades he has hauled his receiving apparatus east and west, north and south through Canada. He has discovered, feature by feature, the thing we knew beforehand, but which we cannot believe until its particulars are made real in words: that we are half spooked and half at home here; that we cannot master the space we have been thrown in, yet are claimed by it and will be at home nowhere else; that we cannot return in time to Europe, yet have learned from it the vocabulary of being human and can at most speak partial sentences of our own in that language.

Dennis Lee, "Running and Dwelling: Homage to Al Purdy", *Saturday Night* LXXXVII (July 1972), 14.

He is deeply and habitually allied with the underdogs in a country and a world that allows bosses to ignore or suppress the underdogs . . . . Along with Milton Acorn he has kept at least some of the nation's poetry at the service of the working man and in the list against middle-class meatballism.

George Bowering, *Al Purdy* (Toronto: Copp Clark, 1970), p. 7.

Can Purdy, whose Canadianism is undoubted,

really distinguish, at say 30,000 feet, our heart-warming, bilingual ice from the pernicious imperialist American ice of Alaska or repressive communist ice of Siberia? I think not.

Mordecai Richler, "Perceptions and Portents: The New Canadian Style", *Saturday Night* LXXXVI, 9 (Sept. 1971), 44.

His intellectual and emotional range is narrower than it needs to be. Although Purdy sees and feels, he does neither with any intensity . . . he turns away, denying his poetry the kind of depth it most lacks.

Ants Reigo, "The Purdy Poem", *Canadian Literature*, No. 79 (Winter 1978), p. 130.

He is desperately and singlemindedly determined to be a foreigner.

George Bowering, "Al Purdy", *Curious* (Toronto: Coach House, 1973).

The flux itself is for Purdy an answer, and a sufficient answer. His grandfather tells him "you don't dast stop/or everything would fall down" and all indications are that Purdy believes him, profoundly. Life is that and nothing more, the movement through — though his imagination longs for it to be more.

Mike Doyle, "Proteus at Roblin Lake", *Canadian Literature*, No. 61 (Summer 1974), p. 16.

Selected Bibliography
Works by Al Purdy

The Enchanted Echo. Vancouver: Clarke and Stuart, 1944.
Pressed on Sand. Toronto: Ryerson, 1955. *(POS)*
Emu, Remember! Fredericton: Fiddlehead, 1956. *(ER)*
The Crafte So Longe to Lerne. Toronto: Ryerson, 1959.
Poems for All the Annettes. Toronto: Contact, 1962.
The Blur in Between. Toronto: Emblem Books, 1963.
The Cariboo Horses. Toronto: McClelland and Stewart, 1965.
North of Summer: Poems from Baffin Island. Toronto: McClelland and Stewart, 1967.
Poems for All the Annettes. Toronto: Anansi, 1968.
Wild Grape Wine. Toronto: McClelland and Stewart, 1968. *(WGW)*
Love in a Burning Building. Toronto: McClelland and Stewart, 1970.
Hiroshima Poems. Trumansburg, N.Y.: Crossing Press, 1972.
Selected Poems. Toronto: McClelland and Stewart, 1972.
On the Bearpaw Sea. Burnaby, B.C.: Blackfish, 1973.
Sex and Death. Toronto: McClelland and Stewart, 1973.
In Search of Owen Roblin. Toronto: McClelland and Stewart, 1974. *(ISOR)*
The Poems of Al Purdy. Toronto: McClelland and Stewart, 1976.

Sundance at Dusk. Toronto: McClelland and Stewart, 1976. *(SD)*

At Marsport Drugstore. Sutton West: Paget Press, 1977.

No Other Country. Toronto: McClelland and Stewart, 1977.

A Handful of Earth. Coatsworth, Ontario: Black Moss Press, 1977.

No Second Spring. Coatsworth, Ontario: Black Moss Press, 1977.

Being Alive: Poems 1958-1978. Toronto: McClelland and Stewart, 1978. *(BA)*

Moths in the Iron Curtain. Sutton West, Ontario: Paget Press, 1979.

Books Edited by Purdy

The New Romans: Candid Canadian Opinions of the U.S. Edmonton: Hurtig, 1968.

Fifteen Winds: A Selection of Modern Canadian Poems. Toronto: Ryerson, 1969.

I've Tasted My Blood: Poems 1956 to 1968. By Milton Acorn. Toronto: Ryerson Press, 1969; also Toronto: Steel Rail, 1978.

Storm Warning: The New Canadian Poets. Toronto: McClelland and Stewart, 1971.

Selected Criticism

Bowering, George. *Al Purdy.* Toronto: Copp Clark, 1970.

Cohn-Sfectu, Ofelia. "The Privilege of Finding an Opening in the Past: Al Purdy and the Tree of Experience", *Queen's Quarterly* LXXXIII (Summer 1976), 262-269.

Doyle Mike. "Proteus at Roblin Lake", *Canadian Literature,* No. 61 (Summer 1974), pp. 7-23.

Duffy, Dennis. "In Defence of North America: The Past in the Poetry of Alfred Purdy", *Journal of Canadian Studies* VI, 2 (May 1971), 17-27.

Lee, Dennis. "Running and Dwelling: Homage to Al Purdy", *Saturday Night,* LXXXVII (July 1972), 14-16.

Lye, John. "The Road to Ameliasburg", *Dalhousie Review,* LVII (Summer 1977), 242-253.

Reigo, Ants. "The Purdy Poem", *Canadian Literature,* No. 79 (Winter 1978), pp. 127-131.

Stevens, Peter. "In the Raw: The Poetry of A.W. Purdy", *Canadian Literature,* No. 28 (Spring 1966), pp. 22-30.

A Note on the Contributor

Laurie Ricou, former Chairman of the English Department at the University of Lethbridge, now teaches at the University of British Columbia. He is the author of *Vertical Man/Horizontal World: Man and Landscape in Canadian Prairie Fiction,* and editor of *Twelve Prairie Poets.* He is currently doing research on Canadian poetry, and on the perception of childhood in Canadian Literature.

Margaret Avison   19

by
Jon Kertzer

The poems of Margaret Avison are often difficult. Although some are conversational in style and direct in meaning, others are puzzling. They compress complicated ideas into a few ambiguous words or a few vivid but unexplained images. They describe strange situations and people; they offer Biblical quotations or historical allusions; they invent words and play with punctuation, spelling and spacing. Some poems are fables or parables: stories that hint at elusive meanings which they refuse to disclose. Others are riddles defying solution, like "Contest", a poem which concludes cryptically:

> Grimly we concede it, who
> would rather do and know,
> until as we are known we know.

The poem never states what we do or what we know, even as it assures us that our knowledge is immense.

In a recent interview, Avison admits that she considers her early poetry too difficult, too "discouraged and inward and thoughtful", and that she now aims for greater "immediacy" in her verse. Her ideal, she says, is to write with the simplicity of a nursery rhyme.[1] But nursery rhymes too can be riddles or parables, and while it is true that her poetry has become less cryptic, it is still dense and intricate, calling for careful thought from the reader. Such intricacy, as Avison commented in several earlier magazine articles, can actually contribute to the value and meaning of a poem. It can force the reader to work, to think, to imagine, and that effort, if provoked and directed by a skillful poet, can make a poem more forceful, thoughtful and imaginative. Modern poetry especially "calls for attack. You pounce, you fasten your teeth in its gristle, you worry it and drag it around in circles, and perhaps you come out on top." And she noted elsewhere that "to penetrate to the essential worth of many writers is a chore, and that the final discovery makes the labor itself a kind of pleasure."[2] The labor to make sense of a poem enhances its significance and our enjoyment. A poem challenges and so promotes understanding. This is the principle of parable and riddle, forms of speech that offer hidden wisdom if only we can puzzle them out. By solving them we sharpen our intelligence. The riddle quoted above plays with the idea of mysterious knowledge acquired only after dogged effort. It asks us how we gain knowledge; what avenues of understanding are open to us. The poem is a contest between competing kinds of knowledge, a struggle for an ultimate wisdom that will illuminate all we do and know. To solve the riddle in the closing lines, we must see it in the context of the whole poem. Through earlier references to Adam and Christ ("The second Adam"), Avison suggests that for her the most luminous understanding comes through the wisdom of Christianity. Men prefer to act rashly with imperfect knowledge ("would rather do and know") until they understand with the redemptive, loving insight that Christ offers ("until as we are know" - by Christ - "we know").

If Avison's poems are sometimes difficult, therefore, it is because she is inquiring into the difficulties of human understanding and perception. If she uses words in playful, puzzling ways, it is because she is concerned with the ways language both permits and hinders understanding. Illumination, in the sense of a powerful, radiant insight, an understanding so brilliant that it clarifies our lives and may even surpass the power of human speech to express, lies at the center of all her poetry. It explains why the image that has dominated her work for forty years is the sun. In her poetry, the sun represents the power of human apprehension at its most acute: the spark of genius, the "golden contemplation" of the brilliant thinker, the "sun-bright gaze" of the visionary, the "inrushing floodlight of imagination" of the poet. The sun permits vision and sustains life. It invigorates the earth in the spring. It dispels the shadows of ignorance, doubt and fear. In her religious poems, the sun is Jesus Christ: the son of God and the "Sun of righteousness" (*Malachi* 4:2). Christ is an "arrowing sunburst" who is "flooding us with . . . risen radiance" and "sunward love". The sun is all these things, and by examining the different ways it illuminates the intricacies of Avison's poetry, we can trace the development of her career.

Margaret Avison began publishing poetry in 1939, and through the 1940's and 1950's contributed poems, articles and reviews to various Canadian and American journals. Some of these poems appeared in her first book, *Winter Sun* (1960), but many have not been republished. During these first twenty years, we find her experimenting with styles and themes, writing in different "voices" as if to discover how her own poetic voice should sound. Sometimes she is solemn, ironic, grim, or comic in tone; but increasingly she adopts a speaking voice. The poems sound as if some one is talking to us, asking us questions, sharing her worries:

> I ask you how can it be thought
> That a little clay house
> Could stop its door
> And stuff its windows forevermore
> With the wet and the wind and the wonderful gray
> Blowing distracted in
> Almost night

> And trains leaving town
> And nine o'clock bells
> And the foghorn blowing far away
> And the ghastly spring wind blowing
> Through thin branches and
> Thin houses and
> Thin ribs
> In a quick sift of
> Precious terrible coldness?

This is Avison's characteristic voice: thoughtful, concerned, melodious, speaking in one, long, carefully crafted sentence. It makes the poem deceptively simple. On first reading, it seems merely a description of a blustery scene. Only a few words — clay, distracted, ribs, sift — and the title, "Death", cause us to look again, and to realize that the fragile house at the mercy of the elements is the human body. Viewed in this way, the question asked by the poet's thoughtful voice becomes another riddle about our ability to withstand life, which is both "wonderful" and "ghastly", and to face death, which is "precious" yet "terrible". Once again, it is a riddle about human understanding. We are asked "how can it be thought": how is it possible to conceive of life and death with all their strength and weakness, desire and fear?

Although it is spring in this poem, the weather is bitter. As the title *Winter Sun* suggests, the season that dominates the earlier poems is cold and bleak, while the sun that offers it heat and vision is feeble. The wintry landscape, though a real place in several poems, usually represents the state of mind in which Avison or the characters in her poems feel frozen. It is a frigid psychological and spiritual state like the one suffered in "Chronic":

> What with the winter solstice
> There is no chance of a strawberry festival
> for months. I cannot think . . . .

In icy mid-winter, there is no chance for celebration or fruitfulness. Life lacks all vitality. It is not even possible to think clearly, as the last line indicates by tapering off into silence, and therefore there is no chance of understanding and so overcoming the disease. This chronic condition prevails because we live in a world "Intent on suicide", as Avison said in her first published poem. Ours is a world devoted to destruction, providing neither sympathy nor love. We are violent and lonely because, confined in ugly cities, we lose contact with nature, a traditional source of vigour and beauty. Nature has a "fierce sub-human peace" that frightens yet attracts us. It is frightening because it is so alien to the human world; it is attractive because it offers the peace and natural wisdom that we desire. It offers the joy of a "strawberry festival". In several poems Avison presents people looking through windows or from observation posts, shut tight in their rooms (and minds), gazing out in hope and fear at a natural scene from which they are separated:

I am inside these days, snug in a job
In one of many varnished offices
Bleak with the wash of daylight
And us, the human pencils wearing blunt.
Soon I'll be out with you,
Another in the lonely unshut world
Where sun blinks hard.

The practice of choosing a vantage point like this is one that Avison develops through her career. In poems like "The Valiant Vacationist", "Perspective" and "New Year's Poem", the perspective establishes the isolation of the individual, directs our attention at the details of the poem, and indicates the need to refine our vision if we are to see clearly. It reveals that that wintry landscape represents both our frozen state of mind and the natural forces that can restore us to health. Thus the phrase "winter sun" indicates both our prison and the means of liberation.

The plight of the lonely individual at the window is also the plight of the world. In several poems, notably "Neverness or The One Ship Beached on One Far Distant Shore", "Dispersed Titles", "Voluptuaries and Others", and "Intra-Political", Avison traces the historical process that has gradually alienated modern man. In them she illustrates how "historical facts fuse with spiritual reality".[3] Changes in history and society, discoveries in science and art are significant because of the way they have changed our view of our inmost selves and our relation to the world we live in. Once that view was richly imaginative and gave our lives value and beauty, but today it is impoverished by reason and rational analysis. We have not only divorced ourselves from nature and its redeeming powers, but in so doing have confined ourselves to one, limited area of human awareness. It is again a problem of knowledge, of how and what we know. Although Avison respects intelligence, she insists that reason alone — which she calls "strait thinking" and the "cramp of understanding" — is not enough. Her own poems appeal to the intellect, but also to our sympathy, emotion and imagination. Reason alone gives a cold, abstract understanding of things. It must be illuminated by imagination, a power that discovers the wonder of the universe. She illustrates the contrast between these two kinds of understanding in "Voluptuaries and Others". The voluptuary is Archimedes in his bath, making a scientific discovery that gives him imaginative insight into the workings of the universe. His discovery is:

The kind of lighting up of the terrain
That leaves aside the whole terrain, really,
But signalizes, and compels, an advance in it.

He illuminates natural law and advances our understanding, but not by explaining away the mysteries of nature or reducing them to rational categories. That, however, is the goal of modern science, which "shows the terrain comprehended", because it "wipes out adjectives, and all shadows". It eliminates all the qualities and mysteries that make the world, not only comprehensible, but wonderful and awesome. And Avison suggests that without wonder and awe our world becomes a winter wasteland.

To explain the need for imaginative understanding and to illustrate the intricacies of its operation, Avison wrote some of her most difficult poems. These include the historical poems noted above and the sonnets "Snow", "Unbroken Lineage", and "Butterfly Bones". In the sonnets she shows the desolate winter of reason animated by the "optic heart". The imagination discovers the marvels of the everyday world making us, like Archimedes, voluptuaries who delight in the sensuousness of experience:

Sedges and wild rice
Chase rivery pewter. The astonished cinders quake
With rhizomes. All ways through the electric air
Trundle candy-bright disks; they are desolate
Toys if the soul's gates seal.

These poems are difficult because their language is so sensuous and fanciful. Through vivid images and playful metaphors they mimic the transformation of vision that is their theme. A river turns to pewter, and sedges chase it through water or through wind that becomes charged, sweet and vibrant. The ground is amazed and invigorated by the life that stirs within it. The reader must realize that his vantage point in this poem is the optic heart which actively recreates and loves, rather than passively observes, what it sees. He must realize that the poetic voice expresses delight in wonders that it discovers by describing them so wonderfully. Thus the imagination discloses the "spiritual reality" present in mere facts; it discovers the spirituality of reality. It illuminates the world through wonder, compassion, love and, ultimately, a sense of the divine. The world becomes miraculous.

In this sense, there is religious awareness present in Avison's early poems, even the most despairing ones. It is felt, for example, in the many references to Christmas: in the dead of winter when the sun is "remote and chilly, but as gold", spiritual hope is born in the person of Christ. Avison reports that in her own life, the rediscovery of Christ occurred on January 4, 1963 when she suddenly became aware of "Jesus of resurrection power . . . sovereign, forgiving, forceful of life".[4] Since then, her poetry has been dominated by this discovery and by the terms that she mentions: resurrection, sovereignty, forgiveness, vigour. She has become an explicitly Christian poet. However, this does not entail a great shift in theme or style in the poems published in *The Dumbfounding* (1966) and *Sunblue* (1978). The shift is in emphasis. The poetic voice grows more confident, sometimes jubilant; the vantage point is less isolated and remote; the source of illumination is more easily identified. The season that dominates the later poems is spring, as the winter sun gives way to "sunblue", the rebirth of the year and the resurrection at Easter:

> Across snow much and sunstriped maples
> honeyed woodsmoke curls and scrolls.
> Sunblue and bud and shoot wait to unlatch
> all lookings-forth, at the implicit touch.

In this quotation from "Released Flow", the snow is melting, the air is sweet and the sap is flowing in the maples. The equivalent of a "strawberry festival" is about to begin: at the sugaring, man will share in the sweet bounty of nature. All these features could have appeared in the earlier poetry. The difference lies in the "implicit touch" that vivifies the scene. It is not just the touch of spring reinvigorating the earth, but the touch of God as well. The divine presence is implied elsewhere in the poem by references to "the extraordinary beyond the hill" and to a "choir" and "scrolls" which turn the country scene into a natural cathedral. The odd phrase "lookings-forth", in the last line, suggests vision and the visionary, looking perhaps at the extraordinary power and glory beyond the hill. In this context, we may be justified in comparing the "implicit touch" to the moment when God first touched Adam and brought him to life. Through all these suggestions the poem hints that the power of nature — a familiar subject in the early poetry — must be sustained and blessed by a greater, supernatural power. Avison scatters such hints through her recent poetry; or she makes the divine touch explicit by incorporating a Biblical echo in the poem. In these ways she demonstrates that simply observing the world sympathetically and imaginatively reveals that it is God's creation. A poem that begins as a description ends as a prayer.

Continuity between early and later poems appears too in Avison's treatment of religious doubt. Her faith in Christ does not turn all her poems into celebrations and prayers. There is still room in them for torment and doubt, especially in *The Dumbfounding* where she examines that joyful-fearful moment when she accepted Christ. That moment offers a new vantage point from which to survey her past suffering and future joy, a point where the darkness of despair meets the light of hope cast by the "Sun of righteousness". She discovers that her pain corresponds to the greater agony undergone by Christ when He was despised, rejected and punished as a man. His humility is a model for her own behaviour, and shows that her suffering need not be in vain, but can be part of a process of purification. By "foresaking all", by accepting her "false-making, burnt-out self" and trusting completely in God, she can be saved from despair just as Christ was resurrected from death. In poems such as "The Word", "Searching and Sounding" and "Natural/Unnatural", she finds that faith can actually be strengthened by doubt. To the believer, "Hope is a dark place / that does not refuse / fear". Hope is vast enough to contain ignorance and fear; hope is necessary precisely because we live in a dark and frightening world. But fear can cleanse the spirit: "the fear of the Lord is clean" says the nineteenth Psalm in a line which Avison interprets in her poem "Ps. 19". "The fear of the Lord is the beginning of knowledge", teaches the *Book of Proverbs:* it can be the start of the quest for enlightenment. Only by going through the darkness can we reach the light. Only by accepting our ignorant, wicked nature can we overcome it. Frequently in these poems, imagery of sun and vision is countered by imagery of darkness, blindness or blindfolds. This last image is appropriate because Christ was blindfolded before the crucifixion, and Avison noted in her own life shortly before her conversion: "I can *feel* the blindfold, the strait jacket — but cannot so far discover where the knot and hooks are to undo them."[5] In her poems — particularly in "The Earth That Falls Away", which is built on the image of a blindfold — she seeks the means of loosening the knots and hooks that obscure her vision:

> Everywhere I look I see emptiness.
> Some snow still has not melted, black
> edging black water-sheeted sidewalk-squares
> that blank you as you watch and walk and wait.

But now she recognizes these dark scenes as painful stages on a pilgrimage that leads to faith.

Her pilgrimage leads through silence as well as through doubt. We have already noted her fascination with the power of words to delight, to communicate ideas and feelings, to spark the imagination. Poetry is a kind of verbal magic whose incantations yield secret knowledge. It "gives words multiple meaning: literal, associative, mimetic, musical", exploiting all the resources of language in order to achieve "an extension of experience to new proportions".[6] But when she is in despair and unable to solve the riddles of her life, her powers of speech falter. When as a Christian poet she wishes to convey the sacredness of the world around her; when she seeks to illuminate the mysteries of Christ's life; when she tries to extend experience until it makes contact with the divine – then words fail her entirely. She is dumbfounded. As a religious poet, she is in a paradoxical position: she is obliged to use ordinary words in extraordinary ways in order to speak about what is inexpressible. Consequently, the experience of darkness outlined above corresponds to an experience of speechlessness, of "wordlessness / plumed along the Dark's way". By passing through darkness, she reaches the sunblue light. By passing through silence, she attains eloquent, lyrical understanding. In several poems ("Words", "The Dumbfounding", "Branches", "Once") the failure of words expresses the faltering of understanding and the painful growth of faith. As part of her struggle to believe she must fall silent, in order to hear a new gospel written in "the new sky's language". Silence purifies her, allowing her to hear the word of the Lord:

> God is, in flesh.
> Now the skies soar
> with song. Heaven utters.

Finally, in the pilgrimage celebrated in Avison's later poetry, she confirms her faith and understanding of God's word in another elaborate way. In the Gospel according to St. John, God is called "The Word": He is the divine power who commanded the creation of the world simply by speaking. In Jesus, "the Word became flesh and dwelt among us" as a humble man. Avison combines these traditional ideas with her belief in the special power of poetry as well as with her love of word play. The result is poetry which is musical, evocative, dense with meaning. In her own fashion, therefore, she is still posing riddles when she says "Let love's word speak plain", in the short elegy "Miniature Biography of One of My Father's Friends". She conveys a great deal in a few words. She refers to her own love and her desire to express it in poetry that is eloquent through its tact and brevity. She speaks of God's love for man and His power to console us in our grief. And she speaks of Christ ("love's word"), who came to earth to offer comfort and salvation. Similarly in the last lines from "The Bible to be Believed", she combines all her ideas about language, eloquence, and silence:

> His final silencing endured
> has sealed the living word:
> now therefore He is voiceful, to be heard,
> free, and of all opening-out the Lord.

Christ's crucifixion ("His final silencing") is expressed as a loss of speech and hope at the moment of greatest despair. But paradoxically, He thereby becomes the "living word" because His sacrifice redeems our sins and secures us eternal life. Therefore He is "voiceful": meaningful, eloquent, jubilant, resounding. His "opening-out" is a disclosure, a revelation, or in the religious term, an apocalypse of all the truths in the Bible, the truths that, the poem declares, are "to be believed".

While not as cryptic as some of her early work, these last poems are still highly intricate. To understand and appreciate them fully, we must recognize their intricacy. We must trace the implications of each word, allusion, and Biblical echo, and admire the craft that has composed them so subtly. All of Margaret Avison's poems require, challenge and encourage the reader's intelligence. They demonstrate that she is one of Canada's most thoughtful and thought provoking poets. Yet she is not coldly intellectual. As we have seen, she is well aware of the limitations and the dangers of the intellect. Rather, she treats ideas sympathetically and passionately. In her poetry, as Robert Gibbs has observed, "Sensation, emotion, and thought fuse."[7] It is this fusion that makes her poems complex, even though her final aim is to "Let love's word speak plain."

[1] "A Conversation with Margaret Avison", University of Toronto Library, videocassette 001085.

[2] *Canadian Forum*, XXIII (September 1943), 143; *Canadian Forum*, XXX (March 1951), 283.

[3] *Canadian Forum*, XXVII (April 1947), 21.

[4] Quoted by Lawrence M. Jones in "A Core of Brilliance: Margaret Avison's Achievement", *Canadian Literature*, 38 (Autumn 1968), p. 51.

[5] *Origin*, IV (January 1962), 11.

[6] *Canadian Forum*, XXVIII (November 1948), 191; *Canadian Forum*, XXIII (September 1943), 143.

[7] Robert Gibbs, review of *The Dumbfounding*, *The Fiddlehead*, No. 70 (Winter 1967), p. 70.

Chronology

1918	Born on April 23 in Galt, Ontario, the daughter of Harold Wilson Avison, a minister, and Mabel Clara (Kirkland) Avison.
	Spent part of her childhood in western Canada.
1939	First published poem, "Gatineau", in *Canadian Poetry Magazine,* IV (December 1939), 19.

1940 Graduated from Victoria College, University of Toronto, B.A. in English.

1940-50 Published poetry in journals and anthologies; worked at various jobs including reviewing, editing, proof-reading, and for various organizations including the Canadian Institute of International Affairs.

1951 Published *History of Ontario*, a children's history text book.

1953 "Night Edition", a short story, published in *Canadian Forum*, XXXII (February 1953), 251-54.

1955 Attended University of Indiana School of Letters.

1956-57 Awarded Guggenheim Fellowship; studied at the University of Chicago Poetry Centre.

1960 Published *Winter Sun*, which received the Governor General's Award for poetry in 1961.

1963 January 4, day of her religious conversion.

Translated Hungarian poetry for *The Plough and the Pen*.

1964 Published *The Research Compendium*, abstracts of theses at the University of Toronto School of Social Work.

Received M.A. from University of Toronto for her thesis: "The Style of Byron's *Don Juan* in Relation to the Newspapers of His Day".

1966 Published *The Dumbfounding*.

1968- Worker at the Women's Missionary Society of the Presbyterian Church.

1978 Published *Sunblue*.

Comments
by Margaret Avison

When he is writing poetry, a person is at his most intense, his most clear-sighted. All his faculties are alert and fused in a single, supreme effort. And the statements he makes at that pressure-point of crystallization must be relatively more valid than the conclusions he may form in his more casual, intellectual, self-conscious moments.
Canadian Forum, XXIV (June 1944), 67.

The precision of Mr. [A.M.] Klein's writing recalls Rubens' painting of lace collars and embroidered vestments, for very rarely does the detail distract one from a poem's total meaning. Like Demosthenes, Mr. Klein knows that everybody's speech is defective, and he has in his humility accepted Demosthenes' corrective pebbles. There are phrases here and there where the pebbles are just a mouthful, for example, the "poised for parabolas" in the very beautiful poem, "Lone Bather". But one almost welcomes these bad moments, because they clearly establish what is wrong with a number of apprentice poets who have learned to mouth the pebbles without realizing what Mr. Klein knows so well – that their whole purpose is to discipline speech into clarity.
Canadian Forum, XXVIII (November 1948), 191.

Any Canadian writer, for example, is aware of a scuffle to find his own words, his own idiom. This generation has grown up with the knowledge that early Canadian poems remain minor poetry because, subject-matter aside, they might have been written in England; some local reservoir remained untapped. Most writers are wary of American poetic idiom now, though certain common features of society and the natural flow from cultural high-pressure areas south of the border make over-wariness an affectation. In trying to find his language-level then, a Canadian poet is trying to assert both an identity and an aesthetic. But the poetic traditions developed elsewhere will never precisely serve his turn.
Poetry, XCIV (June 1959), 182.

The twenties found story-tellers elaborately representational, using a language that was deliberately and traditionally artificial. The revolution impressionism had long since made in painting had not yet had its literary counter-part, but some new way of using words was clearly needed. Two points of departure proved fruitful: how the world seems *to me*, and how I can present the world I see *in its own terms*.
Canadian Forum, XXXIX (March 1960), 276.

There is some corner I have to turn yet, some confronting I have to do — as you would instantly agree, I think, it must come about at the deepest levels in order to find free singing voice. Part of it is a trouble in my aesthetics: that it divorces one from the well [will?] to be "against" any "group". Poetry over against the world - if such could exist, I'd stay on the world's side. . . . In order to find harmony between the "inrushing floodlight of imagination" as writer, with the reader's, I suspect one must listen painfully and long to the experience of living — albeit today an *anti*-poetic one — as amateur listeners know it. Somewhere, in this effort, a wrong self-effacement has taken place in me. I can *feel* the blindfold, the strait jacket – but cannot so far discover where the knots and hooks are to undo them.
Letter to Cid Corman in *Origin*, IV (January 1962), 10-11.

Comments
on Margaret Avison

We hear her called a very intellectual poet, but she begins (and often ends) with the perceiving eye. That eye seems to have been educated on the prairies, even when it looks at the city or the East. Where so much space flows between object and object or between foreground and background, the nature of the picture depends on the focus (long-sighted or short-sighted). . . . Miss Avison likes to stretch and contract and revise our vision, as we watch "the hill and the hoof-pocked dark between / evening star and mushroom".

> Milton Wilson, "The Poetry of Margaret Avison", *Canadian Literature*, No. 2 (Autumn 1959), p. 47.

Subsequent poems during the 40's and 50's, were to explore the ambiguities raised by the question of perceiving, ambiguities of existence and response, inexactnesses which linguistic ambiguities could be employed to convey. So rhyme is largely cast aside, her verse becomes intentionally cryptic. . . . The intellectual response, for all its humanity and variety, continually led to alternatives, unanswered questions, dead ends and dissatisfaction. Words, however useful, were ambivalent, even possibly deceitful, and "Possible" to a mind in search of a liberating absolute, is an unhappy answer. In *The Dumbfounding*, the word becomes much more obviously the Word, a metaphysical source and end, which imbues all.

> William H. New, "The Mind's Eyes (I's) (Ice): the Poetry of Margaret Avison", *Twentieth Century Literature*, XVI (1970), 187, 195-96.

The article concerns the progress of her personal beliefs from the "will to be good" of her early days as a minister's daughter to the present "getting to be where Christ's suffering goes terribly on" of the mature religious poet. She tells how the period between the points — that of church going and Christian service — had given her a "blurry but adequate" portrait of God and a concept of Jesus as "about the best person who ever lived", and how the Bible had become increasingly "opaque" to her as she substituted her invented Christ for the scriptual Person.

She then describes the single most important event in this progress of belief, the occasion of January fourth, 1963, when the "Jesus of resurrection power" revealed Himself to her when she was supposedly alone; says the poet:

> I would not want to have missed what he gave then: the astounding delight of his making himself known at last, sovereign, forgiving, forceful of life.

Under the influence of the refocusing caused by this experience, she looks back upon her previous life and word and notes "how grievously I cut off his way by honouring the artist" and sees her past as a "long willful detour into darkness".

> Lawrence M. Jones, "A Core of Brilliance: Margaret Avison's Achievement", *Canadian Literature*, No. 38 (Autumn 1968), p. 51.

[*The Dumbfounding*] is the richest most original, most fully and deeply engaged and therefore the most significant book of poetry published by a Canadian since the modern movement got under way more than a score of years ago. . . . This quality in Margaret Avison . . . derives from two things: first the peculiar searching intensity of her sensibility and the verbal and metrical adequacy of its expression; and second her synthetic and I think intuitive power of seeing, feeling, *smelling* connections, so that nothing exists alone and nothing is without the significance of everything. Avison's originality, however, is very far removed from the romantic worship of individuality, newness, and difference, and her associational intuition does not lead, as it might with a lesser poet, to transcendentalism or pantheism, but to an affirmation of Christian faith.

> A.J.M. Smith, "Margaret Avison's New Book", *Canadian Forum*, XLVI (September 1966), 132.

Selected Bibliography
Works by Margaret Avison

Poems:

Winter Sun. Toronto: University of Toronto Press, 1960.
The Dumbfounding. New York: Norton, 1966.
Sunblue. Hantsport, N.S.: Lancelot Press, 1978.

Magazine publications:

Combustion, Canadian Forum, Canadian Poetry Magazine, Contemporary Verse, Christianity Today, Credo, Gangila, Here and Now, His, Kenyon Review, Manitoba Arts Review, Origin, Poetry, Queen's Quarterly, Toronto Telegram.

Translations:

The New Reasoner (Summer 1958).
Duczynska, Ilona and Polanyi, Karl, eds. *The Plough and the Pen, Writings from Hungary 1930-1956.* Toronto: McClelland and Stewart, 1963.

Anthologies:

Smith, A.J.M. *The Book of Canadian Poetry.* Toronto: Gage, 1943, 1957.
Sutherland, John. *Other Canadians: An Anthology of the New Poetry in Canada 1940-1946.* Montreal: First Statement Press, 1947.
Klinck, Carl F. and Watters, Reginald E. *Canadian Anthology.* Toronto: Gage, 1955, 1966.
Gustafson, Ralph. *The Penguin Book of Canadian Verse.* Harmondsworth: Penguin, 1958.

Wilson, Milton. *Recent Canadian Verse.* Kingston: Jackson Press, 1959.

Mandel, Eli and Pilon, Jean-Guy. *Poetry 62.* Toronto: Ryerson, 1961.

Wilson, Milton. *Poetry of Mid-Century 1940-1960.* Toronto: McClelland and Stewart, 1964.

Bruce, Phyllis and Geddes, Gary. *Fifteen Canadian Poets.* Toronto: Oxford, 1970.

Nichol, B.P. *The Cosmic Chef and Perloo Memorial Society under the direction of Captain Poetry presents an evening of concrete.* Toronto: Oberon Press, 1970.

Prose (selected):

Review of *New Poems*, by Dylan Thomas. *Canadian Forum*, XXIII (September 1943), 143.

Review of *Day and Night*, by Dorothy Livesay. *Canadian Forum*, XXIV (June 1944), 67.

Review of *The Soldier*, by Conrad Aiken. *Canadian Forum*, XXIV (January 1945), 241.

Review of *Selected Poems*, by Kenneth Patchen and *Residence on Earth and Other Poems*, by Pablo Neruda. *Canadian Forum*, XXVII (April 1947), 21-22.

Review of *The Rocking Chair and Other Poems*, by A.M. Klein. *Canadian Forum*, XXVIII (November 1948), 191.

Review of *The Canticle of the Rose*, by Edith Sitwell. *Canadian Forum*, XXIX (February 1950), 262-63.

Review of *Collected Poems*, by W.B. Yeats. *Canadian Forum*, XXX (February 1951), 261.

Review of *Selected Essays*, by T.S. Eliot, *Canadian Forum*, XXX (March 1951), 282-84.

History of Ontario. Toronto: Gage, 1951.

"Night Edition", *Canadian Forum*, XXXII (March 1953), 251-54.

"Poets in Canada", *Poetry*, XCIV (June 1959), 182-85.

"Callaghan Revisited", *Canadian Forum*, XXXIX (March 1960), 276-77.

The Research Compendium: Reviews and Abstracts of Graduate Research 1942-1962. Toronto: University of Toronto Press, 1964.

"The Style of Byron's *Don Juan* in Relation to the Newspapers of His Day". M.A. Dissertation. University of Toronto, 1964.

Selected Criticism

Colombo, John Robert. "Avison and Wevill", *Canadian Literature*, No. 34 (Autumn 1967), pp. 72-76.

Doerkson, Daniel W. "Search and Discovery: Margaret Avison's Poetry", *Canadian Literature*, No. 60 (Spring 1974), pp. 7-20.

Ghiselin, Brewster. "The Architecture of Vision", *Poetry*, XCIV (1947), 324-28.

Gibbs, Robert. Review of *The Dumbfounding. The Fiddlehead*, No. 70 (Winter 1967), pp. 69-71.

Jones, Lawrence M. "A Core of Brilliance: Margaret Avison's Achievement", *Canadian Literature*, No. 38 (Autumn 1968), pp. 50-57.

Mandel, Eli. Review of *Winter Sun. Queen's Quarterly*, LXVII (1960), 704-05.

Marshall, Tom. *Harsh and Lovely Land.* Vancouver: University of British Columbia Press, 1979.

New, William H. "The Mind's Eyes (I's) (Ice): The Poetry of Margaret Avison", *Twentieth Century Literature*, XVI (1970), 185-202.

Reaney, James. Review of *Winter Sun. Canadian Forum*, XL (March 1961), 284.

Redekop, Ernest. *Margaret Avison.* Toronto: Copp Clark, 1970.

Smith, A.J.M. "Critical Improvisations on Margaret Avison's *Winter Sun*", *Tamarack Review*, No. 18 (Winter 1961), pp. 81-86.

Smith, A.J.M. "Margaret Avison's New Book", *Canadian Forum*, XLVI (September 1966), 132-34.

Wilson, Milton. "The Poetry of Margaret Avison", *Canadian Literature*, No. 2 (Autumn 1959), pp. 47-58.

Zezulka, J.M. "Refusing the Sweet Surrender: Margaret Avison's 'Dispersed Titles' ", *Canadian Poetry*, I (Fall/Winter 1977), 44-53.

Zichy, Francis. "Each in His Prison / Thinking of the Key: Images of Confinement and Liberation in Margaret Avison", *Studies in Canadian Literature*, III (Summer 1978), 232-43.

A Note on the Contributor

Jon Kertzer is an Associate Professor in the Department of English, University of Calgary. His main areas of interest are modern British literature and Canadian literature. He has written on both modern poetry and the modern novel, in particular on: Joseph Conrad, Edward Thomas, A.M. Klein, Marie-Claire Blais, Ernest Buckler, Michael Ondaatje, and Margaret Avison.

Mordecai Richler 20

by
Mark Levene

Courtesy: Jack Clayton.

"The Canadian imagination", Northrop Frye reports, "has passed the stage of exploration and has embarked on that of settlement."[1] In terms of fiction, the process of settlement since the mid-fifties has been exciting and rapid. A number of writers began to build up large bodies of work that grew increasingly complex in philosophical implication, if not always in technical originality. MacLennan, Davies, Laurence, Richler, Munro and Atwood are the figures who have significantly altered the previous cast of English-Canadian fiction with its emphasis on social criticism and its aesthetic hesitations.

Although these novelists have certain themes and attitudes in common, they are highly individual in the images of urban and rural experience they project. Their literary personalities, their public imprints, are also very different. MacLennan is the modest recorder of national tensions, Atwood the flinty, enigmatic poet of gods and ghosts. But only Mordecai Richler has been persistently, even wilfully, controversial in his public assertions as well as in the situations that dominate his fiction.

"You're a stinker who writes garbage about your people", he was told at a synogogue.[2] For this audience history remains an ever-threatening nightmare and literature a weapon that can induce it. Under such pressure the Montreal novels become literary consultations offered by Richler to ubiquitous Nazis and the PLO. Either unwittingly or for his supper Richler also plays Judas at the table of nationalist belief. To some his assaults on the tendency in Canada to inflate our moral and artistic importance are malicious, a repetitive scurrying for American favour and stock-options. Abrasive, alternately arrogant and self-mocking, Richler has made a settled, dispassionate perspective on his work difficult to achieve. "I feel compelled to be an honest witness to what I do know. Involved in this is a recognition of death, a kind of desire for vengeance . . . and a need to be known as well."[3] The "loser's advocate", the vengeful satirist, the scourge of cultural pretensions and orthodoxies should not be expected to have measured, comforting judgments. The risk he takes — if he is not as good as Swift or Lawrence — is that in the end he may seem "a temperamentally ill-natured writer whose art, as essayist or novelist, consists of being as offensive as possible to everyone who comes his way".[4]

Richler shares with other English-Canadian novelists a preoccupation with the inescapability of the past and a disbelief in the free, isolated individual. Like Buckler, Watson, Laurence, and Atwood, Richler (despite his New York intellectualism and stylistic influences) cannot allow his heroes to remain, to affirm, their identities outside some kind of communal bond — family, history, even place. But in a fundamental way Richler's fiction is uncharacteristic. *The Acrobats* (1954) and *Joshua Then and Now* (1980) position their major figures in the aftermath of the Spanish Civil War; *A Choice of Enemies* (1957) depicts left-wing intolerance and the mood of the McCarthy period; Mortimer Griffin in *Cocksure* (1968) is doomed by the rigid individualism and self-containment of his society; Jake Hersh pursues the Horseman pursuing Dr. Mengele, awaits the inevitable "injustice collectors" because he and his contemporaries are "always the wrong age. Ever observers. never participants. The whirlwind elsewhere."[5] The Montreal novels are obviously different, yet the personal strategies they portray must also be seen in the context of Richler's historical obsessions. His insistence on the causes and nightmares of our time was untypical not only of Canadian fiction with its traditional stress on private experience, but of postwar literature in general. When Richler began to write, the retreat from ideology was in full, often undignified, operation. Unlike many other novelists, Richler was not strongly tempted by religion, the special powers of the imagination, or the intricate folds of the psyche. Honest to the guilt of having been spared direct battle in Spain, Normandy, and Palestine, he could not follow his questions about man's values through to piety or a resigned ambivalence. In mood he was closer to Mailer and Camus than to MacLennan, Laurence, or Klein.

Although not a good book in his own eyes, *The Acrobats* remains important because it marked him as a serious novelist and because it initiated the subjects and ideas that drive all of his fiction.[6] One of these ongoing concerns is with the Spanish Civil War as "the last great cause" of the modern age. Throughout his novels the defense of the Spanish republic against Franco, for all the stark violence and betrayals, is regarded as a pure, exact measure of postwar sensibility. Spain represented a clear political choice, the subsequent decade only moral clutter, uncertainty, and depletion. Almost every aspect of Valencian life André Bennett encounters in 1951 suffers in comparison with the past. A rich, vigorous river from the time of Seneca to that of Franco, the Rio Turia now is "a belly of yellow weeds and burnt grass, anaemic sands and stones, trickling mosquito-ridden streams" (p.47). The lives of the characters are similarly diminished. Once a member of a distinguished family, Juanito (who finds another incarnation in *Joshua*) is a pimp, a thief, a male prostitute. Derek, his buyer, actually fought in the civil war, "the only moment of truth he had known" (p.124); his present is loathsome, hovering between vacant affairs and feeble postures.

André, the sub-expressionist son of an implausibly described gentile family in wealthy Westmount, came to Valencia for two reasons: to escape his guilt over the death through abortion of a Jewish girl in Montreal, and because Spain was "where the killing had started", and "you could not paint, not really, so long as men were killing each other so often" (p.56). Like Richler, André is not entirely convinced by Chaim's credo that "salvation is personal" (p.107). He believes that absolute meaning exists, "a shining beauty of a truth" (p. 56), but it cannot be discovered in current political or religious systems. The tension between personal guilt and this instinct for illumination gives André a migraine condition, and he withdraws in fear of madness from the dancing, overarticulate Toni. The resolution he finds is in the recognition of the Nazi, Roger Kraus, as his double and the refusal to submit to his fear of him. The ambiguous tie between hero and antagonist creates a sense of guilt both personal and historical which is larger, more diffuse and suggestive, than the overly specific experience of each one separately. Kraus himself is, however, the most appealing Nazi in modern Jewish fiction. The instrument of his sister's murderous impulses, he would prefer stamp-collecting and skis to the slaughter of Jewish communists. In spirit Theresa is more akin to Richler's later monsters (Karp, Dingleman, Star Maker), though with his barrel chest, spindly legs, and an involuntary capacity for survival, Kraus is their ancestor as well. The ancestry of the novel's style is equally bizarre. Richler had written one "sub-Céline" novel (unpublished) before *The Acrobats*.[7] Here the effect of the French novelist is usually apparent through André's apocalyptic nightmares and his visions of "tossing leaking kidneys heavenwards" (p.141).

The transition from André's historical quest to the Montreal ghetto and Adler family of *Son of a Smaller Hero* (1955) represents a pattern Richler followed in his first four novels — from the place of the individual in the "public" world to his definition within a tightly ordered culture. The predominant influence on the second novel is Lawrence's *Sons and Lovers* both in some striking details (Noah's relationship with his mother and his affair with a Miriam transplanted from England to Montreal) and in its general form as a novel of artistic apprenticeship. At odds with his grandfather, despite their intimacy, and in reaction against the suffocating delusions of his entire family, Noah "was hungering for an anger or a community or a tradition to which he could relate his experience" (p.64). This hunger leads him into Professor Theo Hall's gentile library and Miriam's chaotic emotions. Eventually the search for beauty and freedom drives him towards Europe, his isolated grandfather and ailing, grasping mother left confidently behind.

Although the novel does not doubt the necessity of Noah's hopes, the final emphasis is on the dreadful consequences of his decision. There is no lyrical affirmation of selfhood and artistic potentiality. With Leah's death a corrosive guilt will, we must assume, abort Noah's flight. His "cage" will have none of the felicity or safety he has seen and rejected as the value of the Adler family (p.201). Thus, the novel ends in a parody of the narrative type it had seemed to be. Noah's choice of an independent identity was not made solely within the framework of family and tradition. At Wolf's funeral the rabbi blesses President Eisenhower while cursing the Kremlin, and Noah. Cold War attitudes are never far from the central debates. Aaron Panofsky had gone to Spain and lost his legs; Noah's search on the other hand is private, inward, because no longer are there absolute beliefs, he tells the old Communist, Panofsky (p.88). In fact, Aaron's bitter, angry love for his father is extremely compelling because oblique and understated. Panofsky himself is powerfully rendered, as is Melech's sour reverence and Jenny's production of raisin buns during times of crisis. But Noah's discourses on God, freedom, aunts, and Nazis are intellectually shabby.[8] And the descriptive style is so insistently moral, there are, moreover, so many "smouldering", "prowling" eyes, that it is a wonder the novel is admired with little qualification by a critic like George Woodcock. Set against other instances of modern Jewish fiction — Henry Roth's *Call It Sleep* (1934), Daniel Fuchs' *Williamsburg Trilogy* (1934-7), Bellow's *The Victim* (1947), Adele Wiseman's *The Sacrifice* (1956) — in its approach to immigrant language, its range of conception and felt life, *Son of a Smaller Hero* is clearly meagre.

Among the least known of Richler's works, *A Choice of Enemies* is an evocative, frightening account of the futile choice between politics and the chance of personal fulfilment. At the outset Norman Price is still managing to sustain a balance of commitments. He is at peace with his conscience for having refused to testify for McCarthy, he is a humane, undogmatic Marxist who deeply enjoys his friends, most of them exiled from Hollywood by their leftist attitudes. Above all, Norman reveres his brother, Nicky, for his grace, vigour, and innocence. But the modest equilibrium of his life in London is overturned by the power the past inevitably wields over the present. In the earlier novels the destructiveness of the past seemed largely accidental, not yet a deterministic principle. Here, reflected primarily in the darkness of the war, it becomes an impersonal, unending force that annihilates every motion towards contentment and virtue. The past is honed and narrowed to the figure of the East German refugee, Ernst Haupt, one of the most fascinating and sympathetic portraits in Richler's fiction. Once part of the Hitler and Stalinist tribes, Ernst is compelled now solely by the demands of survival. He has murdered, stolen, lied, prostituted everything but his ability to sing Mozart and Schubert — all in the service of amoral, purposeless endurance. Ernst kills Nicky in a brawl, then makes his way to London where, like a selective plague, he finds Sally, Norman's one remaining hope. As a gesture of good will towards the lovers, Norman makes his choice of enemies, but this, like all his subsequent assertions, is immediately undermined by a nemesis from the past. Gestures have a strange significance for Richler at this time. In another age, identified again with the Spanish Civil War and Norman's father, they had meaning as expressions of complete people. In 1956 they are at best travesties of intention. A gesture of friendship leads to Nicky's death; Karp, haunted by his own corner of the war, goads Norman into a loss of memory, not in malice but out of a perverse sense of loyalty and romance. When he recovers, Norman marries an English girl because it is "time to weed one's private garden", but the "small virtues" he has chosen are illusions (p.215). Vivian perpetuates the destruction that brought Norman to her in the first place. A similar continuity faces Ernst. His survival skills temporarily at bay, Ernst saves the life of a Jewish shopkeeper, then is blackmailed into marriage by the daughter of a Nazi. Her embrace is the final curse of history on him.

With these details Richler brought the subject of personal and historical paralysis into virtually complete pessimism. Each of the three novels is bleaker than the last; nothing the characters can do or feel is untainted, creative in the simplest human terms. Fortunately, by retracing his steps down the Main and St. Urbain Street, perhaps by finding a way to reappraise his entire background, Richler was able to change the tone and style — though not strictly the themes — of his fiction. *The Apprenticeship of Duddy Kravitz* (1959) expands into magnificent, if ambiguous, comedy the halting resolutions of the previous works. Duddy's obsession with his land is a private vision which, for the first time in Richler's fiction, arises from love rather than an intimation of freedom or a groping for stability. The question critics usually pose about the novel is whether Duddy is to be admired or denounced. In Richler's own mind, and in the novel, the answer is clear. "He is supposed to end up, in spite of all the ruthless and rotten things he's done, so that you think, well, yes, this is another human being."[9] Duddy is gullible and conniving, compulsively energetic and malicious, "prepared for instant struggle, the alibi for a crime unremembered already half-born, panting, scratching, and ready to bolt if necessary" (p.176).

Prey to the intellectual stereotypes of the educated, he seeks his identity in the approval and love of family. Capable of selfless devotion to them, Duddy tortures the feelings of Virgil and Yvette who, ironically, already see him as a "somebody". But because they are in essence alien creatures, *goyim*, the trust Duddy has given them cannot be translated into a recognition of their separate reality. He is precisely what Uncle Benjy perceived: a "scheming little bastard" and a "fine, intelligent boy underneath" (p.279). There is little psychological complexity about Duddy's motives. Denied the assurance of genuine parents, he wants to feel worthy of his grandfather's attention. The novel centres not only on the route he takes to fulfil Simcha's dictum that "a man without land is nobody" (p.48), but also on the degree of responsibility we can legitimately attribute to Duddy. Simcha draws him into his life out of bitterness with Benjy, and it is in anger at the failures he shares with his sons that he voices an abstract, ill-considered principle to the seven-year-old boy. Without cruelty or understanding, Simcha has manoeuvred Duddy for his own comfort; he has provided the first instance of confusion between human and social values. The letter Benjy writes his nephew is also unconsciously destructive. It helps to redirect Duddy to acquire the land just as he is beginning to settle awkwardly into the shape of "a gentleman, a *mensh*" (p.279). Less intrusively than in *A Choice of Enemies,* Richler is still emphasizing the erosion caused by "gestures", the ruinous consequences of ordinary, often caring, interference. Duddy forges Virgil's signature, the crime is his, but Simcha, Benjy, and Max moved some of the muscles.

The tones of the conclusion are, therefore, far from straightforward. Duddy expels the Boy Wonder from his land, yet for once Dingleman seems merely an unpleasant man, not a symbolic figure of monstrous evil. Simcha judges his grandson fairly, but is also judged by him for his severe treatment of Benjy. The sense of betrayal Duddy expresses to Yvette, though misdirected, is not a total delusion. These nuances intensify and deepen our sadness at the loss of Duddy's humanity and his submission to a corrupt, abstract, but necessary myth. To some extent, however, the sombreness of Duddy's fate is mitigated by the remarkable comic energy in the novel: the Commencement scene, the screening of "Happy Bar-Mitzvah, Bernie!", the characters of Peter John Friar and Duddy himself in his more endearing moments. Morally *Duddy Kravitz* is close to the earlier novels; technically it points towards the "black comedies" and the later blending of realism and satire in *St. Urbain's Horseman.*[10]

Anti-semitism was the charge often levelled at Richler for *Duddy Kravitz* ("to submit to that or be inhibited by that would be their ultimate triumph", he notes about those who are "beyond the pale"[11]). The most Richler can be accused of in *The Incomparable Atuk* (1963) is a mild spitefulness and prejudice against Toronto's claim to cultural importance. In his own terms "more a spoof" than a full satire animated by grotesque characters and the logic of extreme situations, *Atuk* is obviously a practising of skills, a transitional work.[12] Nevertheless, some of the shots are splendidly executed. Nathan Cohen, who had been patronizing and, one hopes, deliberately obtuse in his 1956 interview with Richler, is splayed here as Seymour Bone, "Canada's Rudest Drama Critic" (p.63). He returns incognito to enjoy the play he had crucified in print the night before. "Canada's Darling" swimmer, Bette Dolan, becomes addicted to the patriotic, genital "help" Atuk has contrived to receive from her (p.23). These episodes, like the picture of the undercover Mountie in drag who comes "to adore his new silk lingerie" (p.75), are enjoyable but have no clear moral centre. More directly linked with Richler's abiding vision of society is his conception of Atuk as a Jew and Buck Twentyman as an emblem of amoral, institutional self-interest. But Atuk's "Jewishness" amounts largely to a sequence of jokes — "For an Eskimo boy to make his mark in this world . . . he must be brighter, better, and faster than other boys" (p.53) — and Twenty-man's menace is too vague, despite the precision of the blade he arranges to fall on Atuk's neck.

The transition to the black comedies was neither sharp nor sudden. "That strain was always present in the novels", Richler has said: for example, the epileptics' magazine in *Duddy Kravitz,* even some of the crowd scenes in *The Acrobats.*[13] Furthermore, *Cocksure* was written as a break from the pressures of completing *St. Urbain's Horseman.* The satires and the "novels of character" are, then, continuous, not separate phases of Richler's career. With *Cocksure* his talents for extravagant farce and grotesque parody are in full, subversive array. Never popular in Canada, the novel's extremes of behaviour and event place it, sometimes uneasily, in the tradition of Swift and Waugh. Richler's earlier characters were all guilty for very specific acts or omissions. In *Cocksure,* trapped by the "life-style" dogmas of a militantly liberated society, Mortimer Griffin is guilty just for what he is. The "square", the "honourable man", for whom divorce and oral sex are not innate truths, he is the "true Jew" exiled and ultimately executed for his differences.[14] The double irony is that the charge of concealing his Jewishness actually precipitates Mortimer's conflicts with the vicious orthodoxies of his pop, swinging, Nazi-infested world.

There are some wildly funny steps in his fall to isolation and martyrdom. Anxious about the ethnically inferior "size of his thingee" (p.86), Mortimer stockpiles a vast quantity of sex aids and becomes a legend with the druggist. He is appalled by the Beatrice Webb school and Miss Ryerson's solution to the educational malaise in England. The novel's sexual comedy is virtually constant, for the simple reason that sex, especially the contemporary, political sort, is an immediate form of control and power. "Now, why do you want to get into bed with me . . . when your father's out?" Joyce asks her eight-year-old son (p.81). But the humour around Mortimer's bland sanity quickly becomes grim. Joyce can grow great clumps of hair, but only the Star Maker, "Blessed Be His Name" (p.5), can propagate himself. "The revolution eats its own", he tells Mortimer. "Capitalism recreates itself" (p.135). With his "spare-parts men" and looking forward to Mortimer's "marvy lymphatic system" (p.133), he is a little bit of everything, ethnic, sexual, financial, the physically indeterminate multi-national. A murderer and a mother-to-be, although he is allowed to say too much, he is not an unimpressive monster.[15] The Star Maker is, of course, thoroughly symbolic — of ultimate survival and individualism — but his effectiveness derives cumulatively from a range of more accessible satirical creations. His absolute devotion to self is the grotesque extension of all the fixed responses and conceptions of behaviour Richler attacks in *Cocksure:* Shalinsky's paranoia, Polly's cinema fantasies, Lord Woodcock's belief in good Germans. The Star Maker is the consequence of a world that has renounced the past and small, human decencies. We comprehend this horror as we acquiesce in the logic of nightmares.

Our assent to *St. Urbain's Horseman* (1971) is richer, more varied, and essentially comforting. Probably Richler's best work, in its intellectual resonance this "novel of character" is among the finest in Canadian literature. It was an extremely difficult book for Richler to write. The structure he developed was more elaborate than before; meditation and event move between past and present instead of following a predominantly linear arrangement. The conception of Jake Hersh was also highly complex. Like Mortimer Griffin, Jake is guilty by nature, by virtue of his temperament and attitudes. But his guilt is more firmly rooted in history. Jake's accidental exclusion from the Spanish Civil War, from the holocaust and Vietnam, intensifies "his Jewish nightmare", invokes the novel's terrible refrain ("Mengele cannot have been there all the time. . . In my opinion, always. Night and day" [p. 67]), and confirms his need of the Horseman.[16] "On those rare evenings when he brimmed over with well-being" (p. 65), the terror struck — of a renewed holocaust, his children butchered, his fragile world destroyed. These visions are intrinsically different from the impositions of history on individual life Richler had created in *The Acrobats* and *A Choice of Enemies.* Central to Jake's reflections on family, career, and "the Germans' second coming" (p.287) is an intense awareness of common mortality, of the rot afflicting all life. Lying beside Nancy, "he could think only of the obtruding bones beneath the wasting flesh" (p.273). The moods of Jake's lamentations modulate from horror at his wife's frailty and anguish at his father's death to ritual surveys of his body's operations.

The novel's preoccupation with human vulnerability is, in fact, one reason for the reappearance of Duddy Kravitz. For Richler the earlier Duddy had "enormous strength in that he's not . . . sufficiently perceptive or sensitive to believe in his own death".[17] Here Duddy too is being "muzzled", shadowed by death. He and Jake are aging, frustrated with the energy and years they have consumed. Duddy can appease his sense of isolation by writing a cheque; however, Jake's payments are larger, a constant process of self-extortion. His guilt, for financial success but artistic mediocrity, for his political safety, for being a rotten son and a mortal father, has two expressions: the acceptance of Harry Stein as an "injustice collector" and the fantasy of Joey Hersh, "the avenging Horseman", veteran of Spain and Palestine, now hunting the tireless Dr. Mengele through the jungles of Paraguay (p.31). Harry is a physical threat whose mind is eaten up by sexual frustration and amoral intelligence, but he exclaims to Jake: "I'm not getting enough of anything, don't you see? And most of the things I want I'm already too old to enjoy" (p.351). This dual claim of mortality and social justice Jake finds impossible to reject.

If Harry is Jake's penance, the Horseman is his strategy for surviving the conflicts between private and historical responsibility. In the earlier novels these categories were absolute and irreconcilable because the choice had to be "real", occurring in the observable world. But like Ibsen and O'Neill before him, Richler has discovered the creativity of illusion. The revelations about Joey's life barely impinge on Jake's imagination since the Horseman serves a purpose beyond immediate, actual experience. He ties together for Jake past, present, and future, Madrid in 1937, Montreal in 1967, the concentration camps and his elegant London home, antitheses that otherwise could not be balanced. Briefly the letter announcing Joey's death makes Jake assume the role of the Jewish defender himself, but if Jake is to endure, the Horseman can only be "presumed dead" (p.436). In imagination and daily life Jake's commitments have to be to family and the work he has yet to create. The reserves of feeling are too low, the years too few, the nightmares too exact, for Jake to become the hunter of evil. So the Horseman continues to ride, the spirit of Jake's virtue and necessary limitations.

Richler's most recent novel, *Joshua Then and Now,* is less unified in tone, character, and narrative method. Parts, notably Reuben's approach to Joshua's sexual education, are spendid comedy, and in the more solemn relationships Richler seems poised to detail qualities of behaviour he had not attempted in the other novels. But he finally withdraws into clichés of Jewish-gentile romance. Indeed, the suspicion grows that all the untidy threads of Joshua's life are being pressed into compact resolutions. The line of monsters from Roger Kraus to Harry Stein runs out in Dr. Mueller who dresses like a cowboy, and Joshua's obsession with the Spanish Civil War is cancelled because the Spaniards now subscribe to tourism and hanker after pornography. "He paused to set his wristwatch to Montreal time. Home time. Family time" (p.397). In Richler's fiction the boundaries of European and Canadian experience, the bonds between youth and age, then and now, were never crossed with such ease, at such little human cost.

[1] Northrop Frye, "Conclusion", *Literary History of Canada: Canadian Literature in English*, gen. ed. and intro., Carl F. Klinck (Toronto: University of Toronto Press, 1965), p. 837.

[2] Richler, "Foreword", *Hunting Tigers Under Glass: Essays and Reports* (London: Panther, 1971), p. 10.

[3] Richler, in *Eleven Canadian Novelists*, Graeme Gibson, interviewer (Toronto: Anansi, 1973), p. 269.

[4] Thomas R. Edwards, review of *Joshua Then and Now*, *The New York Times Book Review* (June 22, 1980) p. 11.

[5] Richler, *St Urbain's Horseman* (New York: Bantam, 1972), p.80. All subsequent references to Richler's works will be included in the text. Other editions cited here are: *The Acrobats* (London: Sphere, 1970); *Son of a Smaller Hero* (Toronto: McClelland and Stewart, 1965); *A Choice of Enemies* (Toronto: McClelland and Stewart, 1977); *The Apprenticeship of Duddy Kravitz* (Harmondsworth: Penguin, 1964); *The Incomparable Atuk* (Toronto: McClelland and Stewart, 1971); *Cocksure* (New York: Bantam, 1969); *Joshua Then and Now* (Toronto: McClelland and Stewart, 1980).

[6] Richler, in Gibson interview, p. 276, p. 291.

[7] Richler, "A Sense of the Ridiculous", *Shovelling Trouble* (London: Quartet, 1973), p. 31.

[8] Cf. G. David Sheps, "The Novels of Mordecai Richler: An Interpretation", *Mordecai Richler*, ed. G. David Sheps (Toronto: McGraw-Hill Ryerson, 1971), p. xviii.

[9] Richler, in Gibson interview, p. 292.

[10] See George Woodcock, "Richler's Wheel of Exile", *The Rejection of Politics* (Toronto: New Press, 1972), p. 145.

[11] Richler, in *Conversations with Canadian Novelists*, 2, Donald Cameron, interviewer (Toronto: Macmillan, 1973), p. 118.

[12] Richler, in "Black Humour: An Interview with Mordecai Richler" by John Metcalf, *Journal of Canadian Fiction*, III, 1 (Winter 1974), 74.

[13] *Ibid.*

[14] *Ibid.*, p. 75. See also Leslie Fiedler, "Some Notes on the Jewish Novel in English", in *Mordecai Richler*, ed. G. David Sheps (Toronto: McGraw-Hill Ryerson, 1971), p. 104.

[15] Cf. George Woodcock, "Richler's Wheel of Exile", *The Rejection of Politics* (Toronto: New Press, 1972), p. 140. See also George Woodcock, *Mordecai Richler* (Toronto: McClelland and Stewart, 1971), p. 53.

[16] See also John Moss, *Sex and Violence in the Canadian Novel: The Ancestral Present* (Toronto: McClelland and Stewart, 1977), p. 135.

[17] Richler, in Gibson interview, p. 290.

Chronology

1931	Born in Montreal 27 January to Moses Isaac Richler and Lily Rosenberg; father worked in junk yard, mother from a literary-religious family.
	Educated at Baron Byng High School and Sir George Williams University.
1951	Leaves university without degree, travels to France and Spain, visits England. Writes at least one unpublished novel. Stories appear in *Points* (Paris).
1953	Returns to Montreal. Revises *The Acrobats*.
1954	Publishes *The Acrobats*, his first novel in print.
1955	Publishes *Son of a Smaller Hero*.
c.1957	Settles in London, England.
1957	Publishes *A Choice of Enemies*.
1959	Receives Canada Council Junior Arts Fellowship.
1959	Publishes *The Apprenticeship of Duddy Kravitz*.
1960	Marries Florence Wood; have 3 sons, 2 daughters.
1961	Guggenheim Fellowship, Creative Writing.
1963	Publishes *The Incomparable Atuk*.
1966	Receives Canada Council Senior Arts Fellowship.
1968	Publishes *Cocksure*.
1968-69	Writer-in-Residence, Sir George Williams University.
1969	Governor General's Award.
1969	Receives *Paris Review* Humour Prize.
1971	Publishes *St. Urbain's Horseman*.
1972	Returns with family to live in Montreal.
1972	Governor General's Award.
1972	Visiting Professor, Carleton University.
1977	Re-visits Spain, publishes travel book.
1980	Publishes *Joshua Then and Now*

Comments by Mordecai Richler

I am not a European writer and I couldn't become one if I stayed here twenty-five years. All my attitudes are Canadian; I'm a Canadian; there's nothing to be done about it.

Cohen interview, 1956 (Sheps, p. 23).

I came back in 1972. I'd been abroad 20 years. I had always intended to return and I felt after I finished *St. Urbain's Horseman* that I couldn't write another novel set in England.

New York Times interview, 1980 (p. 11).

My own novels break down into two categories readily. There are the naturalistic novels and the straight satires and I find it refreshing to go from one to the other. I guess my ultimate interest is in the novel of character really.

Metcalf interview, 1973 (p. 73).

Satire is a pretty difficult thing to write, much more difficult in many ways than *St. Urbain's Horseman.* You forego enlisting the reader's sympathy, and that's a pretty big thing to give up, because you're presenting somebody with the book and you're saying everyone in it is rotten in one way or another and so they don't engage, and it's difficult to keep the reader's attention.
Cameron interview, 1971 (p.119).

Well I think that the greatest novelist in the English language in our time was Evelyn Waugh . . . And I also came very early to like Céline enormously.
Gibson interview, c. 1969 (p. 278).

The style is me, it's there. It's been arrived at, for better or worse. It's only there sporadically in the early work, but then it evolved and that's the way I write.
Cameron interview, 1971 (p. 125).

But something almost nobody has grasped is that running through all my novels, I think, there has been a persistent attempt to make a case for the ostensibly unsympathetic man.
Cameron interview, 1971 (p. 117).

I think there's better writing coming out of Canada now than there was 25 or 30 years ago. I think Alice Munro, Robertson Davies and Margaret Atwood are very talented writers. Of course, there's a lot of nationalist nonsense as well in the country.
New York Times interview, 1980 (p. 22).

There has been a collapse of absolute values, whether that value was God or Marx or gold. We are living at a time when superficially life seems meaningless, and we have to make value judgements all the time, it seems in relation to nothing.
Cohen interview, 1956 (p. 38).

We've lived through two great horrors, in our time, the murder of the Jews and Hiroshima . . . and one must, you know, figure out where he stands in relation to it just as at one time you had to figure out where you stood in relation to the Communist Party.
Cameron interview, 1971 (p. 125).

I write out of a kind of disgust with things as they are . . . .
Gibson interview, c. 1969 (p. 271).

The women in my novels tend to be rather idealized creatures, and not written about with the greatest confidence, I'm afraid.
Gibson interview, c. 1969 (p. 288).

The more we disentangle ourselves from the hypocrisies of our background, the more chaotic our life becomes. Now possibly too much was thrown overboard, and even with its built-in hypocrisies there was a system of some kind in the past.
Gibson interview, c. 1969 (p. 289).

I don't believe in Consciousness I, or Conscious-II, or Consciousness III. That belongs to *Vogue* magazine, like McLuhan. Forget it, it's yesterday's newspaper. Really. We're all going to die, and most things haven't changed. That's what I think, anyway.
Cameron interview, 1971 (p. 126).

Comments on Mordecai Richler

Mordecai Richler is alone [among Canadian novelists] in asserting that he deals with the larger issues of our age, and from the vantage-point of one raised and spiritually tutored in Canada . . . .But is Mordecai Richler really in touch with his time?
Nathan Cohen, 1957 (Sheps, pp. 46-47).

Richler is a *real* writer, which is rare, and even a *good* writer, which is rarer still. In fact, one is so tempted to call him a *great* writer that it is a puzzle, on reading him once again, that one can't. What does Richler lack that distinguishes, say, a Tolstoy?
Barbara Amiel, 1980 (*Maclean's,* p. 51).

He represents the old consciousness, she [Atwood] represents the new. He's still trying to exorcise his past, our past, she's searching through it to find our roots.
Christina Newman, 1972 (*Maclean's,* p. 88).

Richler belongs (as Brian Moore does) in society, and he has enough nerve to refuse alienation.
Hugo McPherson, 1965 (Sheps, p. 120).

One of the most interesting facts about these novels is that the ostensible heroes and the ostensible villains share many qualities.
G. David Sheps, 1970 (p. xv).

If *St. Urbain's Horseman* represents the thematic reconciliation of exile and ghetto . . . it also represents the reconciliation of the two manners that are in conflict or at least in competition in Richler's earlier writings: the fantastic (belonging to his nightmares of grotesque monsters and largely linked to England and the film world) and the realistic (linked — though not exclusively — to the scenes of Montreal life).
George Woodcock, 1971 (*Politics,* pp. 144-145).

Another aspect of his work . . . makes Richler more dangerous than he seems perhaps even to himself: his concern with exile, his compulsion to define all predicaments in terms of that hope-

lessly Jewish concept, and his implicit suggestion that, after all, we are — everyone of us — Jews.
Leslie Fiedler, 1968 (Sheps, p. 104).

Selected Bibliography
Works by Mordecai Richler

Books

The Acrobats. London: André Deutsch, New York: Putnam's, 1954. London: Sphere, 1970.
Son of a Smaller Hero. London: André Deutsch, 1955. Toronto: McClelland and Stewart, 1965.
A Choice of Enemies. London: André Deutsch, 1957. Toronto: McClelland and Stewart, 1977.
The Apprenticeship of Duddy Kravitz. London: André Deutsch, Boston: Little Brown, 1959. Harmondsworth: Penguin, 1964. Toronto: McClelland and Stewart, 1969.
The Incomparable Atuk. London: André Deutsch, Toronto: McClelland and Stewart, 1963; as *Stick Your Neck Out.* New York: Simon and Schuster, 1963.
Cocksure. London: Weidenfeld and Nicolson, Toronto: McClelland and Stewart, New York: Simon and Schuster, 1968. New York: Bantam, 1969.
St. Urbain's Horseman. London: Weidenfeld and Nicolson, Toronto: McClelland and Stewart, New York: Knopf, 1971. New York: Bantam, 1972.
Joshua Then and Now. Toronto: McClelland and Stewart, New York: Knopf, 1980.
The Street (stories). Toronto: McClelland and Stewart, 1969. London: Weidenfeld and Nicolson, 1972.
Hunting Tigers under Glass: Essays and Reports. Toronto: McClelland and Stewart, 1968. London: Weidenfeld and Nicolson, 1969. London: Panther, 1971.
Shovelling Trouble (essays). Toronto: McClelland and Stewart, 1972. London: Quartet, 1973.
Notes on an Endangered Species and Others (essays). New York: Knopf, 1974.
Ed., *Canadian Writing Today.* Harmondsworth: Penguin, 1970.
Jacob Two-Two Meets the Hooded Fang (juvenile). Toronto: McClelland and Stewart, New York: Knopf, 1975.
Images of Spain (travel, photographs by Peter Christopher). Toronto: McClelland and Stewart, New York: Norton, 1977.
Screenplays: *No Love for Johnnie,* 1961; *Life at the Top,* 1965; *The Apprenticeship of Duddy Kravitz,* 1974; *Fun with Dick and Jane,* 1977.

Interviews

Cameron, Donald. "Mordecai Richler: The Reticent Moralist", *Conversations with Canadian Novelists,* 2. Toronto: Macmillan, 1973.
Cohen, Nathan. "A Conversation with Mordecai Richler", *Tamarack Review,* No. 2 (Winter 1957), pp. 6-23 [In Sheps collection.]
Gibson, Graeme. *Eleven Canadian Novelists.* Toronto: Anansi, 1973.
Goodman, Walter. *New York Times Book Review* (June 22, 1980), pp. 11, 22-24.
Metcalf, John. "Black Humour: An Interview with Mordecai Richler", *Journal of Canadian Fiction,* III, 1 (Winter 1974), 73-76.

Selected Criticism

Books

Sheps, G. David, ed. *Mordecai Richler.* Critical Views on Canadian Writers. Toronto: McGraw-Hill Ryerson, 1971.
Woodcock, George. *Mordecai Richler.* Toronto: McClelland and Stewart, 1971.

Parts of Books, Bibliography, and Articles on Richler

Amiel, Barbara. "Desperate Encounters of Middle Age", *Maclean's* (June 9, 1980), p. 51. [Review of *Joshua Then and Now.*]
Cohen, Nathan. "Heroes of the Richler View", *Tamarack Review,* No. 6 (Winter 1958), pp. 47-60. [In Sheps collection.]
Ferns, John. "Sympathy and Judgement in Mordecai Richler's *The Apprenticeship of Duddy Kravitz*", *Journal of Canadian Fiction,* III, 1 (Winter 1974), 77-82.
Fiedler, Leslie. "Some Notes on the Jewish Novel in English", *The Running Man,* I, 2 (July-August 1968), pp. 18-21. [In Sheps collection.]
Kattan, Naim. "Mordecai Richler: Craftsman or Artist", *Canadian Literature,* No. 21 (Summer 1964), pp. 46-51. [In Sheps collection.]
Lecker, Robert and Jack David, eds. *The Annotated Bibliography of Canada's Major Authors,* I, Downsview: ECW Press, 1979.
Mathews, Robin. "Messiah or Judas: Mordecai Richler Comes Home", *Canadian Review,* I, 1 (February 1974), 3-5.
McPherson, Hugo. "Fiction 1940-1960", *Literary History of Canada: Canadian Literature in English.* Gen ed. and intro. Carl F. Klinck. Toronto: University of Toronto Press, 1965, pp. 712-715. [In Sheps collection.]
McSweeney, Kerry. "Revaluing Richler", *Studies in Canadian Literature* (Summer 1979), pp. 120-131.
Moss, John. *Sex and Violence in the Canadian Novel: The Ancestral Present.* Toronto: McClelland and Stewart, 1977.
Newman, Christina. "In Search of a Native Tongue", *Maclean's* (September 1972), p. 88. [Review of *Surfacing* by Margaret Atwood and *Shovelling Trouble* by Richler.]
Scott, Peter Dale. "A Choice of Certainties", *Tamarack Review,* No. 8 (Summer 1958), pp. 73-82. [In Sheps collection.]
Sheps, G. David. "Waiting for Joey: The Theme of the Vicarious in *St. Urbain's Horseman*", *Journal of Canadian Fiction,* III, 1 (Winter 1974), 83-92.
Warkentin, Germaine. "Cocksure: An Abandoned Introduction", *Journal of Canadian Fiction,* IV, 3 (1975) 81-86.
Woodcock, George. "Richler's Wheel of Exile", *The Rejection of Politics.* Toronto: New Press, 1972.

A Note on the Contributor

Born in Winnipeg, Mark Levene was educated at the University of Manitoba (United College), the University of Toronto, and in London, England. He is now Associate Professor of English at Erindale College, University of Toronto, where he teaches Canadian literature and modern fiction. He writes on political and historical literature, particularly the novels of Koestler, Hughes, and Richler.

Margaret Laurence 21

by
Frederick Sweet

Courtesy: Eedie Steiner.

The African Stories

All of Margaret Laurence's African stories involve what was central to African experience when the author was there: the winding down of colonialism and the emergence of independent African countries. Although Laurence shows an acute awareness of the casualties — both African and European — of such social and political upheaval, her stories have a fundamentally optimistic thrust, reflecting both contemporary attitudes and her own idealism at the time. We might begin with her first novel, *This Side Jordan*, which appeared in 1960, and which is set in the Gold Coast in the transitional period of Ghanaian independence. The characters are arranged perhaps somewhat too neatly — in two opposing groups, African on one side, English on the other. The central African character, Nathaniel Amegbe, a teacher, is caught between native African traditions and western mores, and must learn to accommodate himself to a radically new situation while not utterly rejecting the old. Likewise, the English businessman, Johnnie Kestoe, must attempt to come to terms with a past which haunts him; in the process, he discovers, despite himself, the humanity of the Africans he has so despised.

The novel also features the births of two babies, one black, the other white. At the end of *This Side Jordan*, the white woman, Miranda, Johnnie Kestoe's wife, gives birth to a daughter, Mary, and the black woman, Aza, the wife of Nathaniel, has a boy, Joshua. The thematic implication of the births is that hope for the future of Africa is also born — the new Mary comes to bring new love, and the new Joshua will lead his people to "this side of Jordan".

Margaret Laurence has since written of her novel: "In *This Side Jordan* (which I now find out-dated and superficial and yet somehow retrospectively touching) victory for the side of the angels is all but assured .... Jordan the mythical *could* be achieved, if not in Nathaniel's lifetime, then in his son's .... Things have shifted considerably since then."[1]

The same sense of an old order dying and of another being born, with all of the social and political tensions inherent in such epochal transformations, is to be seen in Laurence's collection of African short stories, *The Tomorrow-Tamer and Other Stories,* published in 1963 (nine of the ten stories were previously published in magazines and periodicals from 1956 to 1963). The short story which gives its name to the collection — "The Tomorrow-Tamer" — is an excellent expression of this over-riding concern. When Kofi, a young African, joins a crew of men sent to build a bridge across a jungle river, he is ostracized by his village, since the bridge is seen as a violation of the prerogatives of the river divinity. In the course of his work, Kofi, in an almost mystical exuberance, reaches up to embrace the sky, plunges from the bridge and is drowned in the river below. For the villagers, Kofi's death assumes profound symbolic significance: he is the sacrifice demanded by the river god, and through his sacrificial death, he sanctifies the bridge and wins sainthood for himself. Thus, through one who tries to meet progress head-on, and who pays dearly for his rashness, the works of progress are assimilated into traditional African patterns.

Along with the drama, the pathos and the tragedy that result when two very different civilizations are brought together, these stories also express Margaret Laurence's sense of African warmth, humour, loyalty and sensuousness. Thus, in the following passage from "A Gourdful of Glory", Laurence vividly describes the vitality of the African marketplace:

> As she spread out her wares in front of her stall, Mammii Ama sang. She sang in pidgin, so that every passerby, whatever his language, would understand.
>
> Mammii Ama sell all fine pit,
>   Oh, oh, Mammii Ama.
> She no t'ief you, she no make palavah,
>   Oh, oh Mammii Ama ....
>
> Everywhere there were voices, and sweet singing bodies. Everywhere the market women's laughter, coarse and warm as the touch of a tongue.

Throughout the collection, Laurence displays her remarkable gift for evoking the physical atmosphere of Africa. Here, for example, is part of her description (in "The Perfume Sea") of a small African town drowsing in the mid-day heat:

> Pariah dogs on the road snarled over a cat corpse; then, panting, tongues dribbling, defeated by the sun, they crawled back to a shaded corner, where their scabrous hides were fondled by an old man in a hashish dream. Footsteps on the cracked and scorching pavement lagged .... A donkey brayed disconsolately .... Only the children, the fire and the gleam of them greater even than the harsh glint of the sun, continued to leap and shout as before.

Margaret Laurence's other African works are: *A Tree for Poverty,* a translation of Somali folk-tales; *The Prophet's Camel Bell* (*New Wind in a Dry Land* in the American edition), a journal-travel book describing the Somalis - their character and way of life; and *Long Drums and Cannons,* a critique of Nigerian fiction and drama from 1952 to 1956.

Canadian Works

Before we look closely at each of Laurence's Canadian works—*The Stone Angel; A Jest of God; The Fire-Dwellers; A Bird in the House; The Diviners* — it might be useful to note some of the central themes that inform Laurence's fiction. One of these is the relationship of past to present and future. Laurence has observed that African writers found that it was essential to come to terms with their ancestors and their gods so that they could accept the past and be at peace with the dead. She has since become aware of the same basic pattern in her own work:" ... the attempt to assimilate the past, partly in order to be freed from it, partly in order to try to understand myself and perhaps those of my generation through seeing where we had come from".[2] In another essay, Laurence observes that the onus for choosing what time-span should be selected and how it should be presented lies not so much on her, the author, as on the main character who is the narrative voice. Once that narrative voice has been established, the protagonist autonomously, as it were, "chooses which parts of the personal past, the family past and the ancestral past have to be revealed in order for the present to be realized and the future to happen".[3]

One of the essential lessons to be learned from the past — namely, the idea of survival as an overriding imperative — is a second central theme for Margaret Laurence. Given her Scots-Irish background, with its stern puritan values, as well as the harsh realities of drought, depression and war, it is hardly surprising that survival should be invested with such significance. However, it should be stressed that Laurence does not mean just physical survival, but also "the survival of some human dignity and in the end, the survival of some human warmth and ability to reach out and touch others".[4]

Finally, although Laurence's fiction could hardly be said to be conventionally religious, there is running through her work a deep concern with what invests human life with meaning. Some scholars have noted that Canada, in much of its literature, would seem to be a country of the Old Testament — a country of exile, of alienation, of vindictive divinity; and Laurence concedes that this conception, derived from her Scots-Presbyterian ancestors, is to be found in her work. But she also points to a sense of hope, as well, which may be identified with the New Testament, and which is evidenced, not in formal Christian theology, but rather in the attaining through struggle of what might be termed a secular state of grace — a discovery of the self, a fresh awareness of the individual's relationship to the human community, an experience of freedom. However depressing some aspects of

Margaret Laurence's work may be, there is always, finally, a sense of what is at the root of all true religion — an affirmation of the essential worth of human life.

The Stone Angel

It has been mentioned that one of Margaret Laurence's enduring preoccupations is with the past. In her first Canadian novel, *The Stone Angel*, she began the process of coming to terms with her own roots through her grandparents' generation, the Scots-Presbyterian pioneers who founded and settled western towns like the one Laurence called Manawaka. Her characterization of Hagar in the novel reflects her ambivalence about that generation: on the one hand, inflexible, authoritarian, afraid to show love; on the other hand, indomitable in the face of formidable adversities - battlers, survivors. Thus Hagar, like her father, Jason Currie, is enslaved to a rigid code based on the principle that any evidence of warm emotions, of human dependency, is a sign of intolerable weakness of character, to be suppressed in oneself and deprecated in others; and as a result, Hagar cuts herself off from much of the joy of life — joy in marriage, in children, in social intercourse. And yet it can be argued as well that the strength of will which is a prime function of the code and of Hagar's personality is also the force that keeps her battling for ninety years, and which is still with her at the very end of her life when she steadfastly refuses to "go gentle into that good night".

In writing her novel, Laurence clearly had in mind the Hagar of Genesis as a prototype for her main character. In the Biblical version, Sarai, the wife of Abram, was barren, and suggested that Abram might have a child by her maidservant Hagar. Hagar subsequently became pregnant, and as a result treated Sarai with contempt. At Sarai's instance, Abram sent Hagar into exile in the wilderness where an angel of the Lord appeared to her and announced that she would have a son, Ishmael, who would be "a wild man; his hand will be against every man, and every man's hand against him". In *The Stone Angel*, Hagar expresses contempt for her husband Bram's (i.e., Abram's) first wife Clara, and after years of wrangling and disillusionment, takes her son John — who is said to be "wild as a mustard seed" — with her into exile in Vancouver. But the central exile — the true wilderness — in *The Stone Angel* is the emotional wilderness of Hagar Currie Shipley. Unlike her Biblical prototype, Hagar, until near the end of her life, is self-exiled, and wanders wilfully in the wilderness of pride and social appearances. She is tragic in Northrop Frye's sense of the word - tragic in her utter isolation from other human beings.

With reference to point of view in the novel, Margaret Laurence chose to have Hagar tell us her story herself. This autobiographical approach combines Hagar's experience in the present — a few days in her ninetieth year just before her death - with flashbacks: a chronological sequence of reminiscences throughout the novel stimulated by events in the present. Laurence has herself observed that the use of flashbacks is frequently overworked and clumsy, and certainly some considerable suspension of disbelief is called for in view of the chronological ordering of the flashback material. But the combination of past and present produces that strong feeling of immediacy and of tension which is to be found in the best story-telling. Moreover, it can be argued that Laurence's treatment of past and present in the novel has a thematic significance as well, in that the novel is about more than simply remembering the past — it is about coming to terms with the past. Until the climactic scene with Murray Ferney Lees in the cannery, Hagar is "rampant with memory" — almost obsessed with the past. But when, prompted by the effects of wine and by Lees' story about the death of his own son in a fire, Hagar finally admits her culpability in the death of her beloved son John, she is at last released from her long hidden guilt through her surrogate son's forgiveness. Past and present merge in the person of John Murray Ferney Lees, and never again do we return to the past in the novel. As a result of coming painfully to terms with the most traumatic aspect of her past, Hagar is freed to respond in a more fruitful way to the present — to Mr. Troy, whose singing brings her to full self-awareness ("pride was my wilderness"); to Sandra Wong, with whom she shares laughter; to Marvin, her long-suffering son who has been waiting for over sixty years for what his mother finally grants him: "You've been good to me always. A better son than John." And thus Hagar, at the end of the novel, at last ceases to be the stone angel of the title, and instead becomes a living responsive one who, in blessing her son, also releases herself from her long bondage.

A Jest of God

In *The Stone Angel*, Margaret Laurence succeeds admirably in making us feel what it is to be ninety and dying; in *A Jest of God*, she puts us inside the head of a very different protagonist: a thirty-four year old primary school teacher, unmarried and desperately insecure. Rachel Cameron is a prisoner of her parents: of her dead father, an undertaker who came to prefer the dead to the living, and whose funeral parlour under Rachel's room is a constant reminder of death; and of her mother, blue-rinsed, neurasthenic, superficial, endlessly demanding and circumscribing. Rachel's life is thus a neurotic suspension between womb and tomb, and her story is the story of a woman who is finally forced by circumstance to confront, and thus free herself from, the forces that have paralyzed her will.

The rather unlikely catalyst for change

in Rachel's life is her affair with Nick Kazlik, a Manawaka high-school acquaintance who has returned from Winnipeg to help on his father's farm for the summer. In her sexual relationship with Nick, Rachel discovers not only expression for her long-repressed sexuality, but also the profound depths of her desire to have a child. Laurence, to convey her sense of certain unchanging aspects of human behaviour and personality, once again turns to the Bible for a prototype. The name "Rachel" figures twice in the Old Testament. In Genesis 30, verse 1, Rachel, seeing that she is barren, says to Jacob, "Give me children or else I die." On page 148 of the novel, Rachel Cameron implores Nick to "Give me my children." Later in the novel, Rachel is convinced that she is pregnant by Nick; but a medical examinations reveals not a living foetus but rather a benign tumour. Now we hear the voice of the second Biblical Rachel (Jeremiah 31:15), the type of all grieving mothers: "In Rama was there a voice heard, lamentation and weeping and great mourning, Rachel weeping for her children and would not be comforted, because they are not."

Yet it is during this time of greatest maternal deprivation that Rachel comes to recognize "I am the mother now" to her own mother. She accepts her adult role as a parent to her "elderly child" and, exercising the control which is now hers, decrees that they must leave Manawaka, with its crippling respectability and constantly haunting reminders of death, and journey west to Vancouver. She now acknowledges that she may never have children of her own, only surrogate children, her students: "It may be that my children will always be temporary, never to be held." But, she adds, "So are everyone's." And it is in this acceptance of her future lot, whatever it may be, that we see an evidence of the distance Rachel has travelled towards the elusive goal of maturity: the secular state of grace.

Another measure of Rachel's complex metamorphosis is to be seen in her changing attitude to God. Throughout much of the novel, she sees Him as a cosmic sadist who sits in heaven and views human folly and misadventure as a joke provided for His perverted amusement. At first, the agony of her betrayal both by Nick and by the putative foetus seems to be yet another of the "jests of God". Only in retrospect does Rachel see that what has happened to her may be construed as an act of mercy rather than of malice. Having been broken in spirit so that she can be whole, Rachel is now in a position to see God not as a cruel jester but as One Whose mercy and grace are expressed in ways that are incomprehensible to limited mortals: "God's mercy on reluctant jesters. God's grace on fools. God's pity on God."

The Fire-Dwellers

Stacey Cameron MacAindra, the female protagonist of *The Fire-Dwellers*, is Rachel's sister. She is thirty-nine years old, has been married for sixteen years and has four children. In *A Jest of God*, Rachel voiced inward envy of her sister's settled domestic state; but in this novel we discover just how misplaced such an uninformed envy can be; for in Stacey's mind, her life is chaotic: she is ever conscious of the aging of her body; of the terrors of the world outside her Vancouver home; of her inability to communicate with her harassed salesman husband Mac and with her children, the youngest of whom, Jen, has not yet even spoken.

The form of the novel is rather more complex than that of *The Stone Angel* and *A Jest of God*, including as it does, in Laurence's words, "a certain amount of third person narration as well as Stacey's idiomatic running inner commentary and her somewhat less idiomatic fantasies, dreams, memories".[5] What is most compelling about Stacey is the candid incisiveness of her analysis of her life. She constantly exposes herself to a relentless, and frequently even comic, honesty. We are not long in her mind before we come to feel Stacey's barely controlled panic, and we empathize with her as she attempts to escape her sense of claustrophobia and impending doom, at first through gin, and then through her husband's trucker friend Buckle, whose perverted sexuality is a profound shock to her. She at last finds temporary respite in a brief affair with a young man, Luke, whose name is symbolic of his function in the novel. Like the Biblical Luke, he is a physician to her, helping her to see herself as herself, rather than as an arbitrary compound of wife-mother-housekeeper roles.

Some critics have found the conclusion of the novel a little too pat: Stacey has found a form of sexual catharsis through her affair with Luke; Jen finally begins to speak; her husband frees himself from the perverse sway of his boss, Thor Thorlakson; her son Duncan recovers from the traumatic experience of almost drowning in the ocean. But the most significant development for Stacey is surely her discovery that hers is not an isolated condition: all those around her are also fire-dwellers, experiencing persistent states of emergency. As for herself, she recognizes that the future will hold more crises, more wrenching ordeals of body and spirit — but for now, it is enough to be aware of her family's love and need for her, and of hers for them. The novel ends on a note of what might be termed "tentative confidence": "Temporarily, they are all more or less okay." However different she may be from Hagar and Rachel, Stacey is another of Margaret Laurence's memorable survivors.

A Bird in the House

A Bird in the House is a collection of eight short stories written over a period of seven years. They were initially published separately, but Margaret Laurence has indicated that they were conceived from the beginning as a related group. Concerned primarily with aspects of the Manawaka childhood and adolescence of the female protagonist Vanessa MacLeod, they are, according to the author, the only semi-autobiographical fiction she has ever written.[6] Laurence's own Scots and Irish ancestors can be seen to be represented in the stories by the Connors and the MacLeods, two connected but rival families — the professional MacLeods, portrayed by Vanessa's stiff and unexpressive Grandmother MacLeod; and the pioneering Irish Protestant Connors, whose primary expression is in the person of Vanessa's overbearing maternal grandfather, Grandfather Connor.

The problem of the relationship of time and the narrative voice, which has been alluded to previously, is a primary focus in *A Bird in the House*. The point of view of the narration throughout is that of the mature Vanessa, but at the same time the author must convey a sense of the increasing awareness of a young child growing into adolescence; that is, the narrative voice must speak, as it were, from two points in time simultaneously. This quite formidable technical challenge posed for herself by Margaret Laurence conveys by its very nature something of the complexity of the concepts of past, present and future. It also allows for revaluation of character over the period of the narrator's maturation, and this is particularly significant in the case of the figure who dominates the volume, Vanessa's Grandfather Connor. In the earlier stories, he emerges as a domineering intolerant tyrant (with many of the characteristics to be seen so conspicuously in Jason and Hagar Currie); but later on Vanessa comes to realize that his wilfulness and stubbornness had once been the essential pioneering virtues of endurance and courage. Time had passed him by, leaving him baffled and frustrated. Even more to the point, as the narrator comes to understand both her grandfather and herself better, she acknowledges an affinity with him that would earlier have shocked her: "I had feared and fought the old man, yet he proclaimed himself in my veins."

In addition to charting in an utterly convincing fashion the emotional development of Vanessa, *A Bird in the House* traces the artistic development of a writer. Vanessa's first youthful efforts are floridly romantic treatments of love and death set in far-off and exotic locales, since "both love and death seemed regrettably far from Manawaka". But as time goes by, and as she overhears adult conversations and comes slowly to an awareness, however confused, of the terrifying complexities of love and death in her own

family, Vanessa becomes more and more concerned to capture in her writing the reality of life as it is lived by those around her. The ultimate result of Vanessa's compulsive need to "set it down as it was" is, of course, the collection of stories itself — the expression into authenticity of Margaret Laurence's emotional and artistic maturity.

The Diviners

The Diviners is Margaret Laurence's most ambitious and complex work. We might begin by noting that *The Diviners* pulls together characters, aspects of plot and of theme from the previous Manawaka novels we have discussed. Thus we learn of the fate of the Currie plaid pin (it is now the possession of the female protagonist, Morag Gunn, who may as a result be seen as Hagar's legitimate descendant). There are references to many of the characters who earlier came to vivid life: Stacey (a fellow student of Morag's) and Rachel, their mother and father (the latter of whom was present at the fire in which Piquette Tonnerre and the children perished); the Pearls; the Kazliks; Dr. MacLeod and Vanessa; and the Tonnerres, who now, particularly in the person of Jules, Morag's sometime lover and father of her daughter Pique, achieve a distinctive prominence.

The novel could be said to have three major focuses: the relation of past to present (an abiding concern of Margaret Laurence's work, as we have seen); the relationship of mother and daughter (so conspicuous as well in *A Jest of God*); and the nature of creativity itself. As in *The Stone Angel*, though in a much more sophisticated fashion, we are exposed to two dominant time sequences in the novel. The present deals with a relatively short period, from summer to autumn, in Morag's old Ontario farmhouse. Interspersed throughout, the past is treated chronologically, first in the form of snapshots of Morag's parents, who died when she was very young; then through Memorybank Movies, which introduce us to Morag's frequently tortured childhood experiences as the adopted daughter of Manawaka's garbage collector, Christie Logan, and his grotesquely fat wife Prin; her unsuccessful marriage to a condescending university English professor; her affair with Jules Tonnerre; and her flight with her daughter to England and Scotland in search of her "real" ancestors. Morag comes to realize that her roots lie not in Scotland but in the Manawaka which she so desperately fled, and that her true father is not the ill-remembered figure in the snapshot but disreputable rejected Christie, whose stories and wisdom become increasingly dear to her in retrospect.

That the past and present are inextricable and that there is a repetitive rhythm to human experience is to be seen in the relationship of Morag and Pique. Throughout the novel, Laurence unflinchingly explores the complex tensions of the mother-daughter relationship. When Pique leaves her mother's home at the end of the novel to go in search of the Métis half of her identity, we see that she is repeating the same necessary process Morag herself had earlier experienced; but Morag must attempt to accommodate herself to the difficult reality that *she* is now the parent who must, for a time, be rejected and left behind.

The title of the novel most directly refers to an old man, Royland, whose mysterious faculty of being able to divine for water with a willow wand is quite suddenly taken from him. He is philosophical about the loss, observing that it was in any case a gift for which he was grateful while it lasted. For Morag, there is an inferential association between the art of divining and the nature of the writer's creativity. The latter, she feels, is also a mysterious gift, one which allows the writer to "look ahead into the past, and back into the future, until the silence". In confronting and accepting the possibility that this faculty may be taken from her, Morag, the literary *persona* so closely associated with Margaret Laurence herself, achieves a serenity which may quite appropriately be termed "a state of grace".

1 Margaret Laurence, "Ten Years' Sentences", *Canadian Literature*, No. 46 (1969), p. 12.

2 Margaret Laurence, "Sources", *Mosaic*, III (1970), 81.

3 Margaret Laurence, "Time and the Narrative Voice" in *The Narrative Voice*, ed. J. Metcalf (Toronto: McGraw-Hill Ryerson, 1972), p. 127.

4 Margaret Laurence, "Sources", p. 83.

5 Margaret Laurence, "Ten Years' Sentences", p. 15.

6 Margaret Laurence, "Sources", p. 82; cf. also "Margaret Laurence" in *Eleven Canadian Novelists Interviewed by Graeme Gibson* (Toronto: Anansi, 1973), p. 197: "I have never written anything that is directly autobiographical except for one book of short stories, *A Bird in the House*, which was based on my own childhood, myself as a child, and my family."

Chronology

1926 Jean Margaret Wemyss, born 18 July in Neepawa, Manitoba: daughter of Robert Wemyss and Verna Simpson Wemyss.

1930 Mother died suddenly of acute kidney failure.

1931 Father married mother's elder sister Margaret.

1935 Father died; maternal grandmother died.

1947 Graduated with Honours in English from United College in Winnipeg.

1943 Married Jack Laurence, a graduate in Civil Engineering of the University of Manitoba.

1949 Moved to England.

1950 Moved to Somaliland where Jack Laurence directed dam-building project.

1952 Moved to the Gold Coast; daughter Jocelyn born.

1954 *A Tree for Poverty: Somali Poetry and Prose* published.

1955 Son David born.

1957 Returned to Canada and settled in Vancouver.

1960 *This Side Jordan* published.

1961 Won Beta Sigma Phi Award for best first novel by a Canadian for *This Side Jordan*.

1962 Separated from Jack Laurence; moved to England with children.

1963 *The Prophet's Camel Bell* published (in the U.S. as *New Wind in a Dry Land*).
     The Tomorrow-Tamer published.

1964 *The Stone Angel* published.

1966 *A Jest of God* published; basis for film *Rachel Rachel*.

1967 Awarded the Governor General's Medal for Fiction for *A Jest of God*.

1968 *Long Drums and Cannons: Nigerian Novelists and Dramatists* published.

1969 Returned to Canada; divorced from Jack Laurence; *The Fire-Dwellers* published.

1970 *A Bird in the House* published.
     Jason's Quest (a children's book) published.

1971 Made a Companion of the Order of Canada (highest award given by the Government of Canada).

1974 *The Diviners* published.

1975 Awarded the Governor General's Medal for Fiction for *The Diviners*.

1976 *Heart of a Stranger* (collection of personal essays) published.

1979 *The Olden Days Coat* (a children's book) published. *Six Darn Cows* (a children's book) published.

Comments by Margaret Laurence

I was fortunate in going to Africa when I did - in my eary twenties - because for some years I was so fascinated by the African scene that I was in this way prevented from writing an autobiographical first novel. I don't say there is anything wrong in autobiographical novels, but it would not have been the right thing for me - my view of the prairie from which I had come was still too prejudiced and distorted by closeness.
     "Sources", *Mosaic*, III (1970), 81.

This, then, has been my own attempt to come to terms with the past. I see this process as the gradual one of freeing oneself from the stultifying aspect of the past, while at the same time beginning to see its true value — in the case of my own people (by which I mean the total community, not just my particular family) a determination to survive against whatever odds.
     Ibid., p. 83.

The greatest problem of all is to try and tell enough of your own truth from your own viewpoint, from your own eyes, to be able to go deeply enough. To make the leap of the imagination to get inside another character, and to be able to tell as much of that truth as you can bear to tell, and this is very hard.

Eleven Canadian Novelists Interviewed by Graeme Gibson (Toronto: Anansi, 1973), p. 189.

Personally, apart from simply wanting to create fictions for reasons that I find mysterious, I would hope that with my own fiction, if anything came across at all under the surface, it would be to this effect — that human beings are capable of great communication and love and very often fall very short of this. We simply do not communicate as much or at as deep a level as we are capable, and one would hope through one's characters to point some of these things out.

Ibid., p. 190.

When I first began writing, the theme to me then seemed to be human freedom and in a profound sense it still is human freedom. But this is linked with survival, which, as you say, has to be linked with some kind of growth and I would express this in terms of an inner freedom.

C. Thomas, "A Conversation about Literature: An Interview with Margaret Laurence and Irving Layton", *Journal of Canadian Fiction*, I (1972), 67.

Comments
on Margaret Laurence

Laurence's characters are undistinguished — old ladies, spinster school teachers, housewives, small-town girls, and, most different, writers. Laurence takes these apparently unexceptional people and renders them unique by showing their inner lives animated, tormented, enriched and deepened by their own unfathomed complexities.

J.W. Lennox, "Manawaka and Deptford: Place and Voice", *Journal of Canadian Studies*, XIII (1978), 129.

It is Hagar, with the most defiant and assertive "I" of all, who stands as Laurence's most interesting character. Each of her heroines, however, is memorable in her own way, and this is the direct result of the author's choice of point of view, with emphasis always on the perceptions of the narrator, as she seeks to define her present self through her Manawaka past.

L.M. Gom, "Margaret Laurence and the First Person", *Dalhousie Review*, LV (1975), 250.

Freedom, in Laurence's fiction, is seen to be a gift which is both a mercy bestowed and also a birthright to be won through infinite desire and struggle, like Jacob struggling with the Angel, an archetypal narrative which Laurence takes from Genesis and uses repeatedly in her fiction.

P. Morley, "The Long Trek Home: Margaret Laurence's Stories", *Journal of Canadian Studies*, XI (1976), 20.

In terms of human relationships ..., Laurence repeatedly concerns herself with characters frantic to explain, often frustrated because they cannot find adequate words, because some acts transcend words, or because words themselves are untrustworthy.

T.L. Dombrowski, "Word and Fact: Laurence and the Problem of Language", *Canadian Literature*, No. 80 (1979), p. 50.

Ultimately, what is impressive about her writing is her affirmation, without any sentimentality, of the essential dignity of the human personality. In the finest sense of that word, she is a humanist.

H. Kreisel, "The African Stories of Margaret Laurence", *Canadian Forum*, XLI (1961), 10.

Selected Bibliography
Works by Margaret Laurence

A Tree for Poverty: Somali Poetry and Prose. Nairobi: Eagle Press, 1954.
This Side Jordan. Toronto: McClelland and Stewart, 1960.
The Prophet's Camel Bell. Toronto: McClelland and Stewart, 1963 (in the United States, *New Wind in a Dry Land.* New York: Knopf, 1964).
The Tomorrow-Tamer. Toronto: McClelland and Stewart, 1963.
The Stone Angel. Toronto: McClelland and Stewart, 1964.
A Jest of God. Toronto: McClelland and Stewart, 1966.
Long Drums and Cannons: Nigerian Novelists and Dramatists 1952-1966. London: Macmillan, 1968.
The Fire-Dwellers. Toronto: McClelland and Stewart, 1970.
A Bird in the House. Toronto: McClelland and Stewart, 1970.
Jason's Quest. Toronto: McClelland and Stewart, 1970.
The Diviners. Toronto: McClelland and Stewart, 1974.
Heart of a Stranger. Toronto: McClelland and Stewart, 1976.
The Olden Days Coat. Toronto: McClelland and Stewart, 1979.
Six Darn Cows. Toronto: James Lorimer and Company, 1979.

Selected Criticism

Bailey, N. "Margaret Laurence, Carl Jung and the Manawaka Women", *Studies in Canadian Literature*, II (1977), 306-321.
Blewett, D. "The Unity of the Manawaka Cycle", *Journal of Canadian Studies*, XIII (1978), pp. 31-39.
Bowering, G. "That Fool of a Fear: Notes on *A Jest of*

God", *Canadian Literature*, No. 50 (1971), pp. 41-56.

Callaghan, B. "The Writings of Margaret Laurence", *Tamarack Review*, No. 36 (1965), pp. 45-51.

Cameron, S.D. "Margaret Laurence: The Black Celt Speaks of Freedom" in *Conversations with Canadian Novelists*. Toronto: Macmillan, 1973, pp. 96-115.

Djwa, S. "False Gods and the True Covenant: Thematic Continuity Between Margaret Laurence and Sinclair Ross", *Journal of Canadian Fiction*, I (1972), 43-50.

Dombrowski, J.Q. "Word and Fact: Laurence and the Problem of Language", *Canadian Literature*, No. 80 (1979), pp. 50-62.

Forman, D. and Parameswaran, U. "Echoes and Refrains in the Canadian Novels of Margaret Laurence", *The Centennial Review*, XVI (1972), 233-253.

Gibson, G. "Margaret Laurence" in *Eleven Canadian Novelists Interviewed by Graeme Gibson*. Toronto: Anansi, 1973, pp. 181-208.

Gom. L. "Margaret Laurence and the First Person", *Dalhousie Review*, LV (1975), 236-251.

Gom, L. "Laurence and the Use of Memory", *Canadian Literature*, No. 71 (1976), pp. 48-58.

Gotlieb, P. "On Margaret Laurence", *Tamarack Review*, No. 52 (1969), pp. 76-80.

Grace, S. "A Portrait of the Artist as Laurence Hero", *Journal of Canadian Studies*, XIII (1978), 64-71.

Harlow, R. "Lack of Distance", *Canadian Literature*, No. 31 (1967), pp. 71-72, 74-75.

Hehner, B. "River of Now and Then: Margaret Laurence's Narratives", *Canadian Literature*, No. 74 (1977), pp. 40-57.

Hind-Smith, J. "Margaret Laurence" in *Three Voices*. Toronto: Clarke Irwin, 1975, pp. 3-60.

Hughes, K.J. "Politics and *A Jest of God*", *Journal of Canadian Studies*, XIII (1978), 40-54.

Kertzer, J.M. "*The Stone Angel:* Time and Responsibility", *Dalhousie Review*, LIV (1974), 499-509.

Kreisel, H. "The African Stories of Margaret Laurence", *Canadian Forum*, XLI (1961), 8-10.

Kroetsch, R. "A Conversation with Margaret Laurence" in *Creation*, ed. R. Kroetsch. Toronto: New Press, 1970, pp. 53-63.

Lennox, J.W. "Manawaka and Deptford: Place and Voice", *Journal of Canadian Studies*, XIII (1978), 23-30.

Lever, B. "Manawaka Magic", *Journal of Canadian Fiction*, III (1974), 93-96.

Lever, B. "Nature Imagery in the Canadian Fiction of Margaret Laurence", *Alive*, No. 41 (1975), pp. 20-22.

McLay, C.M. "Everyman is an Island: Isolation in *A Jest of God*", *Canadian Literature*, No. 50 (1971), pp. 57-68.

Metcalf, J., ed. *The Narrative Voice*. Toronto: McGraw-Hill Ryerson, 1972, pp. 126-130.

Morley, P. "The Long Trek Home: Margaret Laurence's Stories", *Journal of Canadian Studies*, XI (1976), 19-26.

—————. "Margaret Laurence's Early Writing: A World in which Others have to be Respected", *Journal of Canadian Studies*, XIII (1978), 13-18.

New, W.H., ed. *Margaret Laurence: The Writer and Her Critics*. Toronto: McGraw-Hill Ryerson, 1977.

—————. "Text and Subtext: Laurence's 'The Merchant of Heaven' ", *Journal of Canadian Studies*, XIII (1978), 19-22.

Osachoff, M.G. "Moral Vision in *The Stone Angel*", *Studies in Canadian Literature*, IV (1979), 139-153.

Pesandro, F. "In a Nameless Land: The Use of Apocalyptic Mythology in the Writings of Margaret Laurence", *Journal of Canadian Fiction*, II (1973), 53-58.

Read, S.G. "The Maze of Life: The Work of Margaret Laurence", *Canadian Literature*, No. 27 (1966), pp. 5-14.

Rosengarten, H.J. "Inescapable Bonds", *Canadian Literature*, No. 35 (1968), pp. 99-100.

Swayze, W. "The Odyssey of Margaret Laurence", *English Quarterly*, III (1970), 7-17.

Thomas, C. *Margaret Laurence*. Toronto: McClelland and Stewart, 1969.

—————. "Proud Lineage: Willa Cather and Margaret Laurence", *Canadian Review of American Studies*, II (1971), 1, 3-12.

—————. "A Conversation about Literature: An Interview with Margaret Laurence and Irving Layton", *Journal of Canadian Fiction*, I (1972), 65-69.

—————. "The Novels of Margaret Laurence", *Studies in the Novel*, IV (1972), 2, 154-164.

—————. "The Short Stories of Margaret Laurence", *World Literature Written in English*, XI (1972), 25-33.

—————. *The Manawaka World of Margaret Laurence*. Toronto: McClelland and Stewart, 1975.

—————. "The Wild Garden and the Manawaka World", *Modern Fiction Studies*, XXII (1976), 401-411.

—————. "The Chariot of Ossian: Myth and Manitoba in *The Diviners*", *Journal of Canadian Studies*, XIII (1978), 55-63.

Thompson, A. "The Wilderness of Pride: Form and Image in *The Stone Angel*", *Journal of Canadian Fiction*, III (1976), 95-110.

Woodcock, G. "Many Solitudes: The Travel Writings of Margaret Laurence", *Journal of Canadian Studies*, XIII (1978), 3-12.

A Note on the Contributor

Frederick Sweet has taught Classics at Bishop's University and English literature at the Canadian Junior College, Lausanne, Switzerland. At present he is a member of the faculty in English and Communications at Seneca College, Toronto.

Margaret Atwood 22

by
Frank Davey

Courtesy: Graeme Gibson.

Margaret Atwood's writing has focussed on the relationships between mankind and nature and between man and woman. From her first major work, the poetry collection *The Circle Game,* to her recent novel *Life Before Man,* she has depicted civilization as tragically hostile to nature, and men and women as at best wary partners. Civilization is the "circle game", the insistent application of geometric form to organic landscape; human love is most often another circle game of

> word-
> plays, calculated ploys
> of the body, the witticisms
> of touch.[1]

Most of the characters of her poetry and fiction neither see themselves as part of the natural world nor feel comfortable within it. Some, like the protagonist of "Progressive Insanities of a Pioneer" (*AC* pp. 36-39), are motivated by arrogance to attempt vainly to "impose" their own patterns upon it — the title suggests that Atwood views even such a motive as "insane". Some, like the girl in "Younger Sister, Going Swimming" (*PU* pp. 66-67), yearn for personal acknowledgement by nature, calling and "signalling" — again vainly — to its impassive hills. Others, like Peter in *The Edible Woman* or the heron-killers of *Surfacing,* dislike nature so strongly that one of their major pleasures is using technology to destroy or replace natural form. Still others seek to ignore nature altogether for fantasy realms of romance or comic-book (Chuck Brewer of *Lady Oracle* dubs himself "The Royal Porcupine", the male protagonist of *Power Politics* would "hang suspended above the city / in blue tights and a red cape, . . . eyes flashing in unison" (*PP* p. 5); Joan Foster in *Lady Oracle* would live in the fantasies of Gothic romance); Lesje Green of *Life Before Man* would live with dinosaurs in "the Cretaceous twilight" (*LBM,* p. 81).

Many of the relationships between men and women in Atwood's work parallel this destructive relationship between mankind and nature, with one of the lovers seeking to control and dominate the other. Perhaps because most of Atwood's work is written from a woman's point of view, and perhaps also because historically it has been men who have directed the technological assault on nature, it is the woman in Atwood who is most often equated with nature and portrayed as victim, and the man who is portrayed as the manipulative oppressor. In *The Circle Game* the lover with "mind's hands that smell / of insecticide and careful soap" (p. 34), the cameraman who insists "that the clouds stop moving" (p. 45), the lover determined to restore "some kind of daily normal order" (p. 70), the map-tracing lover of "The Circle Game", are all male; their "victims" female. In *The Animals in That Country* the insane pioneer of "Progressive Insanities of a Pioneer", the surveyors with "their trail of single reason" (p. 4), the trappers with their "steel circles" and "abstract hunger" (pp. 34-35) are again all male. In both *The Edible Woman* and *Surfacing* the female protagonists are equated with natural forces — Marian MacAlpin with her own rebellious body, *Surfacing's* unnamed narrator with the wilderness landscape. They struggle against technologically oriented men — the former against her lawyer-fiancé with his guns, cameras, and planned career, the latter against a withdrawn father, an exploitive art-teacher, and a lover who embraces her "as though trying to fold up a lawn chair" (*S* p. 146).

We should note however that this pattern of natural woman versus technological man does not conform to Atwood's declared views nor to the more balanced pattern that emerges if we read in her work past its major characters. In *The Edible Woman* Ainsley is as calculating and predatory as Peter. In *Surfacing* the narrator herself has become cold and self-protective; her friend Anna has developed nearly comic preferences for the artificial over the natural. In *The Animals in That Country*, the victims of the Boston Strangler die because "they saw him as a function" ("The Green Man", p. 12), while in contrast Captain Cook abandons his maps and atlases to acknowledge "a new land cleared of geographies" (p. 61).

The usual voice in Atwood's poetry and fiction is that of a woman who has become frightened, alienated, or embittered by her experiences. Some of these women, such as the narrator of *Surfacing*, Mrs. Moodie in *The Journals of Susanna Moodie*, and many of the narrators of Atwood's stories, have developed a deep division between their public and private selves. Their friends, husbands, or lovers know them only as the controlled, predictable persona which they have adopted as camouflage in a world which values order and predictability; their narrations, however, reveal the irrational feelings, opinions, and fears which constitute the real subjective experience of their lives. Others, such as Joan Foster in *Lady Oracle*, Marian in *The Edible Woman*, and the speaker of *Power Politics*, have become glib and superficial in their private thoughts, and thereby display alienation from even their own deepest feelings.

The technique of Atwood's writing is directed toward the revelation of the character of such women, toward capturing their variously laconic, impassive, naive, or sardonic sensibilities. In the poetry the short lines, the precise diction, and the avoidance of description reveals speakers who are as wary and stinting in speech as they are skeptical and ungenerous in love. The modular stanza structure noted by Robin Skelton[2] and the large number of copula verbs[3] suggests speakers who see little hope for change in their world and who feel passive among their experiences. In both the poetry and fiction, flights of Gothic imagery concerning fantasy rescuers, comic-book heroes, or commercial mythology help convey the unconscious fears and wishes of characters who have nearly give up all hope of fulfillment in their actual lives. In the novels, Atwood frequently combines such imagery with abrupt shifts of narrative point of view to indicate sudden schizophrenic shifts between vastly different parts of the narrator's personality. Joan Foster shifts from housewife, to popular author, to secret writer of Costume Gothics; Marian MacAlpin shifts from sensible young woman to a believer in another Gothic world of prohibited foods; *Surfacing's* narrator shifts from competent independent woman to a superstitious believer in an active and intervening nature. Atwood accompanies each shift to the Gothic mode with a shift from first to third-person narration, ostensibly to emphasize the large rift between conscious and unconscious parts of the personality.

Atwood's first book of poems, the privately printed *Double Persephone*, proclaimed a choice between "two immortalities: / one of earth, lake, trees / ... / The other of a world of glass, / Hard marble, carven word." This dichotomy between a static world of order, sculpture, stylized beauty and a natural world of flesh, earth, and temporal process has been the informing dialectic of all her poetry. *The Circle Game* rests on an antithesis between the static schemes of the city planner or game-playing lover and the natural life of the landscape or the woman. *The Animals in that Country* is based on an antithesis between the "ceremonial", "elegant", and "heraldic" animals of static European tradition and the furtive yet real animals of "this country" which "have the faces of animals" (p. 3). *Procedures for Underground* opposes the world of conscious order to "underground", an uncontrollable world of raw natural force. *The Journals of Susanna Moodie* portrays Mrs. Moodie's struggle to defy the "white chaos" of change and seasonal process by her concentration on

> form, geometry, the human
> architecture of the house, square
> closed doors, proved roofbeams
> the logic of windows
> ("The Two Fires", pp. 22-23)

Power Politics portrays the struggle in yet more complex terms as one not only between two lovers, each trying to subjugate the spontaneous "underground" elements within the other, but also between conscious and unconscious parts of each individual. The man would "cauterize" his senses, turn himself "into an impervious glass tower" (p. 32); the woman cries out to him

> Let me stop caring
> about anything but skinless
> wheels and smoothly-
> running money
>
> Get me out of this trap, this
> body, let me be
> like you, closed and useful. (pp. 18-19)

Throughout these books Atwood perceives contemporary men and women as uncomfortable with their bodies, with natural forms, and with the uncertainties created by the passage of time. They would replace biological form with the "skinless wheels" of machinery, would replace the "open" and "underground" world of nature with the "closed" and visible one of fences, houses, maps, and geometry. In short, they would transform a living temporal world into a static spatial one. A recurrent symbol in Atwood for such a transformation is the camera, which literally changes ongoing event into static design. It is such a transformation Marian flees from when Peter tries to photograph her in *The Edible Woman*, and which both the totem poles and the tourists ("the other wooden people") are being subjected to in "Totems" (*CG*, pp. 59-60). The poem "Camera" (*CG*, pp. 45-46) describes a "camera-man" who in his search for an "organized instant" asks reality to "stop," to "hold still":

> you insist that the clouds stop moving
> the wind stop swaying the church
> on its boggy foundations.

"Girl and Horse, 1928" tells of a girl "caught by light / and fixed in that / secret / place where we live, where we believe / nothing can change, grow older". In each of these poems, however, time triumphs over technology. The girl rides away after the photo is taken.

> (on the other side
> of the picture, the instant
> is over, the shadow
> of the tree has moved. You wave,
>
> then turn and ride
> out of sight through the vanished
> orchard, ...
>
> (*PU*, p. 10)

The camera-man discovers that both he and his spatial creation are themselves participants in temporality.

> wherever you partly are
> now, look again
> at your souvenir,
> your glossy square of paper
> before it dissolves completely.
>
> (*CG*, p. 45)

Throughout Atwood's poetry from *Double Persephone* to *You Are Happy*, mankind and nature live in an uneasy tension, the former stalemated in his attempts to end natural change, the latter sufficiently wounded by technology that it flourishes only in the long term. Similarly, when men and women succeed in dominating and paralyzing each other's lives, they find that even their gifts to one another "warp" in their hands "to implements, to manoevers" (*PP* pp. 18-19); yet when they fail they often are still unhappy, yearning for the immortality of such static objects as "doorknobs, moons / glass paperweights" (*PP* p. 56). An abundance of sculptural metaphors — the statues the Gorgon creates in *Double Persephone*, the totem poles of "Totems" (*CG* pp. 59-60), the "heraldic" animals of "The Animals in that Country" (*AC* pp. 2-3), the "5 plaster Indians" of "A Night in the Royal Ontario Museum" (*AC* pp. 20-21), the "glass paperweights" above — attests to man's obsession with avoiding change, process, or growth.

The short stories collected in *Dancing Girls* (1977), which date from 1964 to 1977, focus on the same tenuous relationships between men and women as do many of the poems. The narrators of these stories are nearly all women who have for some reason suppressed all display of personal feeling, and who have therefore experienced an extraordinary separation between their inner and outer selves. Their narratives consist of insights and grievances that are secret even to closest friends. While the women of the poetry frequently struggle to maintain some honest communication with husband or lover, these women have given up such a goal, and feel safe in presenting to a man only a superficial persona.

Unable to disclose her feelings or opinions to anyone, or to verify their reasonableness against the opinions of others, the woman in such stories tends toward suspicion and paranoia. The elderly protagonist of "The War in the Bathroom" becomes convinced another inhabitant of her rooming house is persecuting her and sets out to retaliate. The narrator of "Lives of the Poets" suspects her lover is having an affair but feels paralyzed about attempting to confirm her suspicion. Sarah, the narrator of "The Resplendent Quetzal", obscurely blames her husband for the stillbirth of their baby, and secretly takes birth control pills so she will not have another. When her inner grief and rage momentarily break through, he tells her "This isn't like you", and she in turn is stricken with the fear that she has suddenly become "someone else, someone entirely different, a woman he had never seen before in his life" (*DG* p. 170). The form of the stories reflects this divorce between the inner "someone else" and the social mask. The bulk of the narrative reflects the inner life of the narrator or point of view character; the dialogue and occasional flashbacks communicate the outer reality to which the inner life is only minimally linked. The narrative tone is calm and measured, and variously suggests detachment, loneliness, and grim self-reliance. The consistency of the tone parallels the lack of growth in the characters; the stories depict the predicament of emotional alienation without suggesting resolution. The overall pattern of both the stories and poetry is pessimistic — insight usually leads only to resignation and further repression of the inner self.

Interestingly, Atwood's novels of this period, although characterized by similar divisions between private and public self, by the same tensions between man and nature and between men and women as the poetry, and by the same metaphors of camera, gun, and statue for the desire to thwart natural process, are basically optimistic in outlook. Their narrators grow as a result of their struggles with those who would regularize and imprison them; they emerge from the novels with an expanded sense of personal freedom and potential. The structure characteristic of the poems is that of tragedy — opportunity seized, then fatally lost; the progressively insane "Pioneer", Mrs. Moodie, and the lovers of *Power Politics* all have a chance to achieve greater depth in their lives if they attempt to understand the "aphorisms" which the world beyond their individual selves offers; all choose instead the false security of man-made structures; and although natural process — like the rightful rule of Lear's kingdom — ultimately triumphs, the individual protagonists suffer. The structural pattern of The *Edible Woman, Surfacing,* and *Lady Oracle,* however, is that of comedy — alienation, a healing period of exile, followed by reintegration and return to "natural" order. Here the protagonists choose to listen to the aphorisms, choose to grow, and therefore survive to participate in the restored natural world.

Each of the novels is narrated by a young woman of some sensitivity who, like the characters of the short stories, finds herself alone among pragmatic and superficial people who have mistaken her for one of themselves. In each the woman subconsciously recognizes the threat which this mistake constitutes to her inner life and begins, often against her own conscious intentions, to act out her deepest feelings. In *The Edible Woman* Marian MacAlpin, who has presented herself to her fiancé as a pliant and "sensible" woman, discovers that her body is irrationally refusing food — first meat, then vegetables, and eventually even vitamin pills. In *Surfacing*, the narrator, who has impressed her friends as coolly self-sufficient and organized, finds herself abruptly unable to tolerate man-made shelter and clothing, or mankind itself with its scent of "stale air, bus stations, and nicotine smoke" and "taste of copper wiring or money". In *Lady Oracle*, Joan Foster, who has appeared to her husband as a "normal girl" (p. 214), to her lover as raw material for his fantasies, and to her reading public as glamorous and mysterious, is moved impulsively to feign suicide, flee to Italy, and seek her true identity

within the Costume Gothic novels she has secretly made a career of writing.

In each novel this period of exile in a Shakespearean "green world" of the personal unconscious results in the narrator's acquisition of both healing insights and a sense of having been transformed to a new life. Marian realizes that she has subconsciously feared being "devoured" by people like her fiancé; the narrator of *Surfacing* realizes that all people — even her impassive lover Joe and her uncommunicative parents — were "human". "Something I never gave them credit for" (pp. 189-$90). Joan discovers her pattern of either fleeing from crises or awaiting "rescue" by a strong man, and also her unconscious view of men as simultaneously killers and rescuers.

> Every man I'd ever been involved with, I realized, had had two selves; the man in the tweed coat, my rescuer and possibly a pervert; the Royal Porcupine and his double Chuck Brewer; even Paul whom I'd always believed had a sinister other life I couldn't penetrate.
> (*LO* p. 295)

These insights leave Marian eager to begin life again, and she starts out by baking a satiric woman-shaped cake made, significantly, of "everything new" (*EW* p. 267). They leave the woman of *Surfacing* ready to build a new relationship with her lover — "we can no longer live in spurious peace by avoiding each other, the way it was before, we will have to begin" (p. 192). They bring Joan to face personal responsibility for the first time in her life, as she prepares to return to Canada and accept the consequences of her feigned suicide.

Atwood's most recent writings represent a considerable expansion of her range in both poetry and fiction. The novel *Life Before Man* is her first novel to portray the static and trapped relationships characteristic of her early poetry. The central characters, the married couple Elizabeth and Nate, are well-meaning people who consciously strive for growth in their lives — Elizabeth for increased independence and Nate for deeper relationships and a more fulfilling vocation. But because they never achieve the self-insight of the protagonists of Atwood's other novels — Elizabeth into the contempt for men she has absorbed from her Aunt Muriel, Nate into his worshipful dependency on any woman with whom he becomes involved — they merely repeat indefinitely their past mistakes. The structure of the novel resembles that of Atwood's longer poems; like collaged independent stanzas, short chapters from a variety of viewpoints document the characters' activities on particular days selected from a one-year period. The effect of these juxtaposed chapters is to minimize temporal continuity and to emphasize the repetitive quality of the actions. The novel closes with the characters in new living arrangements but in possession of no greater happiness or understanding than when the book opened. [1] This pattern is the one of contemporary tragedy, so familiar in the work of Williams, Beckett, or Pinter — alienation, struggle, followed by surrender to habitual mistake and limited vision.

In contrast, various poems in Atwood's *Two-Headed Poems* (1978) and an even more recent short story embrace for the first time in these genres the comic, redemptive vision of her first three novels. The poem "April, Radio, Planting, Easter" begins with the speaker in the suspicious, defensive condition we see in so many of Atwood's poems.

> so you fashion yourself a helmet
> of thickened skin
> and move cautiously among the chairs
> prepared for ambush
> impervious to the wiry screams
> and toy pain of others.

But by the conclusion she has not only "lovingly" planted onion seedlings but is announcing the unity of all the planet's living things.

> We do not walk on the earth
> but in it, wading
> in that acid sea
> where flesh is etched from
> molten bone and re-forms.
>
> ...
>
> ...there is no *other*.

A similar movement from negative to affirmative images occurs in "All Bread" which transforms its initial observation "All bread is made of wood / cow dung, packed brown moss, the bodies of dead animals" into an assertion of the sacramental nature of organic matter, and of the commonality of planetary life such a sacrament implies.

> Lift these ashes
> into your mouth, your blood;
> to know what you devour
> is to consecrate it,
> almost. All bread must be broken
> so it can be shared. Together
> we eat the earth.
>
> (*THP*, pp. 108-109)

The poem is reminiscent of the scene in Chapter 23 of *Surfacing* in which the narrator realizes that her identity is tied to the voices of the biological world. [1]

The short story "Missed Crass" (*Chatelaine*, December 1979) makes an even more optimistic statement. It opens in Toronto, several centuries after an atomic war, on a society of "Furts", stolid underground people who are mindlessly repeating the actions which saved them long ago. The usual Atwood themes of static life and closed, circular behaviour are clearly evident. But the focus of the story falls a nine-year-old girl Furt who defies the social paralysis of her people to walk out to the now radiation-free

surface. The girl, who has thus "surfaced" to authentic life much like the heroines of Atwood's first three novels, is welcomed by those few who preceded her — "honor to those whose risk", they say to her, "honor to those who persevere." Such people appear in this story as the redeemers of the human race and, along with the struggling trees, plants, and mysterious Avies, as the redeemers of earth.

"Metamorphosis" — so the narrator of *Surfacing* describes the growth of "pure white" flowers of the sundew from the old flesh of gnats and midges, as she begins to pursue her own transformation through fasting and the shedding of clothing (*S* p. 167). In *Lady Oracle* the metamorphosis of a caterpillar into a butterfly is the ruling metaphor, and is in a way achieved by Joan through her traumatic descent into the unconscious world of her own Costume Gothic fiction. *The Journals of Susanna Moodie* ends with "Resurrection" — a reborn Mrs. Moodie sees the "holy fire" of change around her and announces that "at the last / judgment we shall all be trees" (p. 59). Finally we have the "Avie" of "Missed Crass" — "sometimes they become plants; sometimes they become Changers again . . . . But whatever they become, they sing." The overall design of Atwood's work includes the best and worst of human life — courage as well as dependency, "surfacing" as well as "circle games", hope as well as despair.

[1] The *Circle Game* (Toronto: House of Anansi, 1966), p. 38, this book subsequently cited [CG]. Other references are to *Double Persephone* (Toronto: The Hawkshead Press, 1961) [DP]; *The Animals in that Country* (Toronto: Oxford University Press, 1968) [AC]; *The Journals of Susanna Moodie* (Toronto: Oxford University Press, 1970) [JSM]; *Procedures for Underground* (Toronto: Oxford University Press, 1970) [PU]; *Power Politics* (Toronto: House of Anansi, 1972) [PP]; *You Are Happy* (Toronto: Oxford University Press, 1974) [YAH]; *Two-Headed Poems* (Toronto: Oxford University Press, 1978) [THP]; *The Edible Woman* (Toronto: McClelland and Stewart, 1969) [EW]; *Surfacing* (Toronto: McClelland and Stewart, 1972) [S]; *Lady Oracle* (Toronto: McClelland and Stewart, 1976) [LO]; *Dancing Girls* (Toronto: McClelland and Stewart, 1977) [DG]; and *Life Before Man* (Toronto: McClelland and Stewart, 1979) [LBM].

[2] "Timeless Constructions — A Note on the Poetic Style of Margaret Atwood", *Malahat Review*, No. 41 (January 1977), pp. 107-120.

[3] See my article "Atwood's Gorgon Touch", *Studies in Canadian Literature* II:2 (Summer 1977), 146-163.

Chronology

1939	Born in Ottawa, 18 November, second child of Carl Edmund, an entomologist, and Margaret Dorothy (Killam).
1939-45	Winters in Ottawa; spring, summer, and fall in northern Quebec.
1946	Toronto, where Atwood remains until

graduate school; extended trips to northern Quebec and Ontario continue into the early fifties.

1952-57 Receives first full year of schooling at age 12; works with children at community centre; sister born. Attends Leaside High School, East York.

1957-61 Attends Victoria College, University of Toronto. Studies under Jay Macpherson, Kathleen Coburn, Northrop Frye, Millar MacLure.
Publishes poetry and prose in *Acta Victoriana*, college literary magazine. first publication by a national magazine, *Canadian Forum*, 1959: "Fruition", a poem. Receives B.A., Honours English, 1961.

1961 E.J. Pratt Medal for *Double Persephone*. Continued publication in *Acta Victoriana*, *Canadian Forum*; first publication in *Alphabet, Tamarack Review*.

1961-63 Cambridge, Mass.; studying Victorian literature under Jerome H. Buckley on a Woodrow Wilson Fellowship at Harvard. A.M. (Radcliffe) 1962. Doctoral studies.

1963-64 Toronto; works for market research company; lives near University of Toronto: writes first novel (unpublished) *Up in the Air So Blue*.

1964-65 Vancouver, Lecturer in English at University of British Columbia.

1965-67 Cambridge, Mass.; doctoral studies at Harvard. Governor General's Award for Poetry for *The Circle Game*, 1966. The Centennial Commission Poetry Competition first prize for *The Animals in that Country*, 1967. Marries fellow graduate student and American novelist, James Polk. Uncompleted Ph.D. dissertation "The English Metaphysical Romance".

1967-68 Montreal, Instructor in English at Sir George Williams University; teaches Victorian and American literature. Publication of *The Animals in that Country*, 1968.

1968-70 Edmonton, teaching creative writing at University of Alberta. Works on *The Journals of Susanna Moodie, Procedures for Underground*, and *Power Politics*. The Union Poetry Prize from *Poetry* (Chicago) for five poems from *Procedures for Underground*. *The Edible Woman* published, 1969; works on screenplay. Abandons a novel. Writes *Surfacing* (from approximately December 1969 to August 1970); works on *Up in the Tree* simultaneously.

1970-71 Publication of *The Journals of Susanna Moodie* and *Procedures for Underground*, 1970. Travels in England, France, Italy.

1971-72 Toronto, Assistant Professor of Humanities at York University; teaches Canadian culture; lecture notes form basis of *Survival*. Publication of *Power Politics*, 1971. Works on *Survival*. Editor and board member of House of Anansi Press until 1973.

1972-73 Toronto, Writer-in-Residence, University of Toronto. Publication of *Surfacing, Survival*, 1972. Separation from husband, divorce.

1973-75 Alliston, Ont., where Atwood continues to live with novelist Graeme Gibson. D.Litt., Trent University, 1973. Unpublished playscript, "Grace Marks", produced by CBC Television in January 1974 as *The Servant Girl*, part of the series "The Play's the Thing". Publication of *You Are Happy*, 1974. The Bess Hopkins Prize from *Poetry* (Chicago), 1974, for the animal poems in *You Are Happy*. LL.D., Queen's University, 1974. Cancels official trip to U.S.S.R. (as first Canadian writer invited by that country) in protest of Alexander Solzhenitsyn's expulsion for dissident views, 1974. Begins work on *Lady Oracle*. Member of the Board of Directors of Canadian Civil Liberties Association, 1973-75.

1976 Birth of daughter, Jess. Publication of *Selected Poems* and *Lady Oracle*. The City of Toronto Book Award for *Lady Oracle*.

1977 The Canadian Bookseller's Association Award for *Lady Oracle*. Works with Gibson on a screenplay for *The Diviners* (rejected). Does illustrations for *Up in the Tree*. *Dancing Girls, Days of the Rebels: 1815-1840*, published. St. Lawrence Award for Fiction (given by *Fiction International* and St. Lawrence University for best first collection of short fiction by a North American) for *Dancing Girls*. Works on *Two-Headed Poems*.

1978 Trip to Paris and Australia. Publication of *Two-Headed Poems* and *Up in the Tree*.

1978-79 Winter in Scotland working on *Life Before Man* while Gibson teaches on exchange at the University of Edinburgh. Publication of *Life Before Man*, 1979.

Comments
by Margaret Atwood

The public has given me a personality of not having a public personality. Sometimes they make up things about it like Margaret the Monster and Margaret the Magician and Margaret the Mother. Romantic notions of what's really there keep getting in the way of people's actual view of you.

Quoted in Roy MacGregor, "Atwood's World", *Macleans*, 15 October 1979, p. 66.

A number of things I've done have been attempts at mythological constructions of one kind or another. Taking an historical figure like Susanna Moodie, or a mythological figure as in the third section of *You Are Happy*, and exploring that to see what can come out of it ..... Of course, I am and always have been very interested in female mythological figures, and a lot of my early — very early — writing is about them. The first book I published was a Persephone book, which is another descent into the Underworld. But for a writer, these are patterns that you take off from.

> Quoted in Gail Van Varsveld, "Talking with Atwood", *Room of One's Own*, I, 2 (Summer 1975), 68.

I don't want to know how I write poetry. Poetry is dangerous: talking too much about it, like naming your gods, brings bad luck. I believe that most poets will go to almost any lengths to conceal their own reluctant, scanty insights both from others and from themselves. Paying attention to how you do it is like stopping in the middle of any other totally involving and pleasurable activity to observe yourself suspended in the fatal inner mirror: you may improve your so-called technique, but only at the expense of your so-called soul.

> "Poetic Process", *Field*, No. 4 (Spring 1971), p. 13.

I don't think of poetry as a "rational" activity but as an aural one. My poems usually begin with words or phrases which appeal more because of their sound than their meaning, and the movement and phrasing of a poem are very important to me. But like many modern poets I tend to conceal rhymes by placing them in the middle of lines, and to avoid immediate alliteration and assonance in favor of echoes placed later in the poems. For me, every poem has a texture of sound which is at least as important to me as the "argument".

> Quoted in Joyce Carol Oates, "An Interview with Margaret Atwood", *New York Times Book Review*, 21 May 1978, p. 15.

For a long time, men in literature have been seen as individuals, women merely as examples of a gender; perhaps it is time to take the capital W off Woman. I myself have never known an angel, a harpy, a witch, or an earth mother.

> "The Curse of Eve — Or, What I Learned in School", in Ann B. Shteir, ed., *Women on Women* (Toronto: York University, Press, 1978), p. 22.

To say that you must read your own literature to know who you are, to avoid being a sort of cultural moron, is not the same as saying that you should read nothing else, though the "internationalist" or Canada Last opponents of this notion sometimes think it is .... To know ourselves, we must know our own literature; to know ourselves accurately, we need to know it as part of literature as a whole.

> *Survival: A Thematic Guide to Canadian Literature* (Toronto: House of Anansi, 1972), p. 17.

Comments on Margaret Atwood

No other writer in Canada of Margaret Atwood's generation has so wide a command of the resources of literature, so telling a restraint in their use.

> George Woodcock, "Margaret Atwood: Poet as Novelist", in George Woodcock, ed., *The Canadian Novel in the Twentieth Century* (Toronto: McClelland and Stewart, 1975), p. 327.

Though unmistakeably of this country in her images and tone, as a poet Margaret Atwood has always been more concerned with private than with public ghosts: the crippling boredom that can strangle love; the vicious cycle of self-gratification that tears men and women apart, and, on a more metaphysical level, the stubborn task of reconciling civilization with this land studded with rocks and peopled with indifference.

> Barbara Amiel, "Poetry: Capsule Comments on Canada", *Maclean's*, 15 January 1979, p. 50.

Atwood's technical concerns have far-reaching implications. She is both the archetypal first Canadian, trying to build some shelter or structure against the hostile wilderness, and the archetypal first human waking from the unconscious sleep of evolution.

> Gary Geddes and Phyllis Bruce, "Margaret Atwood", in Gary Geddes and Phyllis Bruce, eds., *15 Canadian Poets* (Toronto: Oxford University Press, 1970), p. 226.

Selected Bibliography
Works by Margaret Atwood
Poetry

Double Persephone. Toronto: Hawkshead Press, 1961.
The Circle Game. Bloomfield Hills, Mich.: Cranbrook Academy of Art, 1964. 18 leaves (incl. 8 plates). [Limited edition of 15 copies, designed, printed and illustrated by Charles Pachter.]
Talismans for Children. Bloomfield Hills, Mich.: Cranbrook Academy of Art, 1965. 6 leaves (col. illus.).

[Limited edition of 10 copies.]

Kaleidoscopes Baroque: a Poem. Bloomfield Hills, Mich.: Cranbrook Academy of Art, 1965. 15 pp. [Limited edition of 20 copies. Col. illus. by Charles Pachter.]

Speeches for Doctor Frankenstein. Bloomfield Hills, Mich.: Cranbrook Academy of Art, 1966. 29 pp. [Limited edition of 15 copies, designed, printed, and color illustrated by Charles Pachter.]

Expeditions: Poems. Bloomfield Hills, Mich.: Cranbrook Academy of Art, 1966. 10 leaves (plates). [Lithographs by Charles Pachter. Limited edition of 15 copies.]

The Circle Game. Toronto: Contact Press, 1966.

The Animals in that Country. Toronto: Oxford University Press, 1968.

What Was in the Garden. Santa Barbara, Calif.: Unicorn Press, 1969. Broadside. [Color illustrated by Charles Pachter. Contained in *Unicorn Folio, Series 3, no. 1, a Canadian Folio.* One of twelve broadsides by Canadian poets.]

Dreams of the Animals, n.p., 197? Broadside (illus.).

The Journals of Susanna Moodie. Toronto: Oxford University Press, 1970.

Procedures for Underground. Toronto: Oxford University Press, 1970.

Power Politics. Toronto: House of Anansi, 1971.

You Are Happy. Toronto: Oxford University Press, 1974.

Selected Poems. Toronto: Oxford University Press, 1976.

Two-Headed Poems. Toronto: Oxford University Press 1978.

Fiction

The Edible Woman. Toronto: McClelland and Stewart, 1969.

Surfacing. Toronto: McClelland and Stewart, 1972.

Lady Oracle. Toronto: McClelland and Stewart, 1976.

Dancing Girls. Toronto: McClelland and Stewart, 1977.

Life Before Man. Toronto: McClelland and Stewart, 1979.

Other Prose

Survival: a Thematic Guide to Canadian Literature. Toronto: House of Anansi, 1972.

"Grace Marks". Unpublished playscript, 1974. 85 pp. [Produced on CBC Television in January 1974 as *The Servant Girl.*]

Days of the Rebels: 1815-1840. Canada's Illustrated Heritage series. Toronto: McClelland and Stewart, 1977.

Up in the Tree. Toronto: McClelland and Stewart, 1978 [Children's book].

Selected Criticism

Davey, Frank. "Atwood's Gorgon Touch", *Studies in Canadian Literature* II, 2 (Summer 1977), 146-163. Reprinted in Jack David, ed., *Brave New Wave* (Windsor: Black Moss Press, 1978), pp. 171-195.

Davidson, Arnold E. and Cathy N. "Margaret Atwood's *Lady Oracle:* The Artist as Escapist and Seer", *Studies in Canadian Literature* III, 2 (Summer 1978), 166-177.

Foster, John Wilson. "The Poetry of Margaret Atwood", *Canadian Literature,* No. 74 (Autumn 1977), pp. 5-20.

Gibson, Graeme. "Margaret Atwood" (interview). In Gibson's *Eleven Canadian Novelists* (Toronto: House of Anansi, 1973), 5-31.

Gibson, Mary Ellis. "A Conversation with Margaret Atwood" *Chicago Review* XXVII, 4 (Spring 1976), 105-113.

Grace Sherill. *Violent Duality: A Study of Margaret Atwood.* Montreal: Vehicule Press, 1980.

Mandel, Eli. "Atwood Gothic", *The Malahat Review,* No. 41 (January 1977), pp. 165-174.

Mansbridge, Francis. "Search for Self in the Novels of Margaret Atwood", *Journal of Canadian Fiction* No. 22 (1978), pp. 106-117.

Marshall, Tom. "Atwood Over and Above Water", *The Malahat Review,* No. 41 (January 1977), pp. 89-94.

Miner, Valerie. "Atwood in Metamorphosis: an Authentic Canadian Fairy Tale", in Myrna Kostash, ed., *Her Own Woman: Profiles of Ten Canadian Women* (Toronto: Macmillan, 1975), pp. 173-194.

Oates, Joyce Carol. "A Conversation with Margaret Atwood", *Ontario Review,* No. 9 (Fall-Winter 1978-79), pp. 5-18.

Rule, Jane. "Life, Liberty, and the Pursuit of Normalcy — the Novels of Margaret Atwood" *The Malahat Review,* No. 41 (January 1977), pp. 42-49.

Schiller, William. "Interview with Margaret Atwood", *Poetry Windsor Poésie,* 11, 3 (Fall 1976), 2-15.

Sillers, Pat. "Power Impinging: Hearing Atwood's Vision" *Studies in Canadian Literature,* IV, 1 (Winter 1979), 59-70.

Skelton, Robin. "Timeless Constructions — a Note on the Poetic Style of Margaret Atwood", *The Malahat Review,* No. 41 (January 1977), pp. 107-120.

Struthers, J.R. "An Interview with Margaret Atwood", *Essays on Canadian Writing,* No. 6 (Spring 1977), 18-27.

Woodcock, George. "Margaret Atwood: Poet as Novelist", in Woodcock, ed., *The Canadian Novel in the Twentieth Century* (Toronto: McClelland and Stewart, 1975), pp. 312-327.

Bibliographical Surveys

Horne, Alan J. "A Preliminary Checklist of Writings by and about Margaret Atwood", *The Malahat Review* No. 41 (January 1977), pp. 195-222.

Horne, Alan J. *Margaret Atwood: An Annotated Bibliography (Prose).* Downsview, Ont.: ECW Press, 1979. Reprinted in Robert Lecker and Jack David, ed., *The Annotated Bibliography of Canada's Major Authors* (Downsview, Ont.: ECW Press, 1979), Vol. I, 13-46.

A Note on the Contributor

Frank Davey is editor of *Open Letter* Professor of English at York University, his books include *Earle Birney* (1971), *From There to Here: a Guide to English-Canadian Literature since 1960* (1974), and *Louis Dudek & Raymond Souster* (1981).

Rudy Wiebe 23

by

Magdalene Redekop

Approaching the fiction of Rudy Wiebe, the reader is confronted with an apparent contradiction between Wiebe's pacifist beliefs and the violence which colours many of his stories. One of his short stories takes the reader into the tormented mind of a rapist as he confronts his terrified victim in her own home. The woman, desperately clutching a Bible as her world falls to pieces around her, is given no chance to speak. The nature of the rapist's violation is left ambiguous; instead, the story draws attention to the fact that her words never manage to 'violate' his world. The fragments that do get past the barrier are immediately drowned in his "stream of consciousness" and the limits of the first person narration become a formal reflection of the man's mental state. The story's reflexive style, its tortured syntax and verbal excesses, capture the narrator's preoccupation with the fact that he is confronting his own depravity. Indeed, his sinister argument goes back to the Biblical story of the fall: "The Devil in the Snake got Eve to eat the

apple by cracking a joke about God and the Devil's been laughing ever since. You laugh and you don't keep the proper things down no more — you get rid of them, right. The stuff's got to be kept down, down where it belongs and not laugh it away, and whatever you do you've got to be able to face it, square face to face and face it right out, and not once do you laugh it away easy."[1]

The man's obsession with his own original sin wipes out the reality of the woman who confronts him, sitting in a chair facing him, like a silent inquisitor, just outside the constricting limits of the story. The actual murder, when it comes, is merely a literal realization of this symbolic act. Although the woman never manages to penetrate the man's obsessive monologue, the implicit message of the story seems clear: only such a dialogue could release the hysterical laughter which lurks beneath the surface of the story and only such laughter could redeem the man from his own self-inflicted hell. The conflicts in Wiebe's fiction are not always of such psychological intensity but 'war', whether literal or symbolic, is a constant element in his fiction and the healing laughter and love of a community (however small) is a constant symbol for the possibility of redemption.

His first novel captures the paradox in its title: *Peace Shall Destroy Many.* The novel concerns the inner conflicts of a young Mennonite in the context of World War II. As is the case with many first novels, the story is autobiographical in theme, if not in content, although the protagonist, Thom Wiens, is by no means a mouthpiece for the novelist. In this novel the values of a small community often militate against the freedom of expression which is vital to the survival of an artist. Since the forces of language and tradition which set that community apart are often seen as constricting, it is fitting that the central figure of authority in the novel is a man called

Deacon Block. The enclosing community may be comforting; more often, in this novel, it seems claustrophobic. Thom Wiens does not go to war but war comes to him in the form of a tension between the desire to remain within the embrace of the community and the urge to respond to the challenges of a larger world. Few young Mennonites could have failed to see, in *Peace Shall Destroy Many,* a reflection of their own internal struggles, but the elders of Wiebe's own church were not amused and the hostile response to the novel led Wiebe to resign his position as editor of the church paper.

In his second novel, *First and Vital Candle,* Wiebe expanded the scope of his fiction to include the conflicts between Indians and white settlers. The theme anticipates the concerns of his last two books, but the novel has serious technical flaws. It was not until the writing of his third novel that Wiebe began a serious apprenticeship in the craft of manipulating fictional voices. Here, in *The Blue Mountains of China,* he returned to the subject of his own people, but with a difference in perspective. The years following the publication of his first novel had led him to discover, as he put it, a "broader concept of being Anabaptist".[2] This fact, along with a maturation in his response to the realities of the contemporary technological society, caused a radical change in perspective. Whereas in the first novel the story, in spite of its third person form, is told from within, in this novel the author is both inside and outside — both immanent and omniscient. In the first novel a small community is seen as a threat to individuality; here the community is viewed almost nostalgically. In *Peace Shall Destroy Many,* violence (aside from the distant fact of World War II) is a result of the stresses from within a confining community. In *The Blue Mountains of China,* violence more often results from the absence of such a community. Indeed, the voices of the external world which seem so seductive in the first novel, now seem associated with the forces responsible for blowing apart any possibility of community. Like more traditional Mennonites, Wiebe now seems to view technology with deep suspicion. With the larger scope of his third novel Wiebe achieved a deepened tragic vision and a clarified conservatism which he later brought to bear on the historical subjects of his last two novels.

The minds of Wiebe's characters, then, seem to serve as battlefields for the clashing of antagonists in a universal dichotomy: man's concept of an ideal confronts the reality which is eternally at war with that vision. The ideal vision is always portrayed within a thoroughly realized context and to this end the reader is moved from Russia, to China, Germany, Paraguay, and Canada. It is interesting to note that, whatever the country, the setting remains geographically constant: the prairie landscape forms a vast panoramic backdrop against which we can see, in relief, the elements of the struggles in which Wiebe demands that his readers engage.

In order to understand the complexity of these struggles and the urgency of Wiebe's challenge it is useful to place his fiction in the context of his own ethnic background. An examination of that background helps to trace the intellectual and historical roots of one central recurring element in his fiction: an idealized community (whether Mennonite, Indian, or Métis) is set off as antithetical to the larger collectivity of the state, whether communist or capitalist. The near vilification of a callous Sir John A. Macdonald in Wiebe's last novel, *The Scorched-Wood People,* is one example; it contrasts clearly with the sympathetic account of Louis Riel's vision of the 'people'. It is the portrayal of his own people which demonstrates most explicitly how deeply his sense of that antithesis is rooted in the fact that he is a Mennonite.

Mennonites were only one part of the anabaptist movement which formed the radical left of the Protestant reformation. The word 'anabaptist' was used derisively to refer to those Protestants who rejected infant baptism and insisted on rebaptism after adult conversion. Since infant baptism was a token of loyalty to the state, it became a symbol of something we now take for granted: the separation of church and state and the religious freedom that goes with it. It seemed to Menno Simons, after whom the movement was named, that the state was antithetically opposed to the church, as evidenced particularly in the fact that states wage war against each other. Mennonites consequently adopted pacifism and nonresistance as central beliefs. They also refused to take oaths of allegiance and they refused to take public office. In its historical context, however, such nonresistance was seen as a threat to the very fabric of society and consequently met with violent opposition. The persecution was brutal. Armed executioners were sent out to hunt down anabaptists and kill them on the spot. In Swabia, an original company of 400 special police (formed in 1528) had to be increased to 1000. More than 5000 anabaptists were killed in the first ten years alone. Eventually, the Dutch and German Mennonites (among them Wiebe's ancestors), escaped to Danzig and Prussia where they were granted religious freedom in exchange for the draining of swampland. Subsequent experiences in Russia served only to reinforce this pattern of persecution.

The experience of suffering and martyrdom has left its mark on Mennonite beliefs and can be seen in Wiebe's portrayal of Riel and Chief Big Bear, both of whom could take an honoured place in *Martyrs' Mirror,* a massive collection of stories written by early Mennonite martyrs. The history of Wiebe's own people supports his novelistic assumption that suffering is inevitable for those who are true to their vision. The vision can never coincide with the comfortable structures of the temporal world since, for Mennonites, ethics is not the same as civic morality. Since the concept of duty, correspondingly, is based on such a separation and may easily lead to civil disobedience, it should be clear that pacifism has very little to do with being passive. Indeed, it is this concept of pacifism which results in that world of constant conflict which is captured in Wiebe's fiction.

Wiebe's fiction demonstrates that the only way to heal the wounds suffered in this constant warfare is by means of the consolation and redemption of the community. The central dichotomy in his novels is not that between the individual and society but rather between two collectivities: the church (which *is* the community) and the world (or the state). Although Mennonites resisted the temptation of utopian beliefs that a perfect community is attainable, they believed that the attempt to approximate the ideal was dependent on separation from the world. For more than 400 years they have tried to maintain such a separation, by means of distinctive traditions, nonconformism, and a separate language. Whenever the separation was threatened, they fled to new frontiers. The resulting fragmentation is dramatized in *The Blue Mountains of China*, which traces the exodus up to the point of collision with the modern urban world.

An understanding of Wiebe's complex background helps to clarify the central place of morality in his art. The word 'religious' has been widely used to define his work but it is generally assumed to mean vaguely 'mystical', or 'transcendental', both terms which fail to reflect the very concrete basis of his Mennonite beliefs. More importantly, however, the label, used so loosely, also fails to do justice to Wiebe's craftsmanship — his mastery of that most concrete of genres: the novel. Professor W.J. Keith has pointed out that Wiebe writes "less about faith itself than about the difficulties of faith and the human matrix out of which faith is born."[3] Wiebe's attempt to provide a realistic depiction of this human world leads him to use a variety of complex fictional techniques. The formal obscurities of his novels are rendered transparent only when the reader has used them as a vehicle for the understanding of the moral vision. There is no substitute for a response to Wiebe's fiction which takes into consideration the total interdependence of his moral theme and his technical achievements. Since his approach to story-telling relies heavily on two basic elements, manipulation of narrative voice and control of time, let us look more closely at these two factors, taking *The Blue Mountains of China* as our primary text.

One of the most crucial decisions made by any writer who sets out to tell a story involves the problem of limitation: he must decide how to frame his story, what perspective to take on events. As Wiebe himself has said, "It is the person who looks at a particular world that counts."[4] Like many modern novelists, Wiebe uses a wide variety of narrative voices which work in counterpoint to create a complex pattern, much the way a film maker would create a montage or an artist a collage. His unusual flexibility in creating this medley of voices comes, to some extent, from the fact that he himself grew up speaking three separate languages: Low German dialect, High German, and English.

The first two chapters of *The Blue Mountains of China* illustrate how the use of separate voices is related both to time and to the moral theme. The novel begins with the voice of an old Mennonite woman, speaking directly to the reader in a voice which is paradoxically both distant and intimate: "I have lived long. So long, it takes me days to remember even parts of it, and some I can't remember at all until I've been thinking over it a little now and then for weeks .... But the Lord led me through so many deep ways and of the world I've seen a little, both north and south. If your eyes stay open and He keeps your head clear you sometimes see so much more than you want of how it is with the world. And if you don't you can thank Him for that, too" (p. 7). The humorous and endearing simplicity of Frieda Friesen's style directly reflects the simplicity of her faith: "....it does come all from God, strength and sickness, want and plenty" (p. 10). The voice of Frieda (her very name is German for 'peace') absorbs and symbolizes the quiet, separate community which makes her faith possible. This simple voice will serve as a guide to the reader who is about to be plunged into a much more confusing world.

Frieda's narrative is retrospective and autobiographical, as reflected in the title of the chapter: "my life: that's as it was (1)". She looks back over a stretch of more than ninety years from the present of the novel (Paraguay, 1967) to her early life in Manitoba. This backward thrust of the narrative is sharply accentuated in the shift from the first to the second chapter, which takes us back to a time when Mennonites were hunted down. At the same time, by its vividly contrasting style, the second chapter draws the reader forward into the story. In this chapter the reader is moved abruptly from the peaceful setting in Paraguay to the Russia of 1929. The first-person reflections of Frieda Friesen are juxtaposed with a third-person stream of consciousness narrative which plunges the reader into the experience of Jakob Friesen. From the first moment, we are forced to share his imprisonment as we are deprived of the expansive plains of Frieda's serene narrative and placed in a tiny cell: "The cell had one opening: the door. Three half steps long, nearly two wide, thirteen rows of sweating stone floor to ceiling"

(p. 12). In a further reversal, Jakob is abruptly released from the prison and returns, in ecstasy, to the open plains and to his home, only to find the farm deserted, his family fled. His radical disorientation is reflected in the fragmentation of the style: ". . . how many sisters do you believe the bible were you october 6 is your name where is your father six you read the bible in they are all gone   jesus has come again and taken them and I am left for hell and the devil and his angels and the place prepared   he could not find me with the GPU   he could not take me. . ." (p. 14).

The reader is challenged to respond to the harsh contrast between chapters one and two. Faced with the baffling complexities and the syntactical confusion of the second chapter, he may wish for a return to the comforting simplicity of the first chapter. Such a return, indeed, will come but it is made clear from the beginning that the only way to move forward in this novel is to move backwards in time. More specifically, the only way back to the present (1967) of Frieda's narrative is by means of an exploration of the past (beginning in 1929). From the vast panorama of Frieda's narrative, where one paragraph can cover a decade, Wiebe moves us to a scene of imprisonment in which time passes with the agonizing slowness of a nightmare. The shift in pacing, a characteristic element of Wiebe's fiction, is effective for reasons that point directly towards his moral theme. In contrasting the old woman's peaceful vision with the young man's hellish experience, Wiebe has encapsulated the theme and made certain that his readers will be aware that any positive affirmation to follow will involve a community ideal. Young Jakob is isolated from the community of Mennonites whose presence resonates in the voice of Frieda Friesen. The ecstatic homecoming after his release, followed by the shock of finding his family gone ("I am left for hell and the devil") provides a shattering picture of hell as the individual self. Divorced from his people, Jakob is no longer human and is catapulted with horrifying speed into his own personal hell. He murders a Russian servant, then is himself murdered.

Even such a cursory analysis of the first two chapters illustrates that Wiebe's use of various narrative voices and his shifts from first person to third person narrative go along with his manipulation of time levels, and that both are inextricably related to his moral theme. The movement backwards in time to the second chapter suggests inversion and reflects the general sense of dislocation and distortion in the novel. At the same time, it anticipates the novel's central affirmation. From the beginning, the voice of Frieda seems to console the reader with the knowledge that the tragedy of the individual will finally be contained in a larger vision of community. Frieda, who is over ninety years old, has arrived at a point of serene understanding. By contrast, the characters who form the focal point of other chapters are caught up in conflict, a conflict which again defines the opposing forces of community and larger world. Inevitably, this triggers flight and exile. Starting with the story of young Jakob, Wiebe takes that strand of Mennonite history forward, following the travels of groups from Russia to Canada. These chapters are interspersed with four instalments that take us back to the voice of Frieda Friesen. The fact that each of her chapters has the same title makes her story seem static, as though to suggest that she has arrived. The reader may even be tempted to think that the myriads of wandering Mennonites in the book will ultimately come home to be embraced by her warm voice.

But the novel's affirmation, in the end, is muted. The thread of Frieda's narrative began the book but it seems unequal to the task of neatly rounding off the book. This is because the pattern of recurring exile is radically altered when it comes into collision with the facts of a modern technological society. In such a homogenized society there are no frontiers left and there seems no way of escaping the fact of mass communication and mass transportation. The final words of Frieda Friesen emphasize the existence of her primitive community in Paraguay on a level separate from the modern North American urban world. She has just returned from a visit to her children in Canada. ". . . I got out of the plane and into the buggy and we drove home the sandy road to Schoenbach. Simons Colony. Stopping at all the villages on the way took longer than coming from New York" (p. 150).

These words are the last the reader hears from Frieda Friesen. We are not told of her death. Her story has no end; it simply stops. We remain conscious of her presence, however, since the last two chapters of the novel bring the remainder of the story up to the time of her life; past is drawn up flush with the present. In these chapters, Wiebe, with relentless honesty, brings his characters up sharply against the barriers to faith set up by an urban, technological society. Television, it turns out, is a more formidable enemy than the Russian police. The last chapter brings together Mennonites from many countries, meeting by chance in a ditch in Canada. They produce varied reactions to the strange figure of John Reimer, a Mennonite who is carrying a cross along the highway. Although Reimer speaks of love and brotherhood, it is made clear that the Mennonite community is permanently splintered.

One central character is left out of the meeting in the ditch: Frieda Friesen. With the sound of her voice still echoing in our minds, we may be tempted to interpret the last chapter as an elegy, a lament for the passing of any possibility of a Mennonite community. But Wiebe does not allow his readers to indulge in simple nostalgia. As a polar opposite to the absent Frieda Friesen,

Reimer and his cross, a potentially embarrassing public spectacle, stand as a challenge to the Mennonite habit of withdrawal, making complacency an impossibility for the reader. The didactic tone of the ending seems to suggest that Wiebe is affirming human and Christian values which transcend those of any insular goup. Some readers have even suggested that these values are a judgement on the values of conservative Mennonites like Frieda Friesen. Such variations in interpretation point to the ambivalence in the ending of this novel. Wiebe's focus on Reimer makes many readers feel that they are being asked to make a choice; yet the novel itself seems to make an absolute choice impossible. Perhaps, in the end, Wiebe himself could not "vote" for either Frieda Friesen or Reimer. His vision of the past is coloured by the reality of the present and the ideals of the future.

The very knowledge that the planes which fly overhead can bring the Mennonite people together, seems both a consolation and a threat since it radically alters the definition of the "separate people". Indeed, since Mennonites have always been known as "die Stillen im Lande" ("the quiet ones in the land"), the very fact that Frieda's story is translated from the Low German into English destroys the wall of separation which was the primary impulse behind the use of a separate language. The result is tension. Since the novel works as a montage, it must be taken in its entirety. When the reader does so, it becomes apparent that there is a tension between the backward-looking memory of Frieda (life "as it was") and the forward-looking movement of the last chapter (which is entitled "On the Way"). Neither past nor future is adequate by itself, and the reader, like the mythological Janus, is forced to look both ways. Only through a discovery of the past, do any of the characters acquire the inner resources to move into the future.

In his last two novels, Wiebe has continued this historical emphasis. The sequence of his novels points directly to the conviction that the gap between the demands of a transcendent vision and the pressures of immediate reality can only be mediated by history – more specifically, by history turned into myth. In *The Blue Mountains of China* it is Frieda Friesen who acts as the family historian. Her grand-daughter laments: "If only Muttchi were here . . . she'd know. She knows everything like this " (p. 208). Frieda is a visionary in the immanent sense of being able to see that the past has pattern and meaning, not in the transcendent sense of hearing voices. In translating her vision from the Low German, Wiebe forges a myth out of the facts of his own silent past.

His next novel, *The Temptations of Big Bear*, accentuates the powerful place of the translator or the craftsman who mediates a vision,

rescuing it from the oblivion of the past. Here the silent nomadic Indian takes the place of the silent wandering Mennonite and Wiebe, removed from the materials of his own familiar past, dwells more on the *process* of meditation. From the opening scene of the novel, the reader is confronted with the fact that sound and vision seem estranged from each other. The first appearance of Big Bear is conveyed in cinematic terms as the Governor observes his approach through a telescope: " 'There's plenty of...' oddly, while it drew a spot closer, the telescope seemed at the same time to push that spot back into a kind of greyish-ringed haze; the Indian swaying gently with the bay horse, 'of time to hunt, it's good he . . .' as if he were very far away, barely moving in a flat, constant green circle at the end of an unbelievably long tunnel, 'he's in time, good, to make treaty.' "[5]

The interrupted syntax of this passage points to the separation of sight and sound. The role of the translator (in this case, Peter Erasmus) is to synchronize the two and the remainder of the novel attempts to do just that by mediating Big Bear's vision of his people. Paradoxically, the result is an increasingly ironic isolation of Big Bear. At his final trial, he is a painfully remote, silent presence, while the voices of the lawyers and translators chatter on. Although he gets his chance to speak and the translator is sympathetic, the reader senses that his listeners have ears but hear not. Big Bear concludes: "A word is power. . . I have said my last words. Who will say a word for my people?" (p. 398).

The translator at the trial, Peter Houri, makes valiant efforts but only succeeds in suggesting to Big Bear that the phrase "her crown and dignity" refers to a lady's hat. The picture and the sound remain separate, as illustrated in Kitty McLean's reaction at the trial: "she found herself trying again and again to focus Big Bear through the outside edge of the judge's egg-shaped glasses..." (p. 381). The picture refuses to focus and the reader's attention is directed more to the misunderstanding than to the vision itself. The final affirmation is a paradoxical one since the picture and the sound are unified only by the novel itself and the only 'simultaneous translator' is the novelist as myth-maker who gives voice to the past.

The Temptations of Big Bear won Wiebe the Governor General's Award for Fiction in 1973. Its fascinations notwithstanding, however, the slow pace makes the experience of reading the novel somewhat like the frustration of watching television with the sound turned off. Here the moral vision and the craft do not find as happy a synthesis as they did in the previous novel. The myth-making process is more clearly focussed in Wiebe's last novel, *The Scorched-Wood People*, where he employs the Métis song-writer Pierre

Falcon to tell the story of Louis Riel and Gabriel Dumont. Once again, however, the reader is left with a picture of isolated figures, contrasting ironically with the vision of community. Like Samuel Reimer in *The Blue Mountains of China*, Louis Riel hears voices. But Falcon draws attention to the fact that it is only when Riel is separated from his people that he hears these voices. The most extreme point of isolation comes during the last chapters when Riel is in his prison cell, awaiting the day of his execution. Bereft of the company of family and friends, Riel, like Jakob Friesen in the earlier novel, might have succumbed to violence. Instead, he channels his energies into writing. Time is against him, however, and like Big Bear he despairs of being able to capture his vision in words. Once again, it is the novelist as myth-maker who achieves that victory. The incoherent fragments of Riel's actual diaries are salvaged by Wiebe and become part of a pattern which snatches life from the very jaws of death. Louis Riel, like Big Bear, transcends his own death by having his story told.

The direction of Wiebe's fiction emerges from this survey of the last three novels. Confronted by the modern technological world, Wiebe's emphasis on the value of community has been transmuted into a conviction about the power of myth. His fiction offers no easy solution to the challenge posed by a contemporary individualistic society. Instead, his novels have moved deeper and deeper into an exploration of the past, perhaps reflecting a conviction that only the past, kept alive in memory, can redeem the present. His novels have mined a rich vein of the Canadian literary tradition, in which Canada is seen as a mosaic of exiled peoples. It is the exploration of his own past which has provided Wiebe with a perspective from which to judge the contemporary world and it may be the threat to the survival of his own people which gives such urgency to his fiction.

[1] Rudy Wiebe, "Did Jesus Ever Laugh?" in *Where is the Voice Coming From?* (Toronto: McClelland and Stewart), 1974, p.66.

[2] Rudy Wiebe, quoted in "Rudy Wiebe: Novelist, Vindicator, and Christian", [anonymous] *Festival Quarterly* (Fall, 1978), p. 31.

[3] W.J. Keith, "Introduction" to Rudy Wiebe, *The Blue Mountains of China* (Toronto: McClelland and Stewart, 1975), p. 1. Subsequent references are to this edition and page references will be incorporated in the text.

[4] Rudy Wiebe, "A Novelist's Personal Notes on Frederick Philip Grove", *University of Toronto Quarterly*, XLVII (Spring 1978), 192.

[5] Rudy Wiebe, *The Temptations of Big Bear* (Toronto: McClelland and Stewart, 1976), p. 14.

Chronology

Comments
by Rudy Wiebe

...to touch this land [the prairie] with words requires an architectural structure; to break into the space of the reader's mind with the space of this western landscape and the people in it you must build a structure of fiction like an engineer builds a bridge or a skyscraper over and into space. A poem, a lyric, will not do. You must lay great black steel lines of fiction, break up that space with huge design and, like the fiction of the Russian steppes, build giant artifact. No song can do that; it must be giant fiction.

"Passage by Land", *Canadian Literature*, No. 48 (Spring 1971), pp. 26-27.

I would like to think of myself as someone who's trying to live what the original Anabaptists were about. They are very contemporary, in a way, because they felt that the social structures that evolved in the west had no sanction. To be an Anabaptist is to be a radical follower of the person of Jesus Christ — that's really what it's about — and Jesus Christ had no use for the social and political structures of his day; he came to *supplant* them.

In an interview with Donald Cameron, recorded in *Conversations with Canadian Novelists, Part Two* (Toronto: Macmillan, 1973), p. 148.

Trusting the 'quintuplet senses', the story teller, too, has been tutoring them, to be his guide through the maze of life and imagination. Through the smoke and darkness and piled up factuality of a hundred years to see a face; to hear, and comprehend, a voice whose verbal language he will never understand; and then to risk himself beyond such seeing, such hearing as he discovers possible, and venture into the finer labyrinths opened by those other senses: touch, to learn the texture of leather, of earth; smell, the tinct of sweetgrass and urine; taste, the golden poplar sap or the hot, raw buffalo liver dipped in gall ....

"On the Trail of Big Bear", *Journal of Canadian Fiction*, III, 2 (Spring 1974), 45.

...the largest quality I find on reading Grove is an old-fashioned one, but one of surpassing importance. It is wisdom. 'True realism,' Grove writes in *It Needs To Be Said*, 'always develops a conflict in such a manner that we see all sides, understand all sides, sympathize with all sides taken separately, and yet cannot tell how that conflict can be avoided which, as it unfolds itself, crushes our sensibilities.' . . . For Grove, artistry is not more important than wisdom; nor does he feel that artistry alone will achieve it. In both these matters I agree with him.

'A Novelist's Personal Notes on Frederick Philip Grove", *University of Toronto Quarterly*, XLVII (Spring 1978), p. 198.

Fiction is always truer than fact in this sense: it is never possible to know all the facts about anything, even the very smallest act. The things done vanish with their doing; they can live only in a living memory, and the true story-teller has the unstoppable longing to capture these acts forever beyond memory. I cannot let this act die because I lived it, because it was lived by someone important to me, because it is an act that is of itself meaningful; there are any number of origins for that passionate emotion which seizes a story-teller and will not let him rest until he has *made*

something out of facts.

"A Novelist's Personal Notes on Frederick Philip Grove", p. 193.

As Robert Kroetsch once said to Margaret Laurence: 'In a sense we haven't got an identity until someone tells our story. The fiction makes us real.' There are still large elements of prairie society that *must* be made real.

"Mermaid Inn", *Toronto Globe & Mail* March 25, 1978), p. 6.

Comments on Rudy Wiebe

Wiebe is religious in the Lawrentian as well as in the Christian sense. That is to say, he is deeply, passionately concerned with values that transcend the material - with the quality of human living.

W.J. Keith, in the introduction to *The Blue Mountains of China* (Toronto: McClelland and Stewart, 1970), p.i.

Wiebe determines to restore to us the history and justice we have lost through spiritual atrophy . . . . He endeavours to bind us together with a place, to regenerate community across time, to make the land breathe with the lives of people who have lived on it, to make us responsible each to all and all to everything that is and was.

John Moss in *Sex and Violence in the Canadian Novel* (Toronto: McClelland and Stewart, 1977), p. 259.

Our history is a history of fragments; God has torn the veil of our people; He hath scattered us in remnants abroad. Wiebe has gathered up the fragments: often, he has grappled with us clumsily, or violently, as we ourselves are a clumsy and a violent people . . . often, he has taken us gently like children by the hand, as we also may be gentle and like children. One would think that, gathering fragments from so many diverse places - from Winnipeg to Siberia to South America - Wiebe would be left with a patchwork quilt. But truly, we are all of the same cloth. Truly, gathered together in our kulak boots and our blistered feet and our imported alligator shoes, we are all one family.

The response of a Mennonite, David Toews, to *The Blue Mountains of China*. Quoted by Hildegard E. Tiessen in "A Mighty Inner River: 'Peace' in the Fiction of Rudy Wiebe", *Journal of Canadian Fiction*. II, 4 (Fall 1973), 71.

With respect to structure, Rudy Wiebe's *The Blue Mountains of China* may be the most demanding novel Canada has yet produced. This is so partly . . . because it is a documentation of a family history reaching back (from 1967) over three generations, tracing several branches over routes of exile through four countries. . . . Wiebe is a Mennonite, and Mennonite family history is itself a living reification of Biblical hermeneutic.

David L. Jeffrey in "Biblical Hermeneutic and Family History in Contemporary Canadian Fiction: Wiebe and Laurence", *Mosaic*, XI, 3 (Spring, 1978), 99.

The novel, traditionally tied to mundane reality in all its concreteness, confusion and complexity and implicitly locating value in the time-bound world of the here and now, presents a profound challenge to any transcendent, timeless vision. Wiebe's solution is bold and sophisticated: he makes narrative itself the problem. . . . The novel itself, multiple and fragmented, highlights the absence of such integrative vision and engages the reader in his own struggle in a narrative wilderness.

Ina Ferris in "Religious Vision and Fictional Form: Rudy Wiebe's *The Blue Mountains of China*", *Mosaic*, XI, 3 (Spring 1978), 79.

Wiebe's Mennonite heritage has fostered a special kind of dry and witty survival humour, not unlike Jewish humour, perhaps because of a similarity of experience undergone by Mennonites and Jews.

Patricia A. Morley in *The Comedians: Hugh Hood and Rudy Wiebe* (Toronto: Clarke, Irwin & Co. Ltd., 1977), p. 7.

Selected Bibliography
Works by Wiebe

Peace Shall Destroy Many. Toronto: McClelland and Stewart, 1962. [Reprinted in the New Canadian Library edition with an introduction by J.M. Robinson, 1972.]

First and Vital Candle. Toronto: McClelland and Stewart, 1966.

The Blue Mountains of China. Toronto: McClelland and Stewart, 1970. [Reprinted in the New Canadian Library edition with an introduction by W.J. Keith, 1975.]

The Temptations of Big Bear. Toronto: McClelland and Stewart, 1973. [Reprinted in the New Canadian Library edition with an introduction by Allan Bevan, 1976.]

Where Is the Voice Coming From? Toronto: McClelland and Stewart, 1974. [Short stories.]

The Scorched-Wood People. Toronto: McClelland and Stewart, 1977.

Far As the Eye Can See. Edmonton: NeWest Press, 1977. [A play written in collaboration with Theatre Passe Muraille.]

Alberta: A Celebration. (With Harry Savage and Tom Radford). Edmonton: Hurtig, 1979. [Short stories.] This bibliography excludes a listing of Wiebe's short stories published in various periodicals, since, with only a few exceptions, these have been anthologized in *Where Is the Voice Coming From?* or incorporated in one of the above novels.

Works Edited by Wiebe

The Story-Makers. Toronto: Macmillan, 1970.

Stories from Western Canada. Toronto: Macmillan, 1972.

Stories from Pacific and Arctic Canada. Toronto: Macmillan, 1974. [Co-edited. Selection of Pacific tales with introduction by Andreas Schroeder; selection of Arctic tales with introduction by Wiebe.]

Double Vision: An Anthology of Twentieth-Century Stories in English. Toronto: Macmillan, 1976.

Getting Here: Stories Selected by Rudy Wiebe. Edmonton: NeWest Press, 1977.

More Stories from Western Canada. [Co-edited with Aritha Van Herk.] Toronto: Macmillan, 1980.

Selected Criticism

Bilan, R.P. "Wiebe and Religious Struggle", *Canadian Literature*, No. 77 (Summer 1978), pp. 50-63.

Cameron, Donald. "Rudy Wiebe: The Moving Stream is Perfectly at Rest", in his *Conversations with Canadian Novelists, Part Two* (Toronto: Macmillan, 1973), pp. 146-60. [Interview.]

Dueck, Allan. "A Sense of the Past", *Journal of Canadian Fiction*, 2 (Fall 1973), pp. 88-91. [Review of *Temptations of Big Bear*.]

Ferris, Ina. "Religious Vision and Fictional Form: Rudy Wiebe's *The Blue Mountains of China*", *Mosaic*, XI, 3 (Spring 1978), 79-85.

Jeffrey, David L. "Biblical Hermeneutic and Family History in Contemporary Canadian Fiction: Wiebe and Laurence", *Mosaic*, XI, 3 (Spring 1978), 87-106.

Mansbridge, Francis. "Wiebe's Sense of Community", *Canadian Literature*, No. 77 (Summer 1978), pp. 42-9.

Melnyk, George. "The Western Canadian Imagination: An Interview with Rudy Wiebe", *Canadian Fiction Magazine*, 12 (Winter 1974), pp. 29-34.

Morley, Patricia A. *The Comedians: Hugh Hood and Rudy Wiebe*. Toronto: Clarke Irwin, 1977.

Moss, John. "Genocide: The White Man's Burden", in *Sex and Violence in the Canadian Novel: The Ancestral Present* (Toronto: McClelland and Stewart, 1977), pp. 256-73.

Taylor, Lauralyn. "*The Temptations of Big Bear*: A Filmic *Novel?*", *Essays on Canadian Writing*, No. 9 (Winter 1977-8), pp. 134-8.

Tefs, Wayne. "Rudy Wiebe: Mystery and Reality", *Mosaic*, XI, 4 (Summer 1978), 155-8.

Tiessen, Hildegaard E. "A Mighty Inner River: Peace in the Fiction of Rudy Wiebe", *Journal of Canadian Fiction*, II (Fall 1973), 71-6.

A Note on the Contributor

Magdalene Redekop grew up in a Mennonite community in Manitoba and now teaches English at the University of Toronto. Although her main area of interest is romantic narrative, her work as Secondary School Liaison Representative has fostered an interest in textbook publishing. Her publications include a biography of Ernest Thompson Seton, written for high school readers.

Alice Munro

by
James Carscallen

Courtesy: Sheila Munro.

As of the middle of 1980, Alice Munro has published four books: two collections of stories, called *Dance of the Happy Shades* (1963) and *Something I've Been Meaning to Tell You* (1974), and two novels, *Lives of Girls and Women* (1971) and *Who Do You Think You Are?* (1978). For the first and last of these she received the Governor General's Award for Fiction. Her biography is very simple. Born in 1931, she grew up in Wingham, Ontario, in Huron County, and went to the University of Western Ontario in London. After two years there she married and moved to the West Coast, where her three daughters were born and where some of her stories are set. Since 1972 she has been living with her second husband in Clinton, Ontario, not far from Wingham. Some factual material from her life and the lives around her appears in her stories — more, perhaps, than most of us are aware. Her father, for instance, was among other things a trapper and a fox-farmer, and her mother suffered from Parkinson's Disease.

The knowledge of these facts, however, will not really help us to understand the stories in which Munro uses them, since it will not tell us why she has picked some facts and left out or changed others. Munro has acknowledged that Del Jordan in *Lives of Girls and Women* is much like her own girlhood self, in her emotions at any rate; but even Del could not have been the way she is if that had not suited the book Munro wanted to write. We need to know, then, what kind of book that is.

Munro is a writer of short stories, and even her novels — to call them that — are, as she has said, sequences of linked stories. The term "short story" can mean just what it says, a story that does not go on for very long; but Munro's stories, like most of those written in the twentieth century, are something more specialized. We might expect *Lives of Girls and Women* to start by giving us some basic information about its characters and setting, and go on from there. If it were a fairy-tale, for example, it would have an opening something like this: "Once upon a time there was a girl called Del Jordan, who lived with her parents at the end of the Flats Road near Jubilee, Ontario; their nearest neighbour was called Benny." Now here is what we actually get: "We spent days along the Wawanash River, helping Uncle Benny fish." Readers nowadays are so used to this kind of opening they may take it for granted, and forget how strange it would sound to someone used only to fairy-tales and the like. But a child hearing it would immediately raise questions: who are "we"? who is Uncle Benny? where is the Wawanash River? Since Munro has done her work carefully, we can pick up what we need to know as we go along, but the narrator is speaking as if we knew it already: it is as if we had just tuned in on a programme that had begun some time before.

We often find the same kind of thing at the end of a Munro story. The chapter "Age of

Faith", for instance, comes to focus on the episode of Major the dog, who has to be shot. We are never told, though, whether Major is actually shot or not – presumably he is, but the narrative breaks off before that happens. The novel as a whole breaks off as Del says "Yes" to Bobby Sherriff: we never find out what happens when she leaves Jubilee (if she does), or even how the visit with Bobby ends. A short story in the special sense is thus like a deliberate fragment; and this characteristic matches another that we find in Munro's work. If you try telling one of her stories to a friend, you may find that it hardly makes a "good story" at all: even if it crystallizes around a striking incident, much of what Munro puts in may be at most loosely related to that incident. "The Flats Road" goes on for some pages not only about Uncle Benny but about everyone else in the neighbourhood, with an anecdote about Sandy Stevenson thrown in. The next chapter is centred on an incident at a funeral, but before and after that it seems to wander in various directions on the general topic of life at Jenkin's Bend. In fact, it sounds less like a pure story than like a reminiscence – we can imagine Del years later thinking it all over, rambling either in her thoughts or out loud to a friend.

One tendency in reminiscence, of course, is to spin out a story or argument in a very continuous way. We can feel this happening with the talkative narrator of "Forgiveness in Families", evidently the kind of person who likes to tell her tale, and would not want the flow of her grievances interrupted. In "The Flats Road", on the other hand, the account of an excited discussion can suddenly turn into information about vixens and the way they used to behave when planes flew over low. When we are thinking things over, something in us wants to break any *line* of thought, and in an extreme case like "The Ottawa Valley" the result is a jumble of separate memories of which the sequence seems hardly to matter. It is true that in this story the narrator herself is puzzled, but she would not be any less so if she arranged her memories as a more continuous story-line. Perhaps it is a different kind of order that she is groping for.

It is significant that the narrator of "The Ottawa Valley" calls her memories "snapshots": she thinks of them, not as stories, though some of them are that as well, but as pictures. A title like "The Flats Road" or "The Ottawa Valley" implies that what we are told adds up to a picture of a locality, and when we call Munro a regional writer, one thing we mean is that her stories, or many of them, add up to a picture of the rural Ontario in which she grew up. The climaxes of a chapter like "The Flats Road" come, not necessarily at crises in the story itself, but at points where the chapter's picture comes together for someone to *see*. We generally use the word "epiphany", which means "appearing", for the

kind of thing that happens when Uncle Benny comes back from Toronto. Events have calmed down; he has time to sit and describe what he experienced, and "we could see it, we could see how it was to be lost there, how it was just not possible to find anything, or go on looking". And what the Jordans see in effect is the Flats Road itself. Uncle Benny has been talking about Toronto, of course, but if we look again we will find that he has described a place much like the house he lives in, or Grenoch Swamp, or his neighbourhood generally. We can even say that Benny *is* the Flats Road — the kind of person who goes with that kind of place. He has brought about an epiphany of the unmanageable world that he lives in and is, and he has thus succeeded in the one way he unconsciously meant to. Del must see this epiphany — which means that she must both see Benny himself and see as Benny sees — if she is to grow beyond the child that he will always be. Other observers in Munro see less well, and since no one within a story can see the whole of it, some of the seeing is always left to the person who is able to see most fully – the reader. But in every case it is seeing that is needed.

Now we can ask what happens when a whole novel is dominated by this concern with seeing – a novel, for instance, in which a girl is slowly learning what she must see to be a writer. A novel like this is usually called a *Bildungsroman*, a German word meaning a novel *(Roman)* of education or formation *(Bildung)*. The best-known in English is James Joyce's *Portrait of the Artist as a Young Man*, and in it you will find the same kind of organization as in Munro's two novels: there are great gaps in time between the chapters, and each of these chapters contains a variety of experiences that come together when the hero, or the reader, sees a meaning in them. This is the kind of story and the kind of book that Munro tends to write, and perhaps we can understand it further if we now go on to ask what it is that we see when we see meaning.

II

The feeling of meaningfulness is not an easy one to understand or explain, but it seems to depend on a sense that two different things are the same or at least alike: as we say, "it's like that" or "that's the way it is". In "The Flats Road", for instance, efforts to catch or keep wild things seem to be the way it is. Del's father is a fox-farmer, foxes being animals that cannot quite be tamed; Del and Owen are trailed across the field by Major, the family dog but an "unsociable" one; Uncle Benny, who likes hunting and fishing, has a yard full of half-wild animals, some in pens and some not. When you think of it, Benny and Madeleine are like half-wild animals too; and each of them is both hunter and hunted in relation to the other one, since Benny catches Madeleine as a bride and later hunts her in Toronto, while from another point of view he himself got caught when he took the lure of an ad in the paper. As we come to see the elements of the chapter in this way, we can respond more fully to details like the screen door in the last scene, with its spring "stretching then snapping back", as if the house as well were a trap. In fact, the less some element in a Munro story has to do with its plot, the more it invites us to feel this relation of likeness. "Age of Faith", for instance, has an opening section about burglary, and something in our minds then wants to see if the rest of the chapter is about burglary too, even though burglars in the strict sense are never mentioned again. The chapter "Who Do You Think You Are?", after being largely about Milton Homer, turns into being about Ralph Gillespie; but Ralph "does" Milton – both mimics him and acts like him – and Rose does Ralph in turn. When we see these correspondences, the chapter starts to come together for us, and we feel that it means something.

But all this seems strange in view of Munro's realism: surely, we may say, she is observing what is there, honestly and accurately, not working it up into sets of parallels. There can be no doubt of Munro's realism or its power, but perhaps it needs to be thought about further. In the first place, we should notice that "realism" can be understood in different ways. One thing we often mean by the word is simply plausibility. In a fairy-tale events often go against our notions of what is likely or even possible, as when a frog turns into a prince on being kissed by a beautiful princess. Munro is playing a game with different rules, and playing it very scrupulously: with only apparent exceptions, there is nothing in her stories that might not happen, and happen without too great an improbability, in the real world. But she often makes us feel, not merely "yes, that could happen", but "that's just what does happen — that's just the way it is". When we respond in this way, we are all the more likely to say that the author has observed truthfully and given us the facts; but this is where some questions arise.

We have seen that Munro's stories are partly factual and partly not, but even if they were entirely factual it would still be impossible to "give the facts" without doing a lot of selecting (as anyone can learn by trying to describe something without omitting any fact about it); and even if it were not impossible to give all the facts, doing this would not by itself create the effect of realism. At the end of *Lives of Girls and Women* Del Jordan is going to try for all the facts about Jubilee, but she will come to feel that she is on the wrong tack. Here, by contrast, is a bit from "The Found Boat", in which two girls cycle down to see a river that has flooded in the spring: "They left the road . . ., and rode right into a field, over a wire fence entirely flattened by the weight of the winter's snow. They coasted a little way before the long grass stopped them, then left their bicycles lying down and went to the water." Even a reader who does not live in the country can experience the pleasure of recognition here, the feeling of "that's the way it is." Yet Munro has not given many details, and if we added or substituted others the passage would not work as well. It looks, then, as if some principle is involved other than that of giving the facts.

For a clue to this principle, we might think of the turns of speech people use in Munro's stories. When Del Jordan's great aunts say "he preferred not" or "doesn't he think he's somebody!" their whole outlook on life is focussed in a single phrase: it is just like them to belittle anyone who tries to be different. Munro has a very sharp ear for phrases of this kind, like Uncle Benny's "I sure will" or Mr. Boyce's "*Con Brio, Miss Farris!*" or Fern Dougherty's "having a good time". Or it may be things people do rather than things they say: Fern absently crooning the aria of which she has forgotten the words, Miss Farris skating around and around in her revealing costume, Jerry Storey nervously creasing and tearing a paper napkin in a restaurant. Like Hugo in "Material", Munro has the knack of hitting on the *typical* detail, the one that sums up the reality it belongs to — even if Mr. Boyce says "*Con brio, Miss Farris!*" only once in his life.

Such detail resonates, as it were, because it suggests a likeness in the way we have been talking about: Jerry Storey's shredded napkin, for example, goes with his way of bringing atrocities and nuclear explosions into the conversation. For the other side of Jerry, we can think of his mother folding and ironing her towels, and keeping Jerry himself like something precious "wrapped up in a drawer". In this last case there is an explicit simile: Jerry is like something wrapped up — something, perhaps, that would secretly like to tear its wrapping apart. The imagery of napkins and towels brings out Jerry's type, and this is also what Del does in the novel she is writing: she reaches from "reality" to "truth", to use her own terms. The Gothic thriller she comes up with has the same kinds of people and events, and the same shape, as what she perceives in Jubilee; but she is trying to make that shape stand out. Her mistake, as she comes to feel, is to bring out the truth of reality to the point where it is not reality any more, and this is what Munro feels she herself did in her early writing. In her mature work she has mastered the art of incorporating truth and reality together – which is not at all easy. Jerry's shredded napkin is entirely plausible, even ordinary, and at the same time tells us the truth about Jerry. We might ask ourselves how the detail from "The Found Boat" tells us the truth about the girls: perhaps a fence has come down in their lives as well, and perhaps something like winter itself has brought it down.

This joining of reality and truth goes on whenever an author chooses one word rather than another. Although the effect of individual words is often easier to feel than to analyze, we can think of the way Del tells us about Jerry's war-stories: "he bombarded me with unbeatable atrocities, annihilating statistics", Del's use of words like "bombard" shows her awareness — conscious or not — that Jerry is fighting his own war, and that she is the enemy. We could say that "bombard" is working like a name here — Del might start to call Jerry "The Bombardier" — and if we turn to names themselves we will find that they are specially important in Munro's kind of writing. A good example is "Del Jordan". "Jordan" is of course a river in Palestine, the one that the Israelites cross into the Promised Land and the one where John the Baptist does his baptizing. Here it is set beside "Del", which sounds rather like "delta" and thus suggests a different river. If we consider "Del" as a short form, we see that it must come from some such name as "Adela", and we notice that Del's mother is called "Ada". Names of this family — which, by the way, includes "Alice" — have the basic meaning of "noble" or "exalted", and awareness of this will affect the kind of suggestion that we take from "Jordan" as well. When, on the other hand, we think of "Del" as "dell", it has a very different effect. One thing to notice here is that the two halves of Del's name can be seen as both opposite and similar in their suggestions - another case of likeness in difference. This is a specially rich name, and we could go further with it, but all Munro's names are worth thinking about. Here are a few important ones from *Lives of Girls and Women:* Benjamin Thomas Poole, Naomi, Miss Farris, Frank Wales, Art Chamberlain, Jerry Storey, Garnet French, Bobby Sherriff. And here are a few titles, all with meanings beyond the obvious ones, taken from Munro's other books: "Walker Brothers Cowboy", "The Peace of Utrecht", "Material", "Marrakesh", "The Ottawa Valley", "Half a Grapefruit", "Providence", "Simon's Luck".

On the same principle, a story itself is like a name when it points to another story: this is always the case, for instance, with the inset anecdotes we find in Munro. The tale of Sandy Stevenson in "The Flats Road" is about a windfall bride who brings disastrous consequences: a poltergeist bedevils Sandy until he has to send her back home. Since Uncle Benny's matrimonial adventure is notably similar, we can say that it is named by Sandy's. In this case both stories are told for us, but a story can also be named by another that is not told at all, and is brought in only by allusion – that is, something in the story we are given hints at the other story without saying so. The title of "Dance of the Happy Shades", for example, is also that of something within it, a piece of music played at a party, and if we know that this piece comes from Gluck's opera *Orfeo,* it leads us to the myth of Orpheus: someone, that is, who sees spirits dancing serenely

in the paradise called Elysium, although he himself cannot stay in the otherworld or bring his dead wife back from it. In a story called "Executioners" we encounter a beautiful girl called Helena, a boy called Howard Troy, and the burning down of the Troy house by — it would seem — another family in Helena's life: it is easy enough to see the parallel here. For one other writing that Munro alludes to, and an extremely important one, we can go back to Jerry Storey and the linens. Jerry belongs to a chapter called "Baptizing", which of course points us to the Bible, and the gospel in particular. In the gospel we also find cloth being torn, cloth used to wrap something precious, and cloth folded up and laid aside. If we think about these correspondences, another question may become more interesting and more disturbing: how is it that Jerry has his barely concealed taste for violence?

Though reflections like these are a natural part of reading and digesting literature, it is true that they may break the immediate spell of a story, and they may also seem to conflict with some of Munro's own statements: that she is concerned with surfaces, not ideas, and that she pictures Joe Phippen's house in "Images", for instance, as a "marvellous, solid, made, final thing" - in other words, as itself and not a "bloodless symbol" of something else. If, then, we want to say "Mrs. Jordan is a figure of hope" or something of the kind, we should not suppose, either that Munro started with the abstract idea of hope and then looked around for somebody to embody it, or that "hope" is an entity by itself: that truth, again in Del's sense, is something other than one side of a coin that has reality for its other side. All the same, there is a problem here: meanings seem to pull apart from things themselves, as Del finds with her novel. For the moment it may be enough for us to remember Munro's image of the solid house: one of her "shining houses", which may also be traps.

III

So far we have looked mainly at Munro's individual stories, though we have seen how a whole *Bildungsroman* has the same "epiphanic" quality as its separate chapters: Del grows up to the point where she begins to see the meaning of her whole life. *Who Do You Think You Are?* gives us essentially the same story with a different time-span, taking Rose from childhood through to middle age. It can even be argued that Munro's independent stories, arranged as we find them in her two collections, take us through the same sequence of steps as the novels, though not everybody might agree. Some account of this sequence, however sketchy, can help us to grasp both Munro's individual stories and the greater story that they fit into.

Munro begins in the beginning: all her

opening stories gesture back toward a time half known from songs and legends, one in which truth and reality had hardly split apart yet. What happened then happens again in this group of stories: someone loses trust and assurance and so turns into an Uncle Benny, helplessly grappling with a chaos in which he can never be at home. Such a person will reach out to whatever seems to offer the peace he has lost, but will never quite capture it, since he is too wounded in his trust to take any real chance. When we have fallen into Uncle Benny's swamp we cannot go back, and the only way to go on is to get inside an ark that will float in the water. This is how we become, as in the next chapter of *Lives of Girls and Women,* ''heirs of the living body'': the physical self and equally the ''social body'', as we say, in while we are also contained and sheltered. But having reached stability in this body, we feel the need to get free — what anyone feels not only at birth but at the age of early emotional crossing to the parent of the other sex, at puberty, and at any other time of severing. The price we pay for independence is isolation: we are free in one way, but the world and other people are now completely alien, ''objects'' that we can only confront.

Now we are at a turning-point: we have become definite, if limited, selves, and set over against us is what we can simply call the other, something that is just as limited even though it may not seem so. Once we have faced this lonely situation, we find ourselves wanting to reach across to the other, and the only way to do that is to accept some kind of law, as we do in school in order to learn. This will mean self-denial, but under the protection of law, school is also a place where there can be an operetta, a play-life in which boys and girls begin to make friends. After various premature tries we are finally baptized into sexual experience, or whatever is like sexual experience: that is, a seemingly direct and total union with the other. And the result, as Munro shows unflinchingly, is tragic: to the extent that it is no more than sexual, or in any different way only the expression of the limited self, the union is incomplete and bound to fail. We may be willing to play games and act parts with one another, but we cannot stop trying to be ''self-created self'', untouchable and secure; and this is because we have to defend ourselves in Uncle Benny's chaos, the condition of mistrust in which we have been lost all the time. Having failed to reach or accept one another, we must now reconcile ourselves to ''real life'', though a state in which everything is an alien object to everything else sounds more like death than life. But all Munro's books have something like the ''epilogue'' at the end of *Lives of Girls and Women:* a time comes, though it is not like other times and stands apart from the book's sequence of events, when we can let the self-created self drown in the mirror that it is, and can glimpse the life of a self beyond

alienation. This glimpse comes through someone like Bobby Sherriff or Miss Marsalles or Ralph Gillespie — a figure who is something of a fool and something of a tempter, but also an innocent friend who invites us to a party. And however brief and insubstantial to the mistrusting self, it is this curious party that offers us a taste of genuine human fellowship and happiness.

This larger story gives us a meaningful shape to which we can fit life in many ways. We can see this shape as that of a child's birth and development up to, and beyond, sexual maturity; we can also see it as the story of a social self - a community or nation. In *Lives of Girls and Women* ''The Flats Road'' hints in various ways at the breaking apart of an older European world and the movement of people - whether conquerors or refugees — out to the chaotic ocean and the chaos of the New World beyond that. We can then, if we like, see the rest of Del Jordan's story as that of Canada (with, for instance, a character called Garnet French at the crisis), as well as that of the western world more generally or indeed the whole human race. We will get distracted the minute we lose a feeling for the book's own mood and terms, but we can assimilate any experience we have had to the shape of its story, and all Munro's books invite us to do just this. In ''Changes and Ceremonies'' we may remember Mr. Boyce's playing the *1812 Overture* — which depicts Napoleon's siege of Moscow — and then saying dismissively to his Canadian pupils, ''I suppose it doesn't make you think of anything.'' Mr. Boyce himself, a recently arrived Englishman, would never think of 1812 as part of Canadian history, but we may well do so in reading this passage; and we can go on to ask ourselves what is like 1812 in the growing up of every boy and girl in Jubilee.

IV

To feel the meaningfulness of Munro's stories, then, we should be willing to let the correspondences they suggest work freely in our minds; we must, however, understand why one of her recent characters draws back from ''horrible, plausible connection'' — the connection we make too readily when we forget how little we know things when we know them merely as objects. Here we should think again of Munro's epilogue stories, which are concerned, as we have seen, with a kind of touching beyond touch — the sense of closeness that joins Rose to Ralph Gillespie, ''one slot over from herself''. To have this kind of closeness, it seems that Rose must be willing to do without other kinds. We all know what it is like to feel close to someone and yet sense that the feeling would be falsified if we expressed it in any direct way, as Rose begins to do with Ralph. While Munro often deals with messages, we find that actual letters in her stories, if written at all, tend to get lost or to say things that are deceptive or disappointing. Yet her characters often experience mysterious intuitions: it is these "messages that cannot be investigated, but have to be relied on" that the narrator muses about in "Winter Wind", a story about the spirit-wind of knowledge that comes only in the winter of isolation or death.

There is a similar winter to pass through in the bringing together of facts, or of facts and patterns, that gives us the feeling of meaningfulness. We have seen how connections enable us to "name" facts, but not how much the connections between facts (not to say facts themselves) are of our own making. As something objective, a fact is just a fact, and any pattern of facts is just a super-fact. No fact in itself is more typical than any other, just as no reality is more real than any other. If some facts seem specially typical, that must be because we find them meaningful: to suppose that this meaningfulness is "there" in the facts by themselves is to offend against their own integrity. It is true that significant connections are there in a story as they cannot be in real life — that, for instance, "The Flats Road" invites us to bring all its hunted animals together by the way it selects and arranges; but here we need to see something further about both art and life.

While Munro's writing has been aptly compared to the special "magic realism" of painters like Chambers and Colville, all realism is magic: it takes us into a wonderland where we see "just facts" but also sense hidden patterns and meet people with oddly appropriate names like "Del Jordan". And all art does the same thing that realism does in its extreme way: art presents something like a dream, as Munro has said her stories do. A dream too seems "just there", yet we sense that it means something, and this is because the person who dreams it unknowingly makes it up: he is both the subject and the object in his dream-experience. If he woke up and understood the dream, he would see that this is so and unite himself and his dream more fully; what he sees while asleep is only a strange hybrid. But now we should think again of what Uncle Benny lost, a life in which, because there was no mistrust, there was no alienation: I and you — subject and object — were one, as we deeply want them to be. If we could wake up from the unknowing that we fell into in the beginning, like little Del Jordan falling down a well of sleep, we would find that I and you have been one all along: as Munro's Spanish Lady comes to realize, we would "see each other for the first time, harmless and still". Real life, then, is also like a dream: in it blank fact is unaccountably haunted by "the qualities of legend", as another of Munro's characters discovers, so that truth and reality meet in a strange connection of the unconnectable. During the "winter" stage of knowing we must

simply bear witness to this dream; but beyond that winter there is a different season in which truth and reality do not violate one another, and we reach this season when we learn that "there" and here are the same. Real life, like a story, is a cryptic and self-contradictory name for a better life that we might wake up to, one in which the self and the other are not strangers. In epiphanic moments, moreover, we may become aware of this name as being a name, and want to reach what it signifies: this is what is happening when Del Jordan, in "The Photographer", senses Bobby Sherriff's final gesture to be "a letter, a whole word, in an alphabet I did not understand".

All Munro's epilogue stories are specially concerned with the same need for understanding, though in other ways these stories are very different. In "The Ottawa Valley", the darkest of them for all its humour, the narrator wants to understand but cannot: clinging to her rights and grievances, she is left with her assortment of fading snapshots, and never quite sees the sick mother who would unite them. In "Who Do You Think You Are?" Rose understands more, though her understanding is presented in terms of communion: this story's concern is with the mysterious comradeship that, after so many years, is still alive, and with the question of telling and mimicking in the light of such a comradeship. "Dance of the Happy Shades" shows us something more like a vision: in the music of the dance the narrator senses a land of grace beyond the land of flies and brick in which she finds herself. Del Jordan also has a vision, but in her case the indirectness of such visions is made very apparent. What Bobby offers her as he rises into the air seems a joke, and one "not so much shared with me as displayed for me" — only a teasing sign of something, like Bobby's unnourishing party fare. But not only will Del soon want to have a more solid meal spread for her: through Bobby's strange "word" she will also want what that meal of reality might become. Del begins to long for a transformed Jubilee, its brute facts all preserved but "held still and held together, radiant, everlasting" — a marvellous house that is both there and here, both substance and name. However impossible such a place may sound, Bobby's odd gesture is not only a joke but a calling and a blessing, to which Del answers "yes"; perhaps, then, she will have her heavenly city in spite of everything, though she has not quite said "thank you".'

What Del receives must also be what she gives, for her calling is to have the transformation of Jubilee take place within her. Del, in other words, is going to be an artist; and an artist of her kind also sounds like a woman having a baby. This comparison points to something important about men and women as they appear in myths and other stories. The men tend to have all the assertiveness and the women all the receptivity, which of course is not true of actual men and women: it holds for our sexual functioning, though even that is more complicated, but not for our functioning as persons. The "woman" in each of us is the self that takes things in: the one that observes and ponders experience, and by understanding turns it into something like a living child that can be given to the world. Thus Munro's story is not just about a girl or a beginning novelist but about all of us: in this way again the special names the universal. Whenever a writer marks off an area of experience to be able to look at it closely, that area becomes a "microcosm": a miniature image of the whole world. Munro likes to write about various particular things — rural southwestern Ontario, Canada, the lives of girls and women; in the same way, she is a writer of short stories and *Bildungsromane*. But because she sees reality with truth we can say simply that she is a great writer, and one who writes about nothing less than human beings.

Chronology

See the opening paragraph of the preceding essay.

Comments
by Alice Munro

The Genesis of a Story:
What you write is an offering; anybody can come and take what they like from it. Nevertheless, I went stubbornly back to the real facts, as I saw them, the real house in the real world [in "Images"], and tried to discover what it was doing in the story and how the story was put together in the first place. . . . When I think of the slanting, patched roof and the stove-pipe, the house as a marvellous, solid, made, final thing, I feel that I have somehow betrayed it, putting it in a story to be extracted this way, as a bloodless symbol. There is a sort of treachery to innocent objects — to houses, chairs, dresses, dishes, and to roads, fields, landscapes — which a writer removes from their natural, dignified obscurity and sets down in print. There they lie, exposed, often shabbily treated, inadequately, badly, clumsily transformed. . . . I do remember how the story started. It started with the picture in my mind of the man met in the woods, coming obliquely down the river-bank, carrying the hatchet, and the child watching him, and the father, unaware, bending over his traps. . . . From this picture the story moved outward, in a dim uncertain way. When this was happening

I was not so much making it as remembering it. I remembered the nurse-cousin, though she was not really there to remember; there was no one original for her. I remembered the trip along the river, to look at traps, with my father, although I had never gone. . . . And it is all deeply, perfectly true to me, as a dream might be true, and all I can say, finally, about the making of a story like this is that it must be made in the same way our dreams are made, truth in them being cast, with what seems to us often a rather high-handed frivolity, in any kind of plausible, implausible, giddy, strange, humdrum terms at all. . . . I have stories that come from inside and outside. ["Dance of the Happy Shades"] is a story that came from outside. But now that I write that, I wonder if it is a true distinction. When I get something from outside — in the form of an anecdote told at a family dinner-party, as this was — I have to see it in my own terms, at once, or it isn't going to be a story, however much in superficial points of interest it might be crying out to be made fiction.

> In "The Colonel's Hash Resettled", in *The Narrative Voice,* ed. John Metcalf (Toronto: McGraw-Hill-Ryerson, 1972), pp. 181-183.

Past and Present:
For there is no doubt in the mind of a good Victorian [Charles Dickens] that the Dark Ages are past. That is another time and another kind of reality; it goes without saying. And this is the reason the whole story [A Child's History of England] has the charm and recklessness and exaggeration of a spell-binding fairytale. . . . Things are not perfect, perhaps they never will be, but it is impossible not to believe in the shining reality of Progress, and to see that men are slowly becoming more civilized, more rational and humane, so that their greatest mistakes, their greatest insanities and brutalities, must surely lie in the past.
I remember the summer I read this, in the isolation of my home. It was 1939.

> "Remember Roger Mortimer," *The Montrealer,* February, 1962, p. 37.

Growing up in Wingham:
We believed there were deep holes in the [Maitland] river. We went looking for them, scared and hopeful, and never found them, but did not stop believing for that. Even now I believe that there were deep holes, ominous beckoning places, but that they have probably silted up. But maybe not all. Because I am still partly convinced that this river — not even the whole river, but this little stretch of it — will provide whatever myths you want, whatever adventures. I name the plants, I name the fish, and every name seems to me triumphant, every leaf and quick fish remarkably valuable. This ordinary place is sufficient, everything here touchable and mysterious

> "Everything Here is Touchable and Mysterious," *Weekend Magazine,* May 11, 1974, p. 33.

Comments on Alice Munro

[On *Lives of Girls and Women:*] In a series of self-contained units, there is an accumulation of a life evolved in that finely mythical past of a small southwestern Ontario town. Liberation from it involves understanding something that must be recaptured and cannibalized, and repeated. Just as the heroine, who has inherited a mound of papers single-mindedly devoted to the family tree, finds. The manuscript is left forgotten in the cellar, a spring flood reduces it to a soggy mess: this brings an end, one accepted with almost brutal relief. But then a new narrator must go through the same deep effort at recapture: the flight from Jubilee, Ont., is the penultimate ending. The real escape perhaps never comes and never should.

O.H.T. Rudzik, *University of Toronto Quarterly* XLI (1972), 314.

The unspoken theory behind WASP behaviour is that if you do not mention something it will go away, or will never happen, or in any case will not mean anything. Do not celebrate too much, and do not mourn loudly. Try not to feel, because feeling brings trouble. Hide yourself behind layers of insensitivity. The best way to do this is to look and act as much as possible like everybody else. . . . If there is a single moral impulse behind Mrs. Munro's work, it's contained in the sentence, "I do not believe things are there to be worked through," [said by Eileen in "Memorial"]: reality must be confronted and felt, however painful it may be. Her narrators are frequently involved in this process: they are trying to break out of the WASP cage of slippery evasions into the clear light of truth.

Robert Fulford, "Solemn Style", *Montreal Star*, June 1, 1974

Sad, grim and always penetrating little pictures of a society in which the new is ever greedily devouring the old, the vulgar and the thrusting elbowing aside the gentle and the humane.

James Brockway, "A Measure of Life", *Books and Bookmen* (August 1974), p. 92.

The young girls in these stories find their role, status, and potential are dictated by their socio-economic and regional background and if they desire a new role they must break these ties.

Patricia Wilson, *Women of Jubilee* 1975, v

Munro deals with nothing more or less heroic than the universal experience of growing up into an awareness of the complexities of human affairs and emotions which constitute experience. The frequent pain and less frequent humour of this process colour her writing and strike a responsive chord in every reader who may have felt that the rough passing from innocence to experience was uniquely his own.

Jill Gardiner, *The Early Short Stories of Alice Munro*, 1973, vii.

Selected Bibliography

D.E. Cook has prepared "Alice Munro: a Checklist (to December 31, 1974)", *Journal of Canadian Fiction*, No. 16 (1976), pp. 131-136. Munro's uncollected early published stories are listed by Cook; her other uncollected publications, apart from stories intended for publication in subsequent books, consist of two articles: "Remember Roger Mortimer: Dickens' *Child's History of England* Remembered", *The Montrealer*, Feb. 1962, 34-37, a reflection on the first book Munro had read; and "Everything Here is Touchable and Mysterious", *Globe and Mail Weekend Magazine*, May 11, 1974, p. 33, a beautiful description of Lower Town outside Wingham. There have been M.A. theses on Munro by Margaret Tanszi (Queen's University, 1972), Claire Duteau (University of Alberta, 1973), Jill Gardiner (University of New Brunswick, 1973), and Patricia Wilson (University of Guelph, 1975). Articles on Munro, in addition to those listed by Cook, include the following: Marcia Allentuck, "Resolution and Independence in the Work of Alice Munro", *World Literature Written in English* XVI (1977), 340-343; Hallvard Dahlie, "Unconsummated Relationships: Isolation and Rejection in Alice Munro's Stories", *World Literature Written in English* XI (1972), 43-48; Eileen Dombrowski, "Down to Death: Alice Munro and Transience", *University of Windsor Review* XIV (1978), 21-29; Juliann E. Fleenor, "Rape Fantasies as Initiation Rite: Female Imagination in *Lives of Girls and Women*", *Room of One's Own*, IV, 4 (1979), 35-49; W.R. Martin, "Alice Munro and James Joyce", *Journal of Canadian Fiction*, No. 24 (1979), pp. 120-126; J.R. Struthers, "Reality and Ordering: the Growth of a Young Artist in *Lives of Girls and Women*", *Essays on Canadian Writing*, No. 3 (Fall, 1975), 32-46. Interviews include those with Mari Stainsby, *British Columbia Library Quarterly*, 35 (July 1971), 27-31; John Metcalf, *Journal of Canadian Fiction*, I (Fall, 1972), 54-62; Graeme Gibson, *Eleven Canadian Novelists*, Toronto, 1973, 241-264; Carole Gerson, *Room of One's Own* IV, 4 (1979), 2-7.

A Note on the Contributor

James Carscallen studied at Toronto and Oxford; he has taught at the University of Waterloo and is at present an Associate Professor of English at Victoria College, University of Toronto. His main area of study is English poetry of the sixteenth and seventeenth centuries, and he has written on Du Bartas, Spenser, Marvell, Vaughan, and Eliot.

Hugh Hood   25

by
J. R. (Tim) Struthers

Courtesy: Sam Tata.

Following the last of his formal education — a Ph.D. in English completed at the University of Toronto in 1955 — Hugh Hood has combined an active career as a university teacher with a prolific and brilliant career as the author of seven ambitious novels, numerous widely-anthologized short stories, and occasional distinguished non-fiction. Hood's choice of the artistic imagination as the subject of his doctoral dissertation, "Theories of Imagination in English Thinkers 1650-1790", anticipated and contributed significantly to his own subsequent career as a creative writer. Hence, the vast scope of knowledge displayed in the dissertation is clearly indicative of the encyclopaedic powers of mind which are conjoined in his imaginative writing with a sophisticated and poetic sense of the delicate stylistic possibilities of English prose. For the material of

his creative writing, Hood has drawn extensively and most characteristically on his own auto-biographical experience and the experience of his own time and place; yet he has shown a remarkable ability to re-create in convincing detail situations which are beyond his experience or which are completely imaginary. Hood remains, as Dennis Duffy observed in 1971 in his pioneering essay entitled "Grace: The Novels of Hugh Hood", "the steadiest viewer of ourselves, in Canada, now",[1] while developing a mode of writing which is completely his own and which many critics have found to be a unique achievement in Canadian fiction. Hood's reputation, in the early 1970 s according to a description given by Kent Thompson in an essay entitled "The Canadian Short Story in English and the Little Magazines: 1971", as "probably the master of the short story in Canada",[2] has been significantly enhanced by the appearance of *Dark Glasses* (1976), *Selected Stories* (1978) and *None Genuine Without This Signature* (1980). Even more impressively, with the publication of *The Swing in the Garden* (1975), *A New Athens* (1977), and *Reservoir Ravine* (1979), the first three novels in *The New Age*, Hood has commenced the most astonishing literary project of our time, a twelve-volume epic series of novels about the meaning of Canadian life in the twentieth century, a master work which he hopes will be of great personal significance to Canadians and which he hopes will take a rightful place amongst the major literary achievements of the world.

In one of several published interviews, Hood has stressed how "D.H. Lawrence said that the novel was the one bright book of life, that it was a kind of gospel, a religious communication".[3] This view is conveyed most clearly in *The New Age* by Hood's choice of the name of his main character, the art historian Matthew Goderich, whose Christian name alludes specifically to the biblical Matthew, author of the first gospel, and whose surname derives in part from *Godes rice*, the kingdom of God. The Trinitarian title of Hood's short story collection *The Fruit Man, The Meat Man & The Manager* (1971) is likewise meant to reflect Hood's religious faith, for, as he explains in another inerview, "The Fruit Man is God proffering the apple, and the Meat Man is Christ incarnate, and the Manager is the Holy Spirit moving the world".[4] The presence of such allegorical names and titles, as well as liturgical elements, epiphanies, and biblical motifs or structures, signifies the creation of a form of fiction — "a secular liturgy",[5] to use Hood's phrase from *Around the Mountain: Scenes from Montreal Life* (1967), or a "secular scripture",[6] to use Northrop Frye's term — which is closely associated with sacred scripture. Hood has discovered a literary method which makes possible a revelation of "the transcendental element dwelling in living things",[7] as he says in his essay "The Ontology of Super-Realism", and which is an appropriate vehicle for communicating his twin religious themes of the promise of Divine Grace and the limits of human capacity. The nature and the coherence of the method, form, themes, and vision of Hood's art strongly reflect his Roman Catholic upbringing, his education in the Catholic school system of Toronto, and the continuing influence of religious belief and practice in his adult life.

In addition to Hood's religious background, there is his bicultural family background — English-Canadian on his father's side, French-Canadian on his mother's side — which has exerted a deep influence on Hood's life, his writing, and his federalist vision of a union of these two cultures within the Canadian identity. Hood's father, Alexander Bridport Hood, was raised in Shelburne, Nova Scotia; and his mother, Margaret Cecile Blagdon, grew up in the French district of Toronto. Hood's father's Nova Scotian background and somewhat tumultuous career figure prominently in Hood's first published novel, *White Figure, White Ground* (1964), which was originally entitled *To His Father's House*, and to a lesser degree in the highly fictionalized portrait of Matthew's father, Andrew Goderich, in *The New Age*. Hood's mother's background is treated in the autobiographical short story "Brother André, Père Lamarche and my Grandmother Eugenie Blagdon", from *The Fruit Man, The Meat Man & The Manager*, and in *Reservoir Ravine*, the third published volume but the earliest chronologically in *The New Age*. Hugh John Blagdon Hood was born in Toronto on April 30, 1928, and in "Recollections of the Works Department", "Where the Myth Touches Us", "Silver Bugles, Cymbals, Golden Silks", and "The End of It" — all of which appeared in his first collection of short stories, *Flying a Red Kite* (1962) — as well as in parts of *White Figure, White Ground*, in the superb title essay of *The Governor's Bridge Is Closed* (1973), and even

more lavishly in *The Swing in the Garden* and *Reservoir Ravine*, Hood has presented, more vividly and more extensively than any other author, his impressions of the city of Toronto and the impact of that city on his own emotional and imaginative life. Hood lived in Toronto until 1955 when he took his first full-time teaching job at Saint Joseph College in Hartford, Connecticut, where he taught until 1961. Meanwhile, on April 22, 1957, Hood married Noreen Mallory, then a designer for the Stratford Festival and for CBC-TV and now a painter, whose home town of Brockville and the surrounding area of eastern Ontario have provided not only a summertime resort for themselves and their four children, but also, and more significantly, an additional *locus* for Hood's fictional universe, as such works as "Three Halves of a House" (from *Flying a Red Kite*) and *A New Athens* testify.

Then in 1961, after teaching for six years in the United States, Hood accepted a teaching position which he continues to hold at the primarily French-speaking Université de Montréal, a move which Hood made in the hope that he would be able "to get back the heritage which mother reacted against"[8] and which led to unexpected and important developments in his nascent career as a writer. If, from a biographical viewpoint, Hood's satiric portrayal of the world of American movies in his second novel, *The Camera Always Lies* (1967), can be said to have been stimulated by close reflection, during his residence in the United States, on certain mendacious, vicious, and violent aspects of American culture and society, then the composition of his next book, *Around the Mountain: Scenes from Montreal Life*, can be said to represent a hymn of praise for his adopted home, which, in reply to a remark identifying him as "a Toronto writer", Hood called "this Best Of All Cities".[9] Hood's appreciation, as Patrick Blandford observes in an essay entitled "Hood *à la mode*: Bicultural Tension in the Works of Hugh Hood", of "the rich heritage of language, religion, and custom which the Québécois contribute to the 'Canadian' identity"[10] is amply expressed in his next two books: *A Game of Touch* (1970), Hood's third novel, which constitutes his most direct and sustained treatment of the themes of biculturalism and separatism and which bears comparison with Hugh MacLennan's famous novel *Two Solitudes* (1945); and *Strength Down Centre: The Jean Béliveau Story* (1970), a book which transcends its popular "sports-biography" label. As Blandford justly argues, the relations between English Canada and French Canada and the search for a resolution of the tensions between the two cultures emerge as a central preoccupation of Hood's ficiton and non-fiction. Sometimes the subject is treated directly, as in *White Figure, White Ground, Around the Mountain, A Game of Touch, Strength Down Centre*, and individual essays in Hood's collection *The Governor's Bridge Is Closed*. However, at other times the subject is treated indirectly by allegorical suggestion, as in the contrast between the corrupt world of American movies and the morally and artistically superior world of French film-making in *The Camera Always Lies* and in the presentation of the Ugeti and Pineal populaces of the mythical third-world country of Leofrica in his fourth novel, *You Cant Get There From Here* (1972).

Along with comprehending the importance to Hood's writing of his religious and personal background, one must gradually learn to appreciate the encyclopaedic and profound dimensions of his literary and ideological background, which, through Hood's love of reading and his continuing study of literature as a professor of English, has formed another essential stratum in his mind and art. The greatest influences on Hood, perhaps, are two English Romantics: Wordsworth, who in the *Lyrical Ballads* looked steadily at incidents and characters from everyday life until the transcendental element dwelling in them was illuminated, and whose long poems like *The Prelude* established him, to use Dennis Duffy's phrase, as "the grand exemplar of this mode of autobiographical definition";[11] and Coleridge, who in such conversation poems as "Frost at Midnight", "The Nightingale", or "The Eolian Harp" showed a gift for meditating freely on a single image, and whose mental powers could encompass and gradually synthesize a very wide and apparently unconnected range of references. Behind Wordsworth and Coleridge and their Romantic theory of the imagination, however, as Hood argued in his Ph.D. dissertation and as he summarizes in the essay "The Ontology of Super-Realism", lies "the theory of abstraction as it was taught by Aristotle and the medieval philosophers",[12] notably St. Thomas Aquinas. The theologian Aquinas and his contemporary, the poet Dante, stand near the head of a long Roman Catholic tradition which extends up through such twentieth-century authors as the Irish short story writer and novelist James Joyce, the French philosopher Jacques Maritain, and the Canadian short story writer and novelist Morley Callaghan. Each of these five authors has had a considerable influence on Hood's artistic theory and practice. In certain ways, Hood's work also aligns itself consciously with the epic tradition — including works by Homer, Dante, Spenser, Milton, Wordsworth, and Joyce — and with two modern *romans fleuves*, Marcel Proust's *A la recherche du temps perdu* and Anthony Powell's *A Dance to the Music of Time*. Such comparisons, it must be emphasized, are neither pretentious nor superficial but are grounded in specific relations — in terms of vision, theme, structure, setting, narrative technique, imagery, or even phrasing — between Hood's works and their predecessors.

The most extensive commentary by Hood on his literary background and his literary method

Courtesy: Sam Tata.

is contained in the interview published in *Before the Flood*.[13] In this interview Hood also clarifies and expands his earlier use of the terms "super-realism"[14] and "documentary fantasy"[15] to describe his characteristic mode of writing. The term "super-realism" draws upon the Latin *"super"* meaning "above" and signifies the way Hood's art expresses his belief that the things of this world, which constitute the artist's proper subject, are informed and illuminated by a transcendental source, the Divine Light of the Holy Ghost which comes down from above.[16] The return process, which Hood in his finest work brilliantly accomplishes, is achieved by what John Mills identifies as the ancient "anagogical method", which "involves an abandonment of the mind to the harmony and radiance of objects in the physical world in order that the mind be guided towards the transcendent source of this harmony and radiance, namely God".[17] Hood, as he says in correspondence with Mills, wants "to be more 'real' than the realists, yet more transcendent than the most vaporous allegorist".[18] To fulfil this double intention he often employs a kind of figurative language known as an emblem, whose function is defined by Hood in a magnificent essay on his childhood reading[19] and is particularly well elucidated by Mills through an analysis of the final emblematic scene of Hood's short story "Flying a Red Kite", where the red kite soaring high above the cemetery is connected with the red stain of crushed raspberries on the little girl's face "as though the little girl had partaken, eucharistically, of a Godhead which the kite 'naturally' represents".[20] Emblems, Hood argues, are as precise as images and at least as meaningful as symbols. "Emblems evoke the world with rich colour and clear definite line, and they name, sign, indicate, point to formal, abstract codes of behaviour, class, worship".[21] In life, the things of this world are informed by a transcendental Being; in the art of "super-realism", they remain so but are also transformed by the artist's imagination. Hence Hood introduces the term "documentary fantasy" in addition to the term "super-realism" in order that we can more wholly understand his work by examining it in at least two complementary perspectives.

"Documentary fantasy", Hood explains, "begins to look like, first of all, the world as a given, as the facts, and then the facts transformed by . . . the fuller range of imagination, which begins to change these matters as a great portraitist does".[22] Hood's fourth novel, an "anatomy"[23] (to use Northrop Frye's term for this sort of form of prose fiction) of the darkly humorous follies and the ultimately destructive evils of world politics in the newly-created country of Leofrica, contains a large amount of apparently factual description; but as the title may suggest, *You Cant Get There From Here* is, in Robert Weaver's words, "entirely exotic and entirely a work of the imagination".[24] Unfortunately, because *You Cant Get There From Here* and the "romance"[25] *The Camera Always Lies* differ in form and setting from what Weaver and many other critics regard as Hood's "most memorable fiction", the stories rooted "in the areas of memory and personal experience",[26] these two works usually have been met with improper expectations and therefore to a large extent have been misunderstood or disregarded. Perhaps *You Cant Get There From Here* can be seen as occupying a place of central importance in Hood's *oeuvre* precisely because it was so completely a work of imagination that it consolidated the earlier development from the more strictly recollective and pleasantly mundane mode of "Recollections of the Works Department" into the more imaginatively autobiographical and sometimes fantastic or visionary mode of *Around the Mountain: Scenes from Montreal Life* and prepared Hood to re-create and to picture the history of his own life and times in a more fictionalized and envisioned and hence conceivably truer way in *The New Age* series than in his earlier autobiographical writings.

In the seven novels and nearly ninety short stories which he published by 1980, Hugh Hood has already shown himself to be a genuinely great artist. Although his innovations may be less conspicuous than some other writers', such subtlety as the handling of narrative point of view, time, and structure in the first trilogy of *The New Age*, such beauty as the inviting Bonnard-like descriptions in "None Genuine Without This Signature or Peaches in the Bathtub" (from the

collection entitled *None Genuine Without This Signature*), and such intelligence as the treatment of the conflicting implications of magical folklore and sacred scripture for human character in "The Woodcutter's Third Son" (from the same collection of short stories) are quietly dazzling. Hood's writing, unlike the achievements of some other important writers in Canada and abroad, is memorable for its surprising variety as well as for its originality and excellence. As further volumes of *The New Age* and possibly more works are composed, Hood will, I expect, have many other delightful surprises to offer.

[1] Dennis Duffy, "Grace: The Novels of Hugh Hood", *Canadian Literature*, No. 47 (Winter 1971), p. 10.

[2] Kent Thompson, "The Canadian Short Story in English and the Little Magazines: 1971", *World Literature Written in English*, XI, 1 (April 1972), 21.

[3] Hugh Hood, "Hugh Hood on the Novel", interviewed by Marianne Lafon, in Marianne Lafon, *The Writer as Communicator* (Montreal: privately printed, 1973), p. 15.

[4] Hugh Hood, "An Interview with Hugh Hood", by J.R. (Tim) Struthers, in J.R. (Tim) Struthers, ed., *Before the Flood: Our Examgination round His Factification for Incamination of Hugh Hood's Work in Progress* (Downsview, Ontario: ECW Press, 1979), p. 38.

[5] Hugh Hood, *Around the Mountain: Scenes from Montreal Life* (Toronto: Peter Martin Associates, 1967), p. 70.

[6] Northrop Frye, *The Secular Scripture: A Study of the Structure of Romance* (Cambridge, Massachusetts: Harvard University Press, 1976).

[7] Hugh Hood, "The Ontology of Super-Realism", in his *The Governor's Bridge Is Closed* (Ottawa: Oberon Press, 1973), p. 130.

[8] Hugh Hood, quoted in Lisa Balfour, "Canadian Author in Search of His Heritage", *The Montreal Star* (June 19, 1965), Sec. Entertainments, p. 6.

[9] Hugh Hood, quoted in Bruce Taylor, "Montreal Days and Nights", *The Montreal Star* (June 16, 1967), p. 4.

[10] Patrick Blandford, "Hood à la mode: Bicultural Tension in the Works of Hugh Hood", in J.R. (Tim) Struthers, ed., *Before the Flood*, p. 145.

[11] Dennis Duffy, "Space/Time and the Matter of Form", in J.R. (Tim) Struthers, ed., *Before the Flood*, p. 141.

[12] Hugh Hood, "The Ontology of Super-Realism", in his *The Governor's Bridge Is Closed*, p. 130.

[13] Hugh Hood, "An Interview with Hugh Hood", by J.R. (Tim) Struthers, in J.R. (Tim) Struthers, ed., *Before the Flood*, pp. 21-93.

[14] Hugh Hood, "The Ontology of Super-Realism", in his *The Governor's Bridge Is Closed*, pp. 126-35.

[15] Hugh Hood, "An Interview with Hugh Hood", by Robert Fulford, *Tamarack Review*, No. 66 (June 1975), p. 77.

[16] Hugh Hood, "An Interview with Hugh Hood", by J.R. (Tim) Struthers, in J.R. (Tim) Struthers, ed., *Before the Flood*, p. 76.

[17] John Mills, "Hugh Hood and the Anagogical Method", in J.R. (Tim) Struthers, ed., *Before the Flood*, p. 100.

[18] Hugh Hood, "Hugh Hood and John Mills in Epistolary Conversation", *The Fiddlehead*, No. 116 (Winter 1978), p. 145.

[19] Hugh Hood, "Before the Flood", in J.R. (Tim) Struthers, ed., *Before the Flood*, pp. 14-17.

[20] John Mills, "Hugh Hood and the Anagogical Method", in J.R. (Tim) Struthers, ed., *Before the Flood*, p. 97.

[21] Hugh Hood, "Before the Flood", in J.R. (Tim) Struthers, ed., *Before the Flood*, p. 15.

[22] Hugh Hood, "An Interview with Hugh Hood", by J.R. (Tim) Struthers, in J.R. (Tim) Struthers, ed., *Before the Flood*, pp. 82-83.

[23] Northrop Frye, *Anatomy of Criticism: Four Essays* (Princeton, New Jersey: Princeton University Press, 1957), pp. 308-12. Also see Hugh Hood, "An Interview with Hugh Hood", by J.R. (Tim)

Struthers, in J.R. (Tim) Struthers, ed., *Before the Flood*, pp. 57, 58, 60-61.

[24] Robert Weaver, "Outsider's Views of Africa and Montreal", review of *You Cant Get There From Here*, by Hugh Hood, and *Going Down Slow*, by John Metcalf, *Saturday Night* (November 1972), p.50.

[25] Northrop Frye, *Anatomy of Criticism*, pp. 304-07. Also see Hugh Hood, "An Interview with Hugh Hood", by J.R. (Tim) Struthers, in J.R. (Tim) Struthers, ed., *Before the Flood*, pp. 57, 59-60.

[26] Robert Weaver, "Outsider's Views of Africa and Montreal", p. 50.

Chronology

1928	Hugh John Blagdon Hood born on April 30 in Toronto, Ontario to Alexander Bridport Hood (1900-1959) and Margaret Cecile Blagdon Hood (1896-1974). Second of three children. Older sister, Barbara Katherine (1925-) and younger brother, Alexander Bridport (1931-).
1934-38	Attended Our Lady of Perpetual Help Parish School in Toronto.
1938-45	Attended De La Salle College "Oaklands" in Toronto.
1945-47	Worked at various jobs.
1947-50	Studied Pass Arts at Saint Michael's College, University of Toronto. Received B. A. degree in 1950.
1950-52	M.A. candidate in English at the School of Graduate Studies, University of Toronto. M. A. thesis entitled "The Architecture of Experience". Received M. A. degree in 1952.
1951-54	Teaching Fellow, University College, University of Toronto.
1954	Wrote part of a novel entitled "The Beginning of Wisdom". Unfinished. No manuscript in existence.
1954-55	Teaching Fellow, Saint Michael's College, University of Toronto.
1952-55	Ph.D. candidate in English at the School of Graduate Studies, University of Toronto. Ph.D. dissertation entitled "Theories of Imagination in English Thinkers 1650-1790". Received Ph.D. degree in 1955.
1955-61	Member of the Department of English, Saint Joseph College, Hartford, Connecticut.
1955-58	Wrote novel entitled "God Rest You Merry". Unpublished.
1957	Married Ruth Noreen Mallory on April 22 in Toronto.
1958	Birth of a daughter, Sarah Barbara, on April 2. Published first short story,

	"The Isolation Booth", in *The Tamarack Review*, No. 9.
1959-60	Wrote novel entitled "Hungry Generations". Unpublished.
1961	Birth of a son, Dwight Alexander, on April 15.
	Left Saint Joseph College to become a member of the Department of English, Université de Montréal, Montreal, Quebec.
1962	Published first book of short stories, *Flying a Red Kite*. Received first of numerous citations in "The Yearbook of the American Short Story" under "Roll of Honor" and "Distinctive Short Stories in American Magazines" for short stories published in 1961, 1962, 1964, 1965, 1966, 1967, 1968, 1969, 1972, 1974.
1963	Birth of a son, John Arthur Mallory, on January 29. *Flying a Red Kite* awarded the Women's Canadian Club of Toronto literary award.
	"The End of It" (published in *The Tamarack Review*, No. 24) awarded the President's Medal, University of Western Ontario, London, Ontario, for the short story category.
1964	Published first novel, *White Figure, White Ground*.
1965	Birth of a daughter, Alexandra Mary, on July 18.
	White Figure, White Ground awarded the Beta Sigma Phi Award for the best first novel by a Canadian.
1966	"Getting to Williamstown" published in Martha Foley and David Burnett, eds., *The Best American Short Stories 1966*.
1968	"It's a Small World", a set of three Expo pieces (published in *The Tamarack Review*, Nos. 44, 45, 46) awarded the President's Medal, University of Western Ontario, London, Ontario, for the general article category.
1970	Formed "The Montreal Storytellers Fiction Performance Group" with John Metcalf, Clark Blaise, Ray Smith, and Ray Fraser. By 1972-73, the group dispersed, as some members accepted appointments in other cities.
1971	Published *The Fruit Man, The Meat Man & The Manager*, the first of nine of Hood's books from Oberon Press.
1974	Province of Ontario Council for the Arts award. Award shared with Alice Munro.
1975	Published *The Swing in the Garden*, the first volume of a projected twelve-volume series of novels entitled *The New Age/Le nouveau siècle*.
1976	*The Swing in the Garden* awarded the City of Toronto 1975 Book Award. Award shared with *Immigrants: A Portrait of the Urban Experience, 1890-*

Comments
by Hugh Hood

My interest in the sound of sentences, in the use of colour words and the names of places, in practical stylistics, showed me that prose fiction might have an abstract element, a purely formal element, even though it continued to be strictly, morally realistic. It might be possible to think of prose fiction the way one thinks of abstract elements in representational painting, or of highly formal music. . . . It's the seeing-into-things, the capacity for meditative abstraction, that interests me about philosophy, the arts and religious practice. I love most in painting an art that exhibits the transcendental element dwelling in living things. I think of this as true super-realism. . . . I'm trying to concentrate on knowable form as it lives in the physical world. These forms are abstract, not in the sense of being inhumanly non-physical but in the sense of communicating the perfection of the essences of things — the formal realities that create things as they are in themselves. A transcendentalist must first study the things of this world, and get as far inside them as possible. . . . That is where I come out: the spirit is totally in the flesh. If you pay close enough attention to things, stare at them, concentrate on them as hard as you can, not just with your intelligence, but with your feelings and instincts, you will begin to apprehend the forms in them. . . . The illuminations in things are there, really and truly there, in those things. They are not run over them by the projective intelligence, and yet there is a sense in which the mind, in uniting itself to things, creates illumination in them. . . . The poetry of Wordsworth supplies us again and again with examples of this imaginative colouring spread over incidents and situations from everyday life. . . . Like Wordsworth,

I have at all times endeavoured to look steadily at my subjects. I hope my gaze has helped to light them up.

Hugh Hood, "The Ontology of Super-Realism".

But let me add that since we started talking, I've been thinking about the name for this sort of writing. It seems to me that some such phrase as 'documentary fantasy' would be about right. You see, I'm trying to give an exact account, in the most precise and credible detail available, of something that is purely imaginary. 'Imaginary' in the sense of 'envisioned' or 'made into art.' To me the words 'real' and 'imaginary' are not in any way opposed to one another. The wholly imaginary is what is most real.

Hugh Hood, "An Interview with Hugh Hood", by Robert Fulford.

I want to be more 'real' than the realists, yet more transcendent than the most vaporous allegorist. In short, I am following what I conceive [to be] the method of Dante. . . . Now let me put it to you that since I am both a realist and a transcendentalist allegorist that I cannot be bound by the forms of ordinary realism.

Hugh Hood, "Hugh Hood and John Mills in Epistolary Conversation".

I really want to endow the country with a great imperishable work of art. . . . I think it would be marvellous for Canada if we had one artist who could move easily and in a familiar converse with Joyce, and Tolstoy, and Proust; and I intend to be that artist if I possibly can; and I am willing to give the rest of my life to it.

Hugh Hood, "An Interview with Hugh Hood", by J.R. (Tim) Struthers.

Comments
on Hugh Hood

Hugh Hood is an extraordinarily productive writer who has not yet — even in Canada where indigenous writers tend, except when ignored altogether, to be overvalued for extra-literary reasons — received either the popular or the critical praise which he deserves. I can suggest at least four possible reasons for this comparative neglect without necessarily denouncing contemporary taste. The first has to do with Hood's rejection of the plain-man notion of plot, narrative, character, and so on which means that readers whose interests lie in being lightly entertained tend to pass him by. Secondly, his work is neither overtly experimental nor even 'modernist', despite his own references to the influence of Joyce and Proust, and he has therefore failed to attract those critics who are interested in attempts to expand the boundaries of fictional form. Thirdly, one does not find, in Hood's work, those rather melancholy themes which are beloved of the taste-makers of Can Lit — no fortress mentalities, survivors, studies of failure, or introspection. Finally, Hood's narratives run counter to the grain of modern fiction in that the authorial stance towards twentieth-century culture is generally uncritical. Alex MacDonald, for instance, of *White Figure, White Ground,* and Matt Goderich, the narrator of *The New Age* series, are successful, joyous men without *angst,* at home in their chosen professions and lucky in their personal relationships. Such protagonists have been rare in serious fiction since the turn of the century and, in fact, sophisticated readers nowadays tend to assume that one defines as 'serious' only those fictional works which explore the lives and psychologies of men at odds with their civilization and environment. It is Hood's great strength as a writer that he forces us to rethink this article of conventional wisdom.

> John Mills, "Hugh Hood and the Ana-gogical Method".

Hugh Hood is a Canadian writer whose work defies easy generalization. Perhaps more than any other writer now publishing in Canada, he is aware of the implications of the recurring problem of a 'Canadian identity', yet his concern is seldom obvious and inevitably, it seems, it is tied to both larger and more particular human problems. He is a complicated craftsman, but his work seems easy to read. He experiments with various prose forms, but does so in such a quiet manner that the experiments do not call attention to themselves. He is a tough moralist, but his work seldom features anything like an obviously dramatic moral confrontation. He is a committed Christian, but he is neither easy nor orthodox about his religion.

> Kent Thompson, "Hood, Hugh (John Blagdon)".

For Hood, then, there is an order to be found in the universe, an order derived from God. He emphasizes his belief that man *can* use his imagination to know the world. It is at this point that we can begin to appreciate the innovative aspects of Hood's world view. He is 'new' precisely because he is so old-fashioned in his belief that art can make sense of experience, and that the artist can learn, by contemplating the forms of the divine in the daily, to connect objects and events existing in various times and places in such a way that a meaningful explanation of life will emerge.

> Robert Lecker, "A Spirit of Communion: *The Swing in the Garden*".

Bibliography
Works by Hugh Hood

"The Architecture of Experience". M. A. thesis, University of Toronto, 1952.

"Theories of Imagination in English Thinkers 1650-1790". Ph.D. dissertation, University of Toronto, 1955.

Flying a Red Kite. Toronto: The Ryerson Press, 1962. Reprinted in paperback 1967.

White Figure, White Ground. Toronto: The Ryerson Press, 1964. Pocket Book Edition. Richmond Hill, Ontario: Simon & Schuster of Canada, 1973.

Around the Mountain: Scenes from Montreal Life. Toronto: Peter Martin Associates, 1967. Reprinted in paperback 1976.

The Camera Always Lies. New York: Harcourt, Brace & World, 1967.

A Game of Touch. Don Mills, Ontario: Longman Canada, 1970.

Strength Down Centre: The Jean Béliveau Story. Scarborough, Ontario: Prentice-Hall of Canada, 1970. *Puissance au centre: Jean Béliveau.* [Translated by Louis Rémillard.] Scarborough, Ontario: Prentice-Hall of Canada, 1970.

The Fruit Man, The Meat Man & The Manager. Ottawa: Oberon Press, 1971.

You Cant Get There From Here. Ottawa: Oberon Press, 1972.

The Governor's Bridge Is Closed. Ottawa: Oberon Press, 1973.

The Swing in the Garden. Part One of *The New Age/Le nouveau siècle.* Ottawa: Oberon Press, 1975.

Dark Glasses. Ottawa: Oberon Press, 1976.

A New Athens. Part Two of *The New Age/Le nouveau siècle.* Ottawa: Oberon Press, 1977.

Selected Stories. Ottawa: Oberon Press, 1978.

Reservoir Ravine. Part Three of *The New Age/Le nouveau siècle.* Ottawa: Oberon Press, 1979.

Scoring: Seymour Segal's Art of Hockey. Paintings by Seymour Segal. Text by Hugh Hood. Ottawa: Oberon Press, 1979.

None Genuine Without This Signature. Downsview. Ontario: ECW Press, 1980.

Selected Criticism

Cameron, Barry. Review of *Dark Glasses, The Fiddle-head,* No. 115 (Fall 1977), pp. 145-47.

Cloutier, Pierre. "All in All in Africa", review of *You Cant Get There From Here, Books in Canada,* November/December 1972, pp. 26-27.

_____. "An Interview with Hugh Hood", *Journal of Canadian Fiction,* II, 1 (Winter 1973), 49-52.

_____. "Space, Time and the Creative Imagination: Hugh Hood's *White Figure, White Ground*", *Journal of Canadian Fiction,* III, 1 (Winter 1974), 60-63.

Duffy, Dennis. "Grace: The Novels of Hugh Hood", *Canadian Literature,* No. 47 (Winter 1971), pp. 10-25. Reprinted in George Woodcock, ed. and introd., *The Canadian Novel in the Twentieth Century: Essays from* Canadian Literature. New Canadian Library, No. 115. Toronto: McClelland and Stewart, 1975.

—————. "A New Athens, the New Jerusalem, a New Atlantis", review of *A New Athens*, *The Fiddlehead*, No. 117 (Spring 1978), pp. 101-08.

Fulford, Robert. "An Interview with Hugh Hood", *Tamarack Review*, No. 66 (June 1975), pp. 65-77.

Garebian, Keith. *Hugh Hood*. Twayne's World Authors Series. Boston: Twayne, forthcoming.

Godfrey, Dave. "Line and Form", review of *White Figure, White Ground*, *Tamarack Review*, No. 35 (Spring 1965), pp. 96-101.

"Hugh Hood and John Mills in Epistolary Conversation", *The Fiddlehead*, No. 116 (Winter 1978), pp. 133-46.

Morley, Patricia A. *The Comedians: Hugh Hood & Rudy Wiebe*. Toronto: Clarke, Irwin, 1977.

Moss, John. *Sex and Violence in the Canadian Novel: The Ancestral Present*. Toronto: McClelland and Stewart, 1977.

New, William H. "Fiction", in Carl F. Klinck, gen. ed. and introd., *Literary History of Canada: Canadian Literature in English*. 2nd ed. Toronto: University of Toronto Press, 1976, Vol. III.

Rollins, Douglas. "The Montreal Storytellers", *Journal of Canadian Fiction*, I, 2 (Spring 1972), 5-6.

Struthers, J.R. (Tim), ed. *Before the Flood: Our Exagmination round His Factification for Incamination of Hugh Hood's Work in Progress*. Downsview, Ontario: ECW Press, 1979.

—————. *Hugh Hood: An Annotated Bibliography*. The Annotated Bibliography of Canada's Major Authors. Ed. Robert Lecker and Jack David. Downsview, Ontario, ECW Press, forthcoming.

Thompson, Kent. Review of *The Fruit Man, The Meat Man & The Manager*, *The Fiddlehead*, No. 92 (Winter 1972), pp. 116-23.

—————. "Hugh Hood and His Expanding Universe", *Journal of Canadian Fiction*, III, 1 (Winter 1974), 55-59.

—————. "Hood, Hugh (John Blagdon)", *Contemporary Novelists*. 2nd ed. (1976).

—————. "Formal Coherence in the Art of Hugh Hood", in Barry Cameron and Michael Dixon, ed. and introd., *Minus Canadian: Penultimate Essays on Literature*, *Studies in Canadian Literature*, II (Summer 1977), 203-12.

A Note on the Contributor

J.R. (Tim) Struthers of London, Ontario is the author of various bibliographies, reviews, interviews, and articles dealing with Canadian literature and with its relation to British and American literature. He edited *Before the Flood*, the first volume of criticism devoted solely to the work of Hugh Hood, and has compiled a lengthy bibliography of works by and on Hood for Volume V of *The Annotated Bibliography of Canada's Major Authors*.

Alden Nowlan

by
Rosalind Eve Conway

Like the protagonist of his novel *Various Persons Named Kevin O'Brien*, Alden Nowlan is many people: a poet, short-story writer, novelist, journalist, playwright, historian and essayist. Yet there is no lack of continuity in his work. The setting is usually a small town or village in Nova Scotia or New Brunswick, and the sensitivity and objectivity of a man who examines and responds to his surroundings is always present. In this profile, Nowlan's poetry, fiction, plays and non-fiction will be discussed. Some of the literary techniques he employs will be surveyed, but the focus will be on his themes.

Nowlan's style has changed over the past 20 years. His earlier poems, particularly those in *A Darkness in the Earth, The Rose and the Puritan, Wind in a Rocky Country* and *Under the Ice*, are short; some are four or eight lines long or less. Many of these poems are written in more traditional forms than his later work; certainly they use more rhyme, half-rhyme and alliteration. Yet amongst many poems written in quatrains and blank verse there are poems written in free verse, and some use the techniques of concrete poetry; even in his earliest poems Nowlan shows that he is conscious of how they appear on the page. Nowlan was in touch with modern poetry through the literary "little magazines". By the time he had written his second chapbook, "The Rose and the Puritan", he had read more widely. Through Fred Cogswell he was introduced to the poetry of Louis Dudek and Irving Layton, whose work in turn led him to the less formal work of the Black Mountain Poets, (Robert Creeley, Charles Olson and Robert Duncan). These poets led him to William Carlos Williams, from whom he learned to let the poem create the form; and perhaps this was how Nowlan acquired his fear of having a fixed style. One sees, progressively, a loosening up in Nowlan's poetry in both form and choice of subject; and this becomes most dramatic by the late 60's when he begins to write longer, more prosaic poems of some subtlety and complexity like "Ypres: 1915" and "Another Poem", in *The Mysterious Naked Man*. The changes in his work were not entirely deliberate; they evolved gradually from his reading. Although his later poems are not usually written in traditional forms, they never "go on too long"; it is clear that a careful craftsman is at work. Indeed, Nowlan constantly revises.

One important aspect of Alden Nowlan's poetry is his use of line-breaks. His earliest poems tend to use heavily end-stopped lines. In *Wind in a Rocky Country* he shows a new flexibility. The following passage from "For Nicholas of all the Russias" shows how he uses run-on lines to elucidate his meaning through qualification:

> Wind in a rocky country and the harvest
> meagre, the sparrows eaten, all the cattle
> gone with the ragged troopers...
> (*Wind in a Rocky Country*, p. 16.)

When Nowlan uses very short lines, the line-breaks often throw emphasis onto the first word of the following line. The use of short lines in modern poetry is most successful when it makes the reader pay more attention to each word the poet has chosen.

In *The Rose and the Puritan*, *Wind in a Rocky Country* and *Under the Ice*, many of the poems show the influence of American poets Edwin Arlington Robinson and Edgar Lee Masters. The inhabitants of Robinson's Tilbury Town, based on Gardiner, Maine, have much in common with the Maritimes townspeople and villagers of Nowlan's poetry and fiction. Robinson chose a sympathetic, psychological approach; like a story-teller, he used third-person narration and traditional forms. Many of Nowlan's poems are reminiscent of those by Robinson; one might compare Nowlan's "Warren Pryor", the story of an unwillingly sophisticated bank teller, with Robinson's "Richard Cory". Masters' work is written in blunt, stark free verse, and its influence can be seen in such poems as "Charlie" and "Carl". However, Masters' people speak for themselves, and so the effect achieved is different. Yet Robinson, Masters and Nowlan all describe the forces which circumscribe the lives of these people; they write about guilt, suffering, disappointment and loneliness. Such powerful subject matter has universal appeal, and these early poems by Nowlan are often anthologized.

In the early volumes there are many poems dealing with Nowlan's family and childhood. Some of these, like "Aunt Jane", "When Like the Tears of Clowns" and "Beginning", are amongst his best known poems. His relatives, like the villagers, are puritans, and deny the flesh, fearing and despising weakness. These are moving and frightening portraits.

Even in Nowlan's early work (one senses) he is at work philosophizing. He thinks of mortality and of how absent God is from our world; he questions people's morality, but he never chastizes them. In his introduction to *Playing the Jesus Game*, Robert Bly compliments Nowlan on "his psychic bravery", his willingness to tear the metaphorical umbrella in the sky that D.H. Lawrence says we use to protect ourselves against chaos. The violent death of the delicate doe in "The Jackers" which so upsets the speaker, probably a very young Nowlan, is juxtaposed with this image:

> Grief was like spoilt bread in the mouth, I bit
> the pillows, though I would not eat;
> lonely as God with pity for her, yet
> dogged by the smell of her frying meat.
> (*Under the Ice*, p. 33.)

Nowlan feelingly describes the deaths of animals, both wild and barnyard. In "A Night Hawk Fell With a Sound Like a Shudder" he writes, "in any hunt I'm with the quarry." The deaths are violent and arbitrary, as in "Hens", in which the partially frozen cock is "calmly"

pecked dead by the hens. In "The Bull Moose" the animal, surrounded by people who are behaving like a mob, is compared to both a "blood god" and a "scaffolded king"; his death, like Christ's, is sacrificial. By anthropomorphizing his animals Nowlan suggests that the violence that is turned on them by man and nature is also readily turned on us, whether it is physical violence or verbal. And all too often the victims are children, as in "Britain Street", which tells of a place where mothers scream their children's names like "curses".

In his poems about violence Nowlan is rooted in realism, and this is particularly evident in *The Things Which Are*, in its many references to bodily injuries. The title itself shows Nowlan's unwillingness to compromise, to prettify. Still, Nowlan admits there are boundaries in "Explanation":

> My best poems
> don't get written,
> because I'm still scared.
> (*The Things Which Are*, p. 45.)

On the other hand, in this volume and in subsequent volumes many poems are not realistic at all. Their setting is in the imagination, and they borrow something from mystery, something from SF and something from romance. Two of the better known examples of this are "July 15" and "The Mysterious Naked Man", in which both men are naked, stripped of civilization, and are perhaps about to start over.

Although Nowlan so often writes of a need to begin again or of the possibility of Armageddon and the destruction of the world, his work is rooted in a love of life. He celebrates involvement. In the title of *Between Tears and Laughter* Alden Nowlan combines two powerful emotions, crying and laughing, as he so often does. In "Johnnie's Poem" he states, "you write poems about what / you feel deepest and hardest" (*Between Tears and Laughter*, p. 50). Throughout Nowlan's work one sees love turn to hate quickly, but turn back again to love; it is indifference which is a crime, as Nowlan makes clear in "The Night Editor's Poem". His recent poems with domestic, and seemingly mundane settings transcend their surroundings because they deal with the very substance of experience, with how people treat one another every day. Nowlan feels joy and wonderment even in his parents reluctantly bringing him into this world. The title of "It's Good to Be Here" is ironically contrasted with the poem's first line in which his mother announces, "I'm in trouble." Yet the title is apt, one realizes, after reading the closing stanza:

> ...I lay curled up,
> my heart beating,
> in the darkness inside her.
> (*Smoked Glass*, p. 71.)

While this profile can only deal with a

limited number of Alden Nowlan's themes, it should be noted that there is much continuity in the subject matter of all his writing. For example, in his three most recent collections of poetry he often focuses on how complex identity is, a topic which is central to his novel and plays, as will be seen.

Nowlan has written two books of fiction, *Miracle at Indian River,* a collection of stories, and *Various Persons Named Kevin O'Brien,* a novel. The setting is a rather impoverished and backward Maritimes of villages, logging camps and sawmills; it is based on the Nova Scotia of Nowlan's youth. Here, as in his poetry, his re-creation of how the people fight and love, work and worship, is vivid and realistic; the dialogue is idiomatic and evocative.

In *Miracle at Indian River* different narrative techniques are employed. Some stories are told by a first-person narrator, and this character varies in his level of sophistication: he may be a reporter, or a naive narrator like a madman or a child. In one story, "At the Edge of the Woods", Nowlan uses the stream-of-consciousness technique, and the reader experiences the workings of the mind of a small, frightened boy. However, the technique used most often is that of narration in the third person. Nevertheless, there is little moralizing; the tone of these stories is sympathetic: Nowlan does not criticize; he describes. His stories, like Morley Callaghan's, are fairly short, opening with one or two paragraphs that succinctly outline the central character and his problem. The character's personality then dictates the plot: there are no twists, no surprise endings. Everything is as ordinary and extraordinary as everyday life.

Several themes run through the stories. The characters' fantasies are subject to the depredations of reality, although they are not always conscious of this. In "Love Letter" Nora moons over her soldier husband, whom she barely knows, and then picks up a young man at the drug store. After their brief escapade she returns to her letter to Ronnie, yet she cannot see she has qualified her love for him. Some of the characters long to attain power: the old man in "The Guide" tells of how he loved to help lost children. He began to pray that they would lose their way, so that he could become their saviour. The parents Nowlan describes are usually incapable of looking after their children properly. Mothers are generally absent or preoccupied; and many of the fathers are alcoholics. In "A Call in December" one anticipates the death of the sickly baby in the DeLaGarde shack. And there is little real gentleness. In "The Glass Roses" Stephen is warned by his rather distant father not to let his logging partner Leka, "The Polack", touch him, although the touching is, ironically, fatherly. Nowlan paints the picture of a brutal

world in which little real communication is possible. Sam Baxter, the shy and aging bachelor in "The Girl Who Went to Mexico", is thrilled with his new subscription to *The Canadian Yeoman* because it leads him to an outside world, one which both entrances and frightens him. He is not used to communicating, but finds himself drawn to the "personal column", through which he locates a lonely, rather eager widow. Although he hides from her for a time, he finally reaches out. There is a victory here that few of Nowlan's characters accomplish. In "The Foreigner" communication becomes impossible; the man speaks in a private language and would be a foreigner anywhere. The attendants of the psychiatric ward strip him and put him in isolation, an ironically ineffective cure. The foreigner is "like a being from another planet"; and alienation is often the subject of Nowlan's work. In the opening of his novel, one learns that Kevin O'Brien feels like an alien.

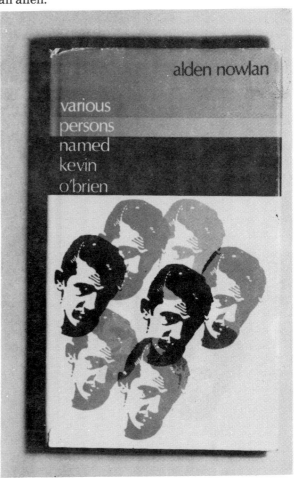

From Various Persons named Kevin O'Brien *by Alden Nowlan.*
©1973 by Clarke, Irwin   Company Limited.
Used by permission.

Various Persons Named Kevin O'Brien consists of eleven chapters, and each is much like a short story, for each focuses on a period of Kevin's life. The chapters are unified through the use of a framework: Kevin's visit to his native village Lockhartville. As events and conversations occur in the present, his mind returns to the past, and the tense shifts. Some of the recollections are narrated in the first person, and it seems that all of these are from the autobiographical manuscripts in Kevin's brief-case. The book begins with his early childhood and ends with a mature Kevin. In the final chapter, as he flies away from Lockhartville he recalls a dance he attended the night before. He thinks of the clannishness and childishness of his cousins egging on the fight, and realizes that he has grown up, while his cousins, in some ways, have remained boys. The novel moves from Kevin's feeling separate from the village to his realization that it accepts him; but now, although he sees it as part of his identity, he can only partially accept it. Kevin's visit is a metaphor for growing up.

The central theme of *Various Persons Named Kevin O'Brien* is that identity is undefinable. It shifts constantly. Even the past changes because one's perceptions of it alter as one ages. The identities of Kevin's village and his mother are also vague; indeed, even Kevin's parentage is questioned. His mother, brother and sister are almost mythical; yet their myths change. In a sense Kevin and his sister Stephanie are also one person, identified by the incorporated public self of their childhood. As Kevin thinks in the opening chapter, in some instances "vagueness is more truthful than accuracy" (p. 4).

Kevin is a dreamer who longs for power, although the realization of its consequences sickens him. The sadism of children and adults who take pleasure in torturing others repulses Kevin. He looks for justice and understanding as a child, and so is often thought a fool. Kevin needs to take control because he feels powerless. Though he has done so by escaping from the village and becoming a reporter, he finds he must do so again, symbolically, at the dance. After landing a successful blow on the man's Adam's apple, he realizes that "his victory had been fortuitous and meaningless" (p. 142). Kevin does not want to be a brute; he wants to be gentle.

One quickly realizes that *Various Persons* is not simply a "fictional memoir" as it is called in the sub-title; it is Nowlan's own memoir. For example, Kevin's grandmother closely resembles Nowlan's Old Em in "Growing Up in Katpesa Creek" in *Double Exposure*. The young Alden, a day-dreamer who longed to be a prophet or a leader, is recreated in Kevin; and both grow up to be reporters and writers. In Nowlan's fiction, as in his non-fiction and poetry, he writes from life.

Nowlan has written several plays with Walter Learning. Two of these, *Frankenstein* and *The Incredible Murder of Cardinal Tosca*,

have been published. *Frankenstein* is a dramatization of Mary Shelley's classic horror story, and as such it is a descendant not only of the novel, but also of the many 20th-century treatments of the tale. The famous assistant from film, Fritz, is here; but he is not deformed physically, or mentally aberrant: he has a conscience, and is a foil for the amoral Victor Frankenstein. Other additions include a group of servants whose comic antics contrast with their masters in a manner reminiscent of Elizabethan and Jacobean drama. Dramatization requires a simplification of the story; and rather than leave certain incidents out, Nowlan and Learning opt to fuse them. The death of Victor's brother William is mingled with the events at De Lacey's cottage, so that a somewhat different — but dramatically equivalent — outcome ensues. Nevertheless, their monster is the same one that Mary Shelley conceived: sensitive, wounded, rejected by his maker, he does not wish to be evil, but to be loved.

In writing about Victor Frankenstein Nowlan again focuses on man's interest in omnipotence. Frankenstein, the Modern Prometheus as Mary Shelley dubbed him, is a rival of God – but so is Satan, and Nowlan and Learning make this clear. In the play as in the novel one finds the same theme: what was done in the name of science was actually done out of pride. He who desires to be the Creator is a destroyer, a usurper trying to undermine God's creation. Victor Frankenstein is evil, and the foulness of the monster is his own foulness. The popular Romantic symbol of the doppelgänger is recalled here: two very different people exist either side by side or in the same body, for in essence they are the same person.

The Incredible Murder of Cardinal Tosca is a Sherlock Holmes adventure. In this apocryphal story Holmes is again dogged by his adversary Moriarty. And these two are also linked alter egos. Just as Victor Frankenstein's monster surprises one with love and gentleness, Moriarty displays integrity and even compassion. There is honour amongst his den of thieves, and he is the originator of it. In contrast, Holmes is not simply the stalwart seeker of justice. He is, at times, cold-blooded, indifferent to the sufferings of others as he pursues his case. It becomes apparent that while crime hurts some people severely, it may sometimes be innocuous – while justice can be deadly.

The play depends upon surprise, sleight-of-hand and a complex denouement. Both *The Incredible Murder* and *Frankenstein* are full of sudden developments and murders; in fact, they are sensationalist. One should not forget that *Hamlet*, in true Jacobean fashion, closes with a stage littered with bodies. Shakespeare knew how to make entertaining plays. Although Nowlan and Learning work, on one level to show the complexity, the doubleness, of human character, on another level they clearly see the stage as arena: the audience has come for fun, and the play-wrights readily provide it. In *The Incredible Murder* they throw in Satanism and a papal secret service to spice up the plot. The plays mix "profit" and "delight", following the tradition of that great dramatist and moralist, Ben Jonson.

Finally, this profile will examine Alden Nowlan's non-fiction. His interest in recording the history of the Maritimes and its people, so evident in his earlier poetry, is offered full expression in both his historical study of Campobello Island and in his essays, collected in *Double Exposure.*

Campobello: The Outer Island is a history of this small New Brunswick island which lies just off the coast of Maine, and which is geographically closer to the U.S. than Canada. Nowlan provides a thoroughly researched history that is anecdotal and amusing. He does not merely record the names of the island's rulers and fisher-men, but looks into their lives, and sometimes, movingly, into their deaths. His portrait of one inhabitant, Franklin Delano Roosevelt, who spent many summers there, is particularly vivid. Nowlan has a knack for bringing history to life.

It is possible that what drew Nowlan's attention to the island was its many identities. Both Welsh and Scots, Canadian and American, it is international yet regional. The complexity of identity that is so often Nowlan's theme is re-called here, just as it is in some of the essays in *Double Exposure.* In "Ladies and Gentlemen, Stompin' Tom Connors!" Nowlan notes that Connors often refers to his younger selves in the third person.

Double Exposure contains several articles recording the history of the Maritimes and its people, and Nowlan's own history. His essays stemming from interviews with various personal-ities like Hank Snow and former Nova Scotia premier Gerald Regan show his interest in draw-ing out their pasts. The essays are, again, an-ecdotal, and, significantly, honest. Nowlan's point-of-view is largely unclouded by the 20th century, and though he states that his rural up-bringing was not unlike one of the 18th century, to attribute his objectivity to this would be simplistic. Nowlan is an original thinker who questions the status quo of both the city and the village.

Alden Nowlan hates smugness, the assur-ance of modern man that there has been progress. In his articles he looks at such diverse issues as incarceration, abortion and food additives. He feels that we are neither worse nor better than our predecessors. We are no more knowledgeable –but simply know different things. The question-ing attitude of the English writer G.K. Chesterton is one Nowlan admires. Alden Nowlan speaks for sincerity, honesty and humility, for facing issues squarely and unhypocritically, and suggests that it might be dangerous to do otherwise. Several essays discuss how haphazard the average man's attitude to politics is, how easily he is swayed. Nowlan asks people to be critical; he complains that most people approach both life and art superficially, assuming under-standing after only a cursory examination.

Although Alden Nowlan is best known for his poetry, it is clear that he works successfully in other genres. A moralist, but not a moralizer, his writing is full of love and sympathy for the Maritimes and its people, and of his great respect for life. In an all too violent and uncaring world, Nowlan is a spokesman for gentleness and under-standing.

Chronology

1933   Born in Stanley (near Windsor), Hants County, Nova Scotia, on 25 January.

1948   Left school at age 15 after 37 days in Grade Five.

c. 1949   Discovered the Regional Library.

c. 1950   First poem accepted by an American "little magazine", *The Bridge,* a mim-eographed publication from Eagle Creek, Oregon.

1952   Moved to Hartland, New Brunswick, to work on *The Observer.*

1957   Met Fred Cogswell, editor of Fiddlehead Poetry Books and professor of English at the University of New Brunswick. He was not only the first poet Nowlan had met, but the first person who read poetry. Cogswell introduced him to the work of various poets, including Raymond Souster, Robinson and Masters. Only one or two poems that pre-date this meeting are still taken seriously by Nowlan.

1958   *The Rose and the Puritan,* a chapbook, published by Cogswell.

1959   *A Darkness in the Earth,* a chapbook, published in California. This was actually written before *The Rose and the Puritan* and before Nowlan's meeting with Cogs-well.

1960   *Wind in a Rocky Country,* a chapbook, published in Toronto.

1961   *Under the Ice,* his first full-length book, published by Ryerson. Nowlan received a Canada Council Junior Arts Fellowship.

1962	*The Things Which Are.*
1963	Married Claudine Orser.
	Moved to Saint John, New Brunswick, to work on *The Telegraph-Journal* as a reporter. Later became the night news editor.
1966	Three operations for cancer of the throat.
1967	*Bread, Wine and Salt,* for which he received the Governor-General's Award for Poetry.
	Guggenheim Fellow· for 67-68; travelled in Ireland and England.
1968	*Miracle at Indian River.*
	Became Writer in Residence at the University of New Brunswick, a position he still holds.
1969	*The Mysterious Naked Man.*
1970	*Playing the Jesus Game: Selected Poems* published in New York with an introduction by Robert Bly.
	Awarded the President's Medal of the University of Western Ontario for the best short story of 1970.
1971	*Between Tears and Laughter.*
	Hon. D.Litt., University of New Brunswick.
1972	Awarded the President's Medal of the University of Western Ontario for the best short story of 1972.
1973	*Various Persons Named Kevin O'Brien.*
1974	*I'm a Stranger Here Myself.*
	With New Brunswick painter Tom Forrestall, *Shaped by this Land.*
1975	*Campobello: The Outer Island.*
1976	With Walter Learning, *Frankenstein.*
	Hon. L1.D., Dalhousie University.
1977	*Smoked Glass,* for which Nowlan won the Canadian Authors' Association Award (excellence in writing with popular appeal).
	Awarded Queen's Silver Jubilee Medal.
1978	*Double Exposure.*
	With Walter Learning, *The Incredible Murder of Cardinal Tosca.*
1979	With Walter Learning, "Full Circle" and "The Runaways", produced by CBC Television.

Comments
by Alden Nowlan

Some critics are uncomfortable because I've worked in so many different genres: poetry, fiction, plays, journalism, history. Of course, in Europe it is taken for granted that a writer will *write*. Not so in North America. I sometimes wish that years ago I had adopted different pseudonyms for different kinds of work – one name for poems, another for plays, a third for journalism. Just to make the critics happy.

But look at almost any English writer's bibliography. You'll find novels, collections of stories, poems, plays, biographies, books about chess, books about cats, books about gardening, detective stories, travel books.

Letter to R.E. Conway, 11 November 1979.

. . . perhaps a poet ought to begin by publishing a book of criticism with all sorts of high-sounding phrases – adumbrate is a very big word with the critics – and then he wouldn't be expected to waste any more time with that sort of thing, he could simply write poems, which is what a poet ought to be doing.

"Alden Nowlan" [Interview], by John Metcalf, *Canadian Literature*, No. 67 (Winter 1975), p. 11.

. . . I don't write poems for an audience. An audience is a crowd. I write poems for one person at a time. I distrust the kind of thing that can be shouted to a crowd. At the end of that road I see the spellbinding orator. I'd rather talk with one person than speechify to a thousand.

"Alden Nowlan", p. 13.

To be a writer you have to run the risk of making a fool of yourself. When I run the risk of sounding prosaic I run the risk deliberately – just as I sometimes deliberately run the risk of sounding sentimental. I think you have to risk sentimentality if you're going to write anything that matters because after all sentimentality is very close to the things that *genuinely* move people – it's not a falsity but simply an exaggeration.

"Alden Nowlan", pp. 14-15.

Usually I do the first version of a poem almost as an exercise in free association except that it's tethered to the point that brought it into being. Sometimes I think of these first versions as first drafts and sometimes I think of them as notes toward a poem. Some of them never go beyond this phase. The rest I throw into a drawer and periodically I dig through a bunch of them and pick out those that appeal to me at the moment and then I work at them as objectively and coldly as possible, almost as if they were somebody else's work. Then when I'm preparing the manuscript for a collection of poems I make further changes in almost every poem that goes into the book, not to make them conform to any theoretical principles but according to Robert Graves' dictum that a poet ought to handle his lines and images and words like a housewife separating the good tomatoes from those that are under-ripe or spoiled.

"Alden Nowlan", p. 8.

No writer can ever be truly successful simply because no work of art, no poem, no story, no novel, no painting, no music can ever be more than a tiny polished fragment from the infinitely and eternally formless reality that inspired it.

In *Sixteen by Twelve*, ed. John Metcalf (Toronto: McGraw-Hill Ryerson, 1970), p. 155.

Comments
on Alden Nowlan

. . . Nowlan is one of the microcosmic-macrocosmic poets, constantly moving within his own world, which is that of the puritanical small towns and the wild logging camps of New Brunswick. In telling his anecdotes, in recording sharp fragments and points of experience, Nowlan combines a concise form with an easy conversational manner and yet at times achieves a super-real intensity of vision which launches personal experience into universality.

George Woodcock, in *Literary History of Canada*, 2nd. ed., vol. 3 (Toronto: Univ. of Toronto Press, 1976), 307.

The voice of the early poems – as is the vision – is more forceful, more heightened, more poetic than the mature voice. The divisions and the ironies of those early poems are starker and are played upon more openly than those of the late poems. The forms are generally tighter. For all their power, the early poems appeal in fairly obvious ways. Nowlan's growth [has been] toward a more complicated, more truly resolved, view of the world . . . .The instrument has had to become more flexible, more subtle, its ironies less stark but more authentically lodged in mature insight.

Robert Gibbs, *The Fiddlehead*, No. 122 (Summer 1979), p. 112. [Review of *Smoked Glass, Double Exposure* and *Poet's Progress.*]

Dedicated honestly and humbly to his art, equally at home in more than one *genre*, Alden Nowlan furnishes an unhip, thoroughly non-academic world with splashes of exquisite insight. A Grade 5 dropout, he has taught himself that the archetypal image . . . is not necessarily a sacred cow but a local breed that he might wryly milk in order to construct a more truthful image . . . .

Keath Fraser, "Notes on Alden Nowlan", *Canadian Literature*, No. 45 (Summer 1970), pp. 50-51.

Surrounded as we are by vague bombast, his details are fantastically clear. His clear direct language is not a transformative language – it's not about one thing turning into another – but a descriptive language, about the way things are.

Robert Bly, in *Playing the Jesus Game: Selected Poems* (Trumansburg, N.Y.: New/Books, 1970), p. 10.

In most of his early poems Alden Nowlan seems guarded, even suspicious, about revealing himself to his readers. He confesses in these poems not the truth about himself but the truth about his neighbours and his environment.

Michael Brian Oliver, *Poet's Progress: The Development of Alden Nowlan's Poetry* (Fredericton: Fiddlehead Poetry Books, 1978), p. 5.

Much of the effectiveness of Nowlan's poetry comes from his ability to paradoxically transform the everyday trivial- even ridiculous –happening into significant patterns.

Oliver, p. 35.

Selected Bibliography
Works by Alden Nowlan

Between Tears and Laughter. Toronto: Clarke, Irwin, 1971.

Bread, Wine and Salt. Toronto: Clarke, Irwin, 1967.

Campobello: The Outer Island. Toronto: Clarke, Irwin, 1975.

A Darkness in the Earth. Eureka, Cal.: Hearse [1959].

Double Exposure. Fredericton: Brunswick Press, 1978.

I'm a Stranger Here Myself. Toronto: Clarke, Irwin, 1974.

Miracle at Indian River. Toronto: Clarke, Irwin, 1968.

The Mysterious Naked Man. Toronto: Clarke, Irwin, 1969.

Playing the Jesus Game: Selected Poems. Trumansburg, N.Y.: New/Books, 1970. [Introduction by Robert Bly. Contains a selection of the early work through *Bread, Wine and Salt* and 26 new poems, most of which are unavailable elsewhere.]

The Rose and the Puritan. Fredericton: Fiddlehead Poetry Books [1958].

Smoked Glass. Toronto: Clarke, Irwin, 1977.

The Things Which Are. Toronto: Contact Press, 1962.

Under the Ice. Toronto: The Ryerson Press, 1961.

Various Persons Named Kevin O'Brien: A Fictional Memoir. Toronto: Clarke, Irwin, 1973.

Wind in a Rocky Country. Toronto: Emblem Books, 1960.

Works by Alden Nowlan and Tom Forrestall

Shaped by this Land. Fredericton: Brunswick Press,

1974. [An extensive collection of Nowlan's poems set in the Maritimes intersperses paintings by New Brunswick artist Forrestall. Most of Nowlan's work is from *Under the Ice*.]

Works by Alden Nowlan and Walter Learning

Frankenstein. Fredericton: Clarke, Irwin, 1976.
The Incredible Murder of Cardinal Tosca. Fredericton: Learning Productions, 1978.

Selected Criticism

Ellis, Glen. "A Conversation with Poets Elizabeth Brewster and Alden Nowlan", Media Centre, University of Toronto, 1972, pt. 2. [Discussion of how Nowlan began to write and the writers who influenced him.]

Fraser, Keath. "Notes on Alden Nowlan", *Canadian Literature,* No. 45 (Summer 1970), pp. 41-51. Deals with both the poetry and the stories.

Metcalf, John. "Alden Nowlan" [Interview], *Canadian Literature,* No. 67 (Winter. 1975), pp. 8-17. [Very useful discussion of his techniques; interesting passage on his use of line-breaks.]

Nowlan, Alden. "Something to Write About", *Canadian Literature,* Nos. 68-69 (Spring-Summer 1976), pp. 7-12. [Discusses his childhood and the early stages of his writing career.]

Oliver, Michael Brian. *Poet's Progress: The Development of Alden Nowlan's Poetry.* Fredericton: Fiddlehead Poetry Books, 1978. [Study of all Nowlan's poetry from 1958-1977. Takes a thematic approach; discusses such topics as puritanism and alienation.]

For more bibliographical information one should consult Frank Davey's *From There to Here* (Erin, Ont.: Press Porcépic, 1974), particularly for the early reviews. Also see Michael Gnarowski's *A Concise Bibliography of English-Canadian Literature,* 2nd ed. (Toronto: McClelland and Stewart, 1978). Various essays by Ernest Buckler, Louis Dudek and others as well as an interview appear in *The Fiddlehead,* No. 81 (August-October 1969), the "Alden Nowlan Feature".

A Note on the Contributor

Rosalind Eve Conway was born in London, England, in 1954. She has done graduate work in Old Icelandic literature at Carleton University, and in Canadian literature at the University of Toronto. Her poetry has been published in numerous magazines, newspapers and anthologies. She is the Reviews Editor of *Writers' Quarterly.*

Robert Kroetsch 27

by

Russell M. Brown

Symbolism may have spent its force, in its present form. But realism is not the answer. Rather a new version of the fabulist *(The* Crow *Journals*[1]*).*

The recent publication of *The* Crow *Journals* has provided readers with the history of composition of Robert Kroetsch's sixth novel, *What the Crow Said*. From the entry that records its first conception, the journal traces the slow growth of Kroetsch's most recent novel, allowing us to see how the initial form of the narrative becomes a kind of armature for the accretions of imagination and intellect. The long creative process to come is anticipated from the outset by Kroetsch when he adds this remark to his first entry: ". . . my own (rural?) experience, basically, expanded

towards the tall tale, the mythological; but always the hard core of detail" *(CJ,* p. 11).

In this comment Kroetsch provides us with a sense of the composite nature of his fiction and of much of his poetry as well. There is always a core of authorial experience, an intensely felt, personal starting point providing the initial impetus to the story. This choice of experience from his own past is more than merely personal, however; it is also a kind of political act, an expression of Kroetsch's conviction that the Canadian artist must give some account of his territory, of his region and place. Moreover, by making new tales out of the particulars embedded in his memory — by giving arrangement and meaning to hailstorms and studhorses, prairie politicians and preachers, rodeos and beer halls - Kroetsch is constantly showing the reader the very process by which such small details, drawn from one's encounters with reality, are transformed into stories, explanations, and myths.

This transformation of a private experience of the past into the public form of tall tale and legend is a process that Kroetsch thinks of as already indigenous to the Canadian West — something which is done daily there, most often in that communal gathering place of western males, the beer hall:

> In the sacred place of the beer parlour, we are allowed to change identities — in our laughter, in our silences, in the stories we tell, in what we remember from the past.[2]

Kroetsch's fiction goes beyond the tall tale in its departure from the realism of its prairie settings, however — beyond the artful lying of the prairie pub. All the novels are given a mythological grounding; each has a subterranean text that grows out of the patterns and allusions introduced into the welter of detail. It is the relationships of these rather different levels of Kroetsch's texts which makes him such a fascinating author to read. His works not only provide the reader with a good story, they also furnish him with stories that seem to expand in significance as he considers them, until each of them seems to aspire to contain all other stories within itself.

Gone Indian, Kroetsch's fourth novel, published in 1973, may be taken as one example of this interplay of narrative levels. The book can be read simply as a comic tall tale, one mixing sexual fantasy and contemporary anxiety in its story of a young graduate student (such as those Kroetsch taught at the time) coming to Canada from the United States in search of a teaching position and a better place to live. The central character is distracted from his goals by a winter carnival, and finally disappears into the north (or perhaps he is killed), riding on a snowmobile with a beautiful woman behind him. Read only at this level of plot, the work is simply a funny, bawdy series of adventures; a more "literary" reading of the novel will reveal a more serious purpose, one that is underscored by literary allusions (to, among other works, Vergil's *Aeneid* and Dante's *La Vita Nuova*) and mythic evocations (of the North American Indian trickster myth, of Ragnarok — the Norse version of apocalypse — and of the large mythic patterns found in *The Golden Bough*) which provide several additional, and interlocking, levels of meaning.

This mythic material is given still greater narrative complexity when we observe the way in which this book is told: it is said to be a series of tapes recorded by Jeremy Sadness for Mark Madham, his graduate advisor, a man with whom he may have many reasons for not being completely honest; Madham then transcribes, edits, and even "corrects" Jeremy's statements before presenting them to us. The distance that this mode of narration puts between us and the story is perhaps increased even more when we realize that Professor Madham shares a good deal of his biography with Kroetsch (including his home address). We become intensely aware of the author's vivid presence in his work — playful and ironic, himself engaged in the same struggle as his characters, that of seeking meaning and coherence in apparent chaos.

. . .

Kroetsch published his first novel, *But We Are Exiles*, in 1965, after a few early short stories. Closer to the realistic tradition than the fiction which follows it, the book nevertheless shows its author already at work mythologizing his materials. Even though Kroetsch later characterized the novel as inconsistent with his subsequent work,[3] it remains a book worth reading both on its own merits and for its initial expresion of themes and patterns of the fiction to come. For example, *Exiles* provides the first of Kroetsch's treatments of male sexuality; it is one of a series of accounts of the irrationality, the competition between men, the flight from domesticity, and

the self-destructive behaviour that seems to be an inevitable part of man's sexual identity. (Later novels will go further in suggesting the pleasures that draw man into sexuality despite the pain.) Also central to Kroetsch's first novel is the intense awareness of mortality that is present in all of his work — an awareness that makes itself felt both as a fear and as an attraction, and that often takes the form of some irredeemable blood guilt for the protagonist. Finally, the fact that a journey is central to the story (or rather two journeys, since the novel has a double-narrative structure) looks forward to the many voyages and quests which structure Kroetsch's books — whether made by horse across the prairies, by raft through the Alberta badlands, or by snowmobile into the unknown north.

Kroetsch's drive to build his novels out of personal experience is particularly apparent in this first novel. After he completed his undergraduate degree at the University of Alberta, believing that an aspiring writer needed "Experience with a capital E" and that such experience should involve adventure and hardship, he travelled north to work as a labourer on the Fort Smith portage and then sailed on the Mackenzie river boats for two seasons. In *The Crow Journals*, he describes witnessing a death at Norman Wells when fumes in the hold of a barge exploded:

> Joe's skin falling off as he kept on crawling up the ladder, his hair burnt off, his clothes gone, except for his belt and his boots and his jockey shorts. Joe dead and still climbing, talking (*CJ*, p.27).

This event becomes the source of *But We Are Exiles;* as the incident which occurs just before the novel opens, it provides the psychic starting point for Peter Guy's final voyage up the Mackenzie River as well as for the inward journey he makes to confront his past.

The story of Peter Guy and Mike Hornyak (the man who dies) is not, however, allowed to exist only on a realistic level, as a tragic event considered in the context of a complex web of human emotion. By providing an epigraph from Ovid's account of Narcissus, Kroetsch suggests that Hornyak is a double-figure for Guy, a kind of mirror image who lures the Narcissus-like protagonist to his watery destruction. The story, which begins with Guy peering at his reflection as he tries to look into the depths of the river into which Hornyak's body has disappeared, gradually reveals that in the past Guy has fled to the North when he caught sight of the reflected image of Hornyak making love to Kettle Fraser, Guy's fiancée. Guy has been trapped in the past by that reflection and, just as Narcissus abandoned Echo, so he has abandoned Kettle because of it. Now, as Hornyak's widow, she is abandoned again because Guy is preoccupied with his own feelings about the dead man and with his responsibility tor Hornyak's death. The conclusion of the novel, in which Guy leaves his boat to take the place of Hornyak's body on the barge being towed behind it, and then floats off into darkness and storm, was disliked by some early readers, but it is appropriate to the mythic structure of the novel: Guy, like Narcissus, is absorbed by his external image. The conclusion also provides a satisfactory close to the surface narrative of the novel once the reader recognizes the compulsive patterns of behaviour that have shaped the inner lives of Peter, Kettle, and Hornyak.

In the fiction that comes after *But We Are Exiles,* psychology of character becomes less important, as comic elements — not only the humorous exaggeration characteristic of the tall tale, but also the hollow chuckle of black comedy — begin to predominate. This development comes partly because of Kroetsch's growing conviction that laughter is the only appropriate response to a universe that he increasingly saw as either random or inexplicable.[4] The publication, in 1966, of *Words of My Roaring* thus initiates a continuing exploration of man's role in a cosmic order that seems less governed by reason than his reason tells him it ought to be.

Words of My Roaring is the first book of a loose trilogy (Kroetsch prefers to call it a triptych) which, continued by *The Studhorse Man* and concluded by *Gone Indian*, is collectively entitled *Out West.* The connections between the three novels are not narrative ones, and the only clear link is the character of John J. Backstrom: protagonist of the first book, he is alluded to in the second, and makes a brief appearance in the third. The real unity of the trilogy is provided by landscape: all three books are set in and around the imaginary Alberta towns of Notikeewin, Burkhardt, and Coulee Hill.

The entire trilogy is a recapitulation of modern prairie history, with each novel moving the reader forward in time — from the depression thirties through the postwar forties and into the present. Each era is a moment of great change in the Canadian West and in society as a whole. Indeed, in response to these historical transitions, each novel might be said to chronicle an ironic search for some kind of Eden, for a redemption variously sought in political action *(Words)*, in sex and the continuity of the species *(Studhorse Man)*, and in the reclamation of pastoral nature *(Gone Indian).*

Paradoxically all three books offer apocalyptic visions along with their Edenic quests. In *Words of My Roaring*, when Backstrom encounters an eccentric prophet who predicts the end of the world, the reader recognizes what Backstrom cannot, that the world order out of which he has emerged, and with which he is struggling, has already *been* ended by drought and depression. Similarly in *The Studhorse Man*, Hazard Lepage

finds that his profession of travelling from farm to farm to breed his stallion to local mares is no longer required: the day of the horse is waning, technology is ascendant. Moreover the final technological advance glimpsed at the end of that novel, the birth control pill (its production ironically abetted by Hazard's stallion), will bring about the end of a number of traditional social structures. In *Gone Indian*, a house that stands out on the prairies is given the name "Worlds End": presuming that an apostrophe has been left out by the sign painter, Jeremy does not notice the intentional ambiguity. The sign not only proclaims the prairie as in some sense the end of the world, it also reminds us that worlds do indeed end — an appropriate reminder in a novel full of events which suggest that the competitive ethic may be coming to an end, and thus that the society which has characterized the West since the Renaissance may at last be at a close.

The Studhorse Man, the centre of the *Out West* trilogy, is a work that for many readers remains Kroetsch's most successful and fascinating novel. Indeed this winner of the 1969 Governor General's Award seems likely to become one of the undisputed classics of Canadian fiction. Since it may be taken as generally representative of Kroetsch's writing, a somewhat fuller consideration of that novel at this point will suggest the richness of all of Kroetsch's narratives. *The Studhorse Man* follows Hazard Lepage, the last of the prairie studhorse men, on the annual circle he makes servicing mares. Because Poseidon, the magnificent blue stallion with which he travels, is the last of a line of great Lepage horses, Hazard's yearly trip has become something more than a means of earning his livelihood: he is now on an obsessive search for a perfect mare to ensure the continuation of the breed. Ironically, Hazard's journey carries him away from Martha Proudfoot, the fiancée whom he has kept waiting for thirteen years and who has the mares he needs. Martha's mares are no answer, because she opposes his project and has "sworn she would only marry him when he abandoned the folly of trying to perpetuate his own breed of horse".[5]

The search for a suitable mate for Poseidon leads Hazard through a kaleidoscopic series of encounters, comic and surreal, in which *his* services seem to be in more demand than those of his stallion. Acquiring a strange travelling companion, a man named Eugene Utter, Hazard eventually turns back toward Coulee Hill where Martha waits in her rooming house, but he encounters only disaster when he arrives. Caught in a fire, he is declared dead until — in a scene indebted to D.H. Lawrence's *The Man Who Died* — Martha's caresses bring him back to life. In the episode which follows, Hazard is killed indeed, a victim of Poseidon's hooves during a confrontation with Martha's young cousin, Demeter Proudfoot (the mad narrator of the novel, he is Hazard's rival for Martha). After Hazard's death, Utter marries Martha and leaves Demeter to manage the production of "Pregnant Mare's Urine" (a source of estrogen) with the help of Poseidon. The novel closes with the news that Martha has given birth to Hazard's posthumous child, a daughter named Demeter Lepage.

Some of the levels of meaning in this story of Hazard's failed search for the continuity of his line are more evident and accessible than others. The whole is quite evidently a fable about the final end of the way of life that produced the myth of the American West, with Hazard and his mighty stallion as distorted images of the cowboy and his faithful horse. Alberta is seen (accurately) as the last stronghold of the cowboy ethos, and World War II as the historic moment which marked the last practical use of the horse. Unfortunately for Hazard, the war ends as the novel opens:

> "For Christ sake listen," Tad said. " . . . Once gas rationing is over and tractors are back on the market, you won't be able to give a horse away" (SM, pp. 13-14).

The novel also works as a parable which warns against the dangers of the quest for an unattainable ideal. But it simultaneously suggests that man's sexual drive and restless energies nevertheless inevitably lead him on one version of this quest, carrying him away from the comfortable world of home and family in the never-to-be-satisfied search for the perfect mate and the ultimate lay. Seen in these terms, Hazard is not only the last of the westerners, he is also one of the last of an old order of "macho" male, the end of the line for man as sexual aggressor and adventurer free to range where his caprice and his lust for experience take him while his faithful woman waits patiently at home. Poseidon, who frequently drags Hazard along despite the man's efforts to direct the beast, becomes an emblematic embodiment of this kind of male sexuality: the stallion is like a self-willed phallus that leaves its owner no choice but to go where he is led. "Martha", the name of Hazard's fiancée, is a word sometimes used to describe women pre-occupied with domestic tasks; thus Martha Proudfoot stands for the domestic life from which Hazard is in unacknowledged flight. Hazard's death is the inescapable result of the meeting of these irreconcilable forces — the male drive for reckless adventure (hazard) and the female instinct for home. The fact that Poseidon's sexual energies are, at the end of this novel, channelled into furnishing hormones for birth control pills not only suggests some harnessing of male sexuality in the emerging, post-Western, world order but also points to a new freeing of female sexuality, and thus to an end of the double standard which has perpetuated the male-female conflict.

Even though his sexual quest may be destructive for Hazard, Kroetsch also suggests that this is the way man has always responded to his recognition of his own mortality. For Hazard, reminders of death are everywhere, beginning with the opening scene in which the studhorse man, wanting to raise money by finding bones for the war effort, succeeds only in digging a pit that resembles his own grave. He finds it difficult to begin his journey immediately thereafter ("The thought of departing was somehow and suddenly unbearable" [SM, p. 8]), partly because even a grave-like hole is more comforting than the open road and partly because, like all such trips, this voyage will carry him closer to the real grave, closer to the end of life and the unknown and unknowable void that waits there. When, a few pages later, Poseidon drags Hazard toward "a patch of darkness that was darker than all the black around him" (SM, p. 17), we glimpse the final end toward which the studhorse man is being propelled throughout the novel.

Man's chief consolations while on this dark journey are suggested by the results of the chaos that Hazard's and Poseidon's visit to Edmonton cause:

> Bosses, because they could not get home, were compelled to spend the night caring for secretaries who could not get home . . . Soldiers proved willing to occupy the cars that had been abandoned; nor did they suffer the darkness alone, what with many typists and housewives transforming fear into merriment (SM, p. 29).

"Transforming fear into merriment" could be taken as the motto of Kroetsch's fiction: while it chronicles the dark goal, it suggests that there is comedy in the journey there and that companionship will help us, because it is better not to suffer alone.

However, while Hazard's journey may be full of both merriment and companionship, Demeter, the narrator, who waits with his cousin Martha in Coulee Hill, is a solitary figure. In love with his older cousin, he views Hazard as a threatening competitor. As he attempts to reconstruct the events that lead to Hazard's death, his narration becomes a parody of biography and scholarship: we learn that he has followed Hazard's earlier paths, handled objects Hazard once held, even measured the railway ties of a train station his subject has visited — "trying to get some sense of the response our hero must have known when he himself encountered that sudden and alien world" (SM, p. 24).

Because Demeter feels such a complex mix of emotions — admiration as well as jealousy — for the man whose life he recounts, the reader suspects the accuracy of his account. Such doubts are reinforced in several places — especially when, at the opening of the ninth chapter, we see Demeter in the act of composition: he shows us a few of the fragmented and disordered "facts" he has collected on 3 x 5 note cards and then proceeds to build these into an elaborate but entirely hypothetical tale.

This narration serves to make the novel a work about the creation of fiction and about the artist's presence in his work. Demeter may be telling us Hazard's story in his own defense, an act of self-justification because of the guilt he feels over the death of the older man, but at the same time his story allows him to call into being the hero that he needs, a hero who compensates for his own lacks: a reckless phallic male whose imagined existence makes up for Demeter's unexciting bookish life. This relationship between the teller and his subject suggests that the artist is involved in a kind of projection in his act of creation; since Kroetsch thinks of fiction as public myth-making as well as private wish-fulfillment, Demeter is also performing a function of which Kroetsch has spoken as one incumbent on the Canadian (especially the western) writer: he is seeking to invent his mythology, to find names for what surrounds him, and to create figures and shapes to fill his new — and still empty landscape. Thus the act of artistic creation, like the act of sex (and Kroetsch frequently associates the two) may itself be a source of needed companionship. Demeter, unable to find comfort in *either* Martha or the open road, can create his companions in the act of story telling. The fact, however, that Demeter tells his tale from a madhouse suggests the dangers of living *only* an imaginative life.

So far these comments deal only with the primary narrative of *The Studhorse Man.* In *The* Crow *Journals,* Kroetsch describes a two-stage method of composition. In the entry for May 4, 1976, some two years after he has begun *What the Crow Said,* he writes: ". . . the novel exists. It is quite literally here, on my desk. Now, in another year, I can write it." His precise meaning is made clearer in that same entry: "I hate this writing of a first draft more than anything else. Now I can begin what Joyce called the 'layering'; the exploration of implication, the play with design." Another year and a half passes while Kroetsch revises his manuscript; he will not correct final galleys until June, 1978 — some four years after the book was begun.

When we look closely at *The Studhorse Man,* we can see what designs and implications Kroetsch's careful layering produced there. Full understanding of such works depends on the reader's recognition of at least some of the several mythic stories called to mind by the novel. Discovery of them thus becomes part of the reader's experience of the novel, a confirmation of a statement made in *Badlands,* which could serve as a reading guide for all of this fiction: "There are no truths, only correspondences."[6] These correspondences not only enlarge the dimensions of the novel — and indeed of one's sense of all

human action — they link Kroetsch to the mythopoeic impulse in Canadian writing and to the modernist discovery of the continuities of myth as well. At the same time, since much of the mythic material in *The Studhorse Man* serves to parody the myth that it calls up, these correspondences contribute to the comedy of the novel and speak to Kroetsch's sense that for the *post-modern* writer parody may be the central act. Thus in *The Studhorse Man* even the smallest gestures may, on the one hand, take on great and sometimes hidden significance while, on the other, they seem wildly improbable and comically inappropriate.

The most striking and important of the mythic parallels contained in *The Studhorse Man* is one with Homer's *Odyssey.* Hazard, journeying across the open prairies after World War II, delaying a return to his potential home with Martha and Demeter, recalls for us Odysseus on his way home from the Trojan War to his wife Penelope and his son Telemachus. The name of Hazard's horse helps make the analogy with the Odyssean story explicit, because it is that of the sea god Poseidon — the god responsible for the problems and delays that Odysseus himself experienced.

In utilizing the Homeric story as an organizing pattern, Kroetsch locates himself in a twentieth century tradition that has two important predecessors, one a Canadian and one not: James Joyce and Hugh MacLennan. In *Ulysses,* Joyce's elaborate parallels with the *Odyssey* brought about the first general recognition of the potential inherent in mythic material for the modern writer. Like *Ulysses,* Kroetsch's *Studhorse Man* seems to offer an event analogous to every one of those found in Homer — although no critic has yet provided a thorough discussion of this aspect of *The Studhorse Man,* and those who have dealt with it are in some disagreement.[7]

Joyce's *Ulysses* itself has a comic and even a parodic dimension, the inevitable result of seeing analogies between events originally cast in an epic and heroic mode now recast in a more realistic and mundane one; *The Studhorse Man,* however, greatly enlarges on the element of parody in the recasting of myth in modern terms. In Kroetsch's novel the Odyssean myth is not simply reduced (as when Penelope's suitor-ridden castle becomes Martha's small town boarding house), but is often completely inverted. Where Telemachus goes in search of Odysseus in order to find his missing father, and where Stephen Dedalus may be seen to be seeking a symbolic father in Leopold Bloom, Demeter is in search of Hazard partly because he wants to capture the man (in the pages of his book) and partly because he wants to kill his symbolic father and take his place.

Because of George Woodcock's famous essay, "A Nation's Odyssey",[8] the use of Homeric material in *The Studhorse Man* also calls to mind the fiction of Hugh MacLennan. Woodcock argues that the pattern of the *Odyssey* was central to MacLennan's first novel, *Barometer Rising,* and that it became "the great unifying myth of his novels". Moreover, "the *Odyssey* was the product of a people in the process of becoming aware of itself" and MacLennan therefore "appropriately used the myth to illuminate the growth of a Canadian national consciousness".[9]

Kroetsch, in his training to be a novelist, went to McGill to study with MacLennan, who at that time seemed to epitomize the successful Canadian writer. Kroetsch found, however, that his own instincts as an author pulled him in directions very different from the rather old-fashioned and realistic approach to fiction that characterized his mentor, and he left after one school year. The parody of the *Odyssey* in *The Studhorse Man* may therefore also serve Kroetsch as a conscious response to, and a consideration of his own place in, the Canadian literary tradition. Kroetsch both recognizes that he has experienced many of the same environmental and literary influences as MacLennan and shows that he is free to handle them in his own way: by recasting the *Odyssey* story he both affirms its importance to moderns and to Canadians while wittingly suggesting that it may have meanings that were previously unrecognized. In fact, Kroetsch is demonstrating his ability to outdo both these writers of the generation of the fathers by showing how much potential lay unexamined in the Odyssean materials.

Kroetsch's exploration of the Odysseus story may be said to go well beyond those of Mac-Lennan and Joyce, because there is so much knowledgeable scholarship buried in the depths of his novel. Kroetsch has based *The Studhorse Man* not merely on Homer's *Odyssey,* but on an exhaustive awareness of the whole body of mythic material relevant to Odysseus and to the supernatural world through which he moves. The giving of the name "Poseidon" to Hazard's studhorse — to take but one example — does more than simply signal Homeric parallels. It provides patterns of association with the larger mythic account of the sea god: Poseidon is the god said to have invented the bridle and to have created the horse;[10] he himself frequently took on the form of a stallion in his aggressive pursuit of a mate.[11]

The complexity of Kroetsch's mythic layering becomes still more apparent when we note that in one version of the myth of Poseidon, the god is said to have pursued Demeter, the goddess of fertility, until she wearied and transformed herself into a mare. An awareness of this incident leads us to investigate in turn the several significances of the Demeter myth in the novel: ultimately the Demeter-Persephone story — which has great importance in ancient Greek religious beliefs — turns out to provide additional mythic

context for Kroetsch's novel, and even for the whole trilogy (Persephone is the middle name of the woman Backstrom takes for a lover in *The Words of My Roaring*).

The myth of Demeter and Persphone leads us still further, to a consideration of the Eleusinian mysteries, a Greek ritual held in honour of the two goddesses, one which still remains partly shrouded in secrecy. The mysteries of Eleusis, an initiation ceremony in which Socrates is said to have participated, provided an experience which was meant to duplicate that of death and rebirth; it entailed a symbolic cleansing of the initiate (which may suggest why, in *The Studhorse Man,* Demeter narrates his entire story from a bathtub), promised the revelation of esoteric wisdom, and celebrated the birth of a sacred child — all events central to *The Studhorse Man.*

Both the Eleusinian mysteries and the larger Demeter-Persephone myths have their origin in agricultural ceremonies and respond to the seasonal pattern of the yearly cycle. Their presence thus leads us to consider the still larger context of what Sir James Frazer called in *The Golden Bough* the vegetation myth: the various stories of dying and reborn gods and kings. Frazer links this myth to the sense that is common to all primitive agriculturally-based societies: the belief that each year the world dies and is reborn (generally with the help of various sacrificial rituals and much sympathetic magic on man's part). T.S. Eliot used Frazer's account of the vegetation mythos as his mythic framework in *The Waste Land,* and Kroetsch seems to have found in it a way of giving large structural patterns to his triptych as well. Backstrom, the unifying figure of the *Out West* books, is partly analogous to Bacchus, the god whose sacrificial death and rebirth is a central example of the vegetation myth. Both Backstrom and Hazard are bringers of fertility to the land (Backstrom runs for political office on a crazy promise to bring rain to the dessicated prairies). Hazard's whole career is based on the seasonal cycle of fertility, and his life and death — which may permit the beginning of a new order with a new studhorse man (Demeter? Utter?) in charge — has several points of resemblance to that of primitive kings who ruled over tribes with agriculture rituals, kings who were sacrificed after a designated period of power to ensure fertility for the land and to allow a new ruler to begin a new cycle in the life of his people.

The story of the sacrifice of the old ruler is given additional meaning in *The Studhorse Man* because it is associated there with the myth of Oedipus, the struggle of son to overcome father. Demeter's last name, Proudfoot, is a possible English translation of Oedipus; his rivalry with Hazard is part of a pattern of sexual competition between men of two different generations that runs through much of Kroetsch's fiction.[12]

There are, moreover, still other myths which are relevant. Kroetsch has himself several times called attention to the importance of the North American Indian trickster mythology.[13] Awareness of the trickster cycles with their stories of penises that separate from the body to have their own comic adventures provides additional context for the sexual satire in the novel, and it also suggests much about the world vision of the fiction. Consideration of the trickster mythology, in turn, eventually brings us back to the *Odyssey*, since Homer's Odysseus is one of the first trickster heroes in literature.

The way in which it is possible for the reader to continue to discover so many ever-enriching meanings in *The Studhorse Man* (we are still far from exhausting its possibilities) has much to do with the novel's attractions and vitality. Kroetsch's work has come closer than that of any other modern writer to recreating an effect like that of original mythic story. *The Studhorse Man* may be seen to be what Carl Karényi calls a *mythologem* — a mythic formation out of which "a torrent of mythological pictures streams out" and from which powerful and "satisfying" meaning unfolds that cannot be recast in any other language.[14] It has been fashionable of late among some critics to talk of "intertextuality" — the effect of an awareness of one story on another. By bringing together so many stories, all working in concert to become one story, Kroetsch is involved in an extended investigation of such intertextuality. *The Studhorse Man* is a product of this investigation: it is a *tour de force* of its kind.

In the novels that come after the *Out West* trilogy — *Badlands* and *What the Crow Said* — this kind of intertextuality and mythic grounding has continued to be an important feature of Kroetsch's writing, but neither of these works seems to have utilized the same complexity of interconnected levels and juxtaposed allusion that characterizes the novels of the trilogy. Instead, *What the Crow Said* suggests that Kroetsch is now interested in exploring new directions. Responding to recent South American writers such as Gabriel Garcia Marquez, the events he chronicles are more fabulous than in any of his previous fiction. He abandons the investigation of narrative perspective and utilizes an almost ununified, loosely episodic structure which owes much more to the tall tale tradition than does any of his earlier fiction. Kroetsch himself referred to the book as his attempt to "deconstruct" the novel.

Since 1975, poetry has occupied an increasingly large part of Kroetsch's attention. *The Ledger* (1975), *Seed Catalogue* (1977), and *The Sad Phoenician* (1979) form part of an ongoing long poem, *Field Notes*, which is built up through the juxtaposition of fragments, interpolation of documents, and the uses of memory, anecdote, response and meditation to form a poetic whole that will reside in the tradition of such long poetic texts as Ezra Pound's *Cantos*, Charles Olson's *Maximus Poems*, and William Carlos Williams' *Paterson*. While it is obviously too early to speak of the whole work, some features of Kroetsch's poem in process such as the use of the physical objects of seed catalogue and family ledger — artifacts which themselves contain a kind of found poetry and to which the poet can append his own series of complex reflections — have turned out to be extremely effective.

Like the fiction, Kroetsch's poetry has sought to transform the daily objects of rural Canada into the substance of dreams. Engaged in this act of transformation, the poetry and the fiction have generated their own remarkable mythic version of history which not only stretches from creation to Apocalypse but brings the two events together, showing them to be two aspects of a single universal and ongoing moment. Kroetsch's work may present some challenges for the reader, but the energy of his vision is intense.

[1] Robert Kroetsch, *The Crow Journals* (Edmonton: NeWest Press, 1980), p. 11. Further references to this work are included in the text and identified as *CJ*.

[2] Kroetsch, "One for the Road: An Introduction", in Glen Sorestad, *Prairie Pub Poems* (Saskatoon: Thistledown Press, 1976), p. 7.

[3] Russell M. Brown, "An Interview with Robert Kroetsch", *University of Windsor Review*, VIII, 2 (1972), 8.

[4] *Ibid.*

[5] Kroetsch, *The Studhorse Man* (Toronto: Macmillan, 1969). Page references are given to the Pocket Books edition further references are identified in the text as *SM*.

[6] Kroetsch, *Badlands* (Toronto: General Publishing, 1975), p. 45.

[7] See Russell M. Brown, "Odyssean Quest", *Canadian Literature*, No. 45 (1970), pp. 88-90, and W.H. New, "The Studhorse Quests", in *Articulating West* (Toronto: new press, 1972), pp. 179-86.

[8] George Woodcock, "A Nation's Odyssey", *Canadian Literature*, No. 10 (1961), pp. 7-18; reprinted in *Odysseus Ever Returning* (Toronto: McClelland and Steward, 1970), pp. 12-23. The thesis of this article provides much of the argument of Woodcock's 1969 monograph on MacLennan.

[9] Woodcock, *Hugh MacLennan* (Toronto: Copp Clark, 1969), p. 52.

[10] Robert Graves, *The Greek Myths* (Baltimore: Penguin, 1955), Vol. I, p. 60.

[11] K. Karényi, *Zeus and Hera* (Princeton, N.J. Princeton University Press, 1975), pp. 66-68.

[12] See Brown, "Odyssean Quest", p. 88 and "An Interview", p. 18.

[13] See Brown, "An Interview", p. 6 and Donald Cameron, "The American Experience and the Canadian Voice", in *Conversations with Canadian Novelists* (Toronto: Macmillan, 1973), Vol I, 89-90. See also the "Old Man Stories" which open Kroetsch's book of poetry, *The Stone Hammer Poems* (Nanaimo, B.C.: Oolichan Books, 1975), pp. 1-21.

[14] C. Karényi, "Prologomena", in C.J. Jung and C. Karényi, *Essays on a Science of Mythology* (Princeton, N.J.: Princeton University Press, 1969), p. 3.

Chronology

ca. 1830 Kroetsch family came to the New World, settled in Bruce County, Ontario.

1926 Robert Kroetsch born, the first of five children (the others are all girls); of Paul Kroetsch who moved to Alberta from Ontario and Hilda Weller Kroetsch, a native Albertan whose parents emigrated from the American midwest; in Heisler, a small farming and coal-mining town (1926 pop.: ca. 200). Paul Kroetsch farmed around 1,000 acres, mostly with horse power.

1932-44 Attended Heisler Public School grades 1-11.

1944-45 Graduated from Red Deer High School.

1945-48 Attended University of Alberta where he completed a general B.A. majoring in English and Philosphy.

1948 Flew north to the Slave River to work as a labourer on the Fort Smith Portage.

1948-50 Worked on the Mackenzie River during the shipping season; traveled during the winters (to California and elsewhere).

1951 Worked briefly on Hudson Bay for a catering company; traveled to Montreal "seeking my fortune. Didn't find it. Instead, went broke." Returned to the North.

1951-54 Information and education specialist for the United States Air Force, Goose Bay, Labrador.

1954 Attended Bread Loaf School of English (Middlebury College), Vermont during summer.

1954-55 Attended McGill University, taking two courses, one of them with Hugh MacLennan. Began work on a novel about Mackenzie River experiences.

1955 Returned to Bread Loaf School. Met Jane Lewis. "That Yellow Prairie Sky" published in *Macleans*.

1956 Married Jane Lewis and traveled to Mexico and San Francisco. (Kroetsch has two daughters and is now divorced). Returned to Bread Loaf and completed M.A. degree (Middlebury College).

1956-61 Attended University of Iowa, was a participant in the writer's workshop there. Received Ph.D. in 1961.

1961 Began teaching in the English department at the State University of New York at Binghamton.

1962 Returned briefly to the Mackenzie for research for novel about his experiences there.

1965 First novel, *But We Are Exiles* (about a crew of a riverboat on the Mackenzie River), published.

1966 Publication of *Words of My Roaring*.

1967 Spent several months in Alberta writing a travel book and researching *The Studhorse Man*.

1968 Publication of *Alberta*. Spent several months in England writing *The Studhorse Man*.

1969 *The Studhorse Man* published, received Governor General's Award for Fiction.

1973 Publication of *Gone Indian*.

1975 Publication of *Bad Lands, The Stone Hammer Poems,* and *The Ledger.* Writer-in-residence at University of Calgary in the fall.

1976-77 Writer-in-residence at University of Lethbridge and University of Manitoba. *Seed Catalogue* published.

1977-78 Returned to SUNY Binghamton for final year of teaching there.

1978-79 Professor in English Department at University of Manitoba. *What the Crow Said* published.

1979-80 At University of Calgary.

1980- At University of Manitoba.

Comments
by Robert Kroetsch

In a sense, we haven't got any identity until somebody tells our story. The fiction makes us real.

> In a conversation with Margaret Laurence, recorded in *Creation,* ed. Robert Kroetsch (Toronto: new press, 1970), p. 63.

I'm very much involved in the significance of landscape, especially my experience of western landscape: the kind of undefined vastness of it with points of reference within that vastness — like a house, for instance, or a river. The western landscape is one without boundaries quite often. So you have the experience within a kind of chaos, yet you have to order it somehow to survive. I'm particularly interested in the kinds of ordering we do on that landscape.

> In an interview with Russell Brown, in *University of Windsor Review*, 7, No. 2 (1972), p. 2.

Living here - even as you watch the sequence of American elections, you develop a sense of irony, of *déjà vu.* They seem so desperately serious about it; yet in their 'free elections' there isn't any way to vote for anything that would make even slight alterations in the existing system. But the Americans involved manage to be innocent each time the election ritual begins. I think we've got a sense of memory that's different from theirs, and maybe again a sense of futility, I don't know. The Canadian sense of history is something that needs much exploring . . . .Perhaps I speak as a westerner. In the rhetoric of prairie politics — in the voices of Riel, Tommy Douglas, Aberhart, Diefenbaker — we go from Eden to the

Apocalypse in one easy leap. They never quite knew whether it's the end or the beginning.

> In an interview with Donald Cameron, in *Conversations with Canadian Novelists* (Toronto: Macmillan, 1973), p. 84.

I remember working on "That Yellow Prairie Sky" — and it was my first published full-length story. I had come back from Labrador. I was living in Montreal. I sat down to write about my adventures in the north, but instead I found myself writing about my memories of the west. And at that time I though I was working with the problem of language — how to record a spoken language. In a sense we speak a new language in Canada. But as I look back on the story now — remembering the remembering — I see I was wrestling with that western problem that goes back to the homesteaders: do I stay or do I leave?

> In a conversation with Margaret Laurence, recorded in *Creation*, ed. Robert Kroetsch (Toronto: new press, 1970), pp. 53-54.

I'm intrigued by the way in which the world hints of meaning. That's exactly where my imagination encounters and counters both experience and language. Where there is a *hint* of meaning. If there was a genuinely apparent meaning, then you'd simply elaborate it, I suppose. If there was no meaning, maybe you'd be able to quit. But the fiction writer has a nagging suspicion that there might, or might not, be a meaning. That's exactly where I'm at. That's why I have to go back, so compulsively, and check details . . . Not only do I go down the Red Deer River; I go outside and feel the sun on my neck — and in either case the darkness is there with a counter-proposal. I resist the traditional realistic novel because experience is always pestering me with this insinuation of meaning.

> In an interview with Geoff Hancock, in *Canadian Fiction Magazine,* Nos. 24-25 (1977), p. 44.

The world of technocracy is especially a world of noise: sophisticated noise, exciting noise, destructive noise. Consider contemporary music. But I find in the Canadian writers whom I know personally a peculiar will towards silence. Something that on the surface looks like a will towards failure.

This silence — this impulse towards the natural, the *uncreated*, if you will — is summed up by the north. The north is not a typical American frontier, a natural world to be conquered and exploited. Rather, in spite of inroads, it remains a true wilderness, a continuing presence. We don't want to conquer it. Sometimes we want it to conquer us. And we don't have to go there literally in order to draw sustenance from it, any more than the American had to go literally to the west. It presses southward into the Canadian consciousness.

The settled part of Canada becomes a borderland then, and a borderland is a place of interaction. This is, characteristically, a good place to look for poets, painters — for man as artist.

> In "The Canadian Writer and the American Literary Tradition", *English Quarterly,* IV (1971), 46.

Iconoclasm comes naturally to me. A loose generalization obviously is that creation and destruction go hand in hand. But my destruction takes the form of trying to make an old story work, for instance having to almost destroy the old story to tell the new one. Or of breaking with forms more and more, of parody, and that sort of thing.

> In an interview with Robert Enright and Denis Cooley, in *Arts Manitoba*, I, 1 (1977), 35.

At one time I considered it the task of the Canadian writer to give names to his experience, to be the namer. I now suspect that, on the contrary, it is his task to un-name. . . .

The Canadian writer's particular predicament is that he works with a language, within a literature, that appears to be authentically his own, and not a borrowing. But just as there was in the Latin word a concealed Greek experience, so there is in the Canadian word a concealed other experience, sometimes British, sometimes American. . . . In recent Canadian fiction the major writers resolve the paradox — the painful tension between appearance and authenticity — by the radical process of demythologyzing the systems that threaten to define them. Or, more comprehensively, they uninvent the world.

> In "Unhiding the Hidden: Recent Canadian Fiction", *Journal of Canadian Fiction,* III, 3 (1974), 43.

There is, in much Canadian writing, a tension between, on the one hand, the desperate need to count, to list, to catalogue — as Whitman did for America in the 19th century — and, on the other hand, the terrible modern suspicion that the counting is being done in a slightly mad dream —

> In "The Canadian Writer and the American Literary Tradition", p. 49.

. . . there's a notion of game theory and of picture theory in language. Game theory is the conception of language as a serious game, picture theory of language as identical with reality. Now I think at various times in literature, we've emphasized one or the other. The whole realistic movement was based on the notion of language as picture. In our own time there's been this tremendous move to language as game — in John Barth for example. Typically I would suggest that the fascinating place is that place right between the two. Again that's a kind of Canadian notion. There's the borderland again.

In Russell Brown, p. 16.

The basic grammatical pair in the story-line (the energy-line) of prairie fiction is house: horse. To be *on* a horse is to move: motion into distance. To be *in* a house is to be fixed: a centring unto stasis. Horse is masculine. House is feminine. Horse: house. Masculine: feminine. On: in. Motion: stasis. A woman ain't supposed to move. Pleasure: duty. The most obvious resolution of the dialectic, however temporary, is in the horse-house. Not the barn (though a version of resolution does take place there), but whores'-house. Western movies use that resolution. Sheila Watson treats of that resolution in *The Double Hook*. [Willa Cather's] Antonia Shimerda is un-housed, almost into whoredom. [Sinclair Ross's] Philip Bentley is unhorsed into housedom.

In "Fear of Women in Prairie Fiction: Erotics of Space", *Canadian Forum*, October-November 1978, p. 22.

Comments on Robert Kroetsch

In Kroetsch's vision of reality confronted by itself, the possessed and the possessor, the pursued and the pursuer, ultimately are one. It is the disturbing vision of an existential romance in which, through the violence of sexuality and death the past is redeemed — and discovered to be a void.

John Moss, in "Canadian Frontiers: Sexuality and Violence from Richardson to Kroetsch", *Journal of Canadian Fiction*, II, 3 (1973), 38.

The sense of a fragmentary, chaotic universe which has pervaded so much of Canadian writing since 1960 receives nowhere more powerful expression than in the novels of Robert Kroetsch. All aspects of these novels imply an immensely vital and unmappable world. Their narrative structures take unpredictable shifts and turns, and invariably terminate in ambiguity. Their language exuberantly interbreeds the bawdy, the literary, the poetic, and the colloquial. Their settings — northern Alberta and the Northwest Territories — appear as mythologic, Protean regions, regions where every journey a man takes is a voyage of discovery into both his unknown self and his unknowable environment.

Frank Davey, in *From There to Here* (Erin, Ont.: Press Porcépic, 1974), p. 155.

Kroetsch, who co-edits *Boundary 2*, subtitled "A Journal of Postmodern Literature", has often commented on his practice in writing, and one sees that a particular approach to his work necessarily involves its techniques as an adjunct to its themes. The epigraph to *Gone Indian*, from Frederick Jackson Turner — "For a moment, at the frontier, the bonds of custom are broken and unrestraint is triumphant" — is appropriate as theme and stylistic metaphor.

Louis K. MacKendrick, in "Robert Kroetsch and the Modern Canadian Novel of Exhaustion", *Essays on Canadian Writing*, No. 11 (1978), p. 17.

Kroetsch's revolt against the techniques of the prairie realists is part of a larger effort to jar the language out of familiar contexts which reinforce that hidden, other experience. His irony, often so comprehensive as to leave readers feeling lost, bewildered, hostile, is a deliberate attempt to unsettle all settled expectations about the experience he is recreating.

Dick Harrison, in *Unnamed Country: The Struggle for a Canadian Prairie Fiction* (Edmonton: University of Alberta Press, 1977), p. 209.

Kroetsch discovers a symbolic richness in an empty vastness which has so often defied the imagination. But further, Kroetsch articulates new comprehension of the prairie landscape, both embracing the destructive nullity of his environment and defying it by a comic ebullience which celebrates man and life. 'How do we fit our time and our place?' is the question Kroetsch poses to himself. His fiction has the conviction of the 'simple necessity' which he recognizes will dictate his answer.

Laurie Ricou, in *Vertical Man/Horizontal World: Man and Landscape in Prairie Fiction* (Vancouver: University of British Columbia Press, 1973), p. 136.

What parody means, of course, is the conscious imitation of a form or idea so as to make the 'original' appear ridiculous: a comic yoking of two versions of the same thing, a high (serious) and a low (ridiculous). Linking of pairs is perhaps the most recurrent and noticeable element in all of Kroetsch's work, from the Narcissus myth — man and his mirror image — in *But We Are Exiles*, through the many linked pairs that the increasingly picaresque mode of his succeeding novels calls for, the man-woman pairs and antithesis of all his books, to the antiphonal structure of his poem, *The Ledger*.

Ann Mandel, in "Uninventing Structures: Cultural Criticism and the Novels of Robert Kroetsch", *Open Letter*, Third Series, No. 8 (1978), pp. 59-60.

In *The Ledger* and *Seed Catalogue* the most important milieu is voice. Kroetsch wants us to hear the language of a place. This means replacing (putting back, finding) sounds which have been lost; it means the creation of an atmosphere in which words and stories are reinstated to the original significance. But how can this be done?

By repeatedly calling up phrases or fragments of speech in different contexts, Kroetsch allows the text to resonate itself into a union of echoes.

Robert Lecker, "Robert Kroetsch's Poetry", *Open Letter*, Third Series, No. 8 (1978), pp. 81-81.

Selected Bibliography
Works by Robert Kroetsch

But We Are Exiles. Toronto: Macmillan of Canada, 1965.
The Words of My Roaring. Toronto: Macmillan of Canada, 1966.
Alberta. Toronto: Macmillan of Canada, 1968.
The Studhorse Man. Toronto: Macmillan of Canada, 1969.
Gone Indian. Toronto: new press, 1973.
Badlands. Toronto: new press, 1975.
The Stone Hammer Poems. Nanaimo, B.C.: Oolichan Books, 1975.
The Ledger. London, Ont.: Applegarth Follies, 1975.
Seed Catalogue. Manitoba: Turnstone Press, 1977.
What the Crow Said. Don Mills: General Publishing. 1978.
The Sad Phoenician. Toronto: Coach House Press, 1979.
The Crow Journals. Edmonton: NeWest Press, 1980.

Works Edited by Kroetsch

Boundary 2: A Journal of Post-Modern Literature. (Kroetsch was one of the two founding editors of the journal published at S U N Y Binghamton: he is now fiction editor.)
Creation. Toronto: new press, 1970.

Articles by Kroestch: a selected list

"The Canadian Writer and the American Literary Tradition", *English Quarterly*, IV (1971), 45-49.
"Unhiding the Hidden: Recent Canadian Fiction", *Journal of Canadian Fiction*, III, 3 (1974), 43-45.
"Voice/in prose: effing the ineffable", *freeLance*, VII, 2 (1976), 35-36.
"Fear of Women in Prairie Fiction: Erotics of Space", *Canadian Forum*, October-November 1978, pp. 22-27.
"Contemporary Standards in the Canadian Novel", *Essays on Canadian Writing*, No. 20 (1981).

Interviews with Kroetsch

"A Conversation with Margaret Laurence", in *Creation*, ed. Robert Kroetsch. Toronto: new press, 1970.
Brown, Russell M. "An Interview with Robert Kroetsch", *University of Windsor Review*, VIII, 2 (1972), 1-18.
Cameron, Donald. "Robert Kroetsch: The American Experience and the Canadian Voice", in *Conversations with Canadian Novelists*, Vol. I. Toronto: Macmillan, 1973, 81-95.
Enright, Robert and Dennis Cooley. "Uncovering Our Dream World: An Interview with Robert Kroetsch", *Arts Manitoba*, I (1977), 32-39. Reprinted in *Essays in Canadian Writing*, No. 18/19 (1980), pp. 21-32.

Hancock, Geoff. "An Interview with Robert Kroetsch", *Canadian Fiction Magazine*, No. 24/25 (1977), pp. 33-52.

Selected Criticism

Bessai, Diane. Review of *Gone Indian, Lakehead University Review*, VII (1974), 156-159.
Brown, Russell M. Review of *Gone Indian, Canadian Literature*, No. 61 (1974), pp. 103-104.
_____. Review of *The Studhorse Man, Canadian Literature*, No. 45 (1970), pp. 88-90.
Davidson, Arnold E. "History, Myth, and Time in Robert Kroetsch's *Badlands*", *Studies in Canadian Literature*, V (1980), 127-137.
Harrison, Dick. *Unnamed Country.* Edmonton: University of Alberta Press, 1977, pp. 182-189, pp. 205-212 *et passim*.
Harvey, Connie, "Tear-Glazed Vision of Laughter", *Essays on Canadian Writing*, No. 11 (1978), pp. 28-54.
Lecker, Robert. "Robert Kroetsch's Poetry", *Open Letter*, 3rd Series, No. 8 (1978), pp. 72-88.
MacKendrick, Louis K. "Robert Kroetsch and the Modern Canadian Novel of Exhaustion", *Essays on Canadian Writing*, No. 11 (1978), pp. 10-27.
Mandel, Ann. "On Kroetsch's Uninventing Structures: Cultural Criticism and the Novels of Robert Kroetsch", *Open Letter*, 3rd Series, No. 8 (1978), pp. 52-71.
Mandel, Eli. Review of *Creation, University of Toronto Quarterly*, XL (1971), 316-318.
_____. "Romance and Realism in Western Canadian Fiction", in *Prairie Perspectives 2*, ed. Anthony W. Rasporich and Henry C. Klassen. Toronto: Holt, Rinehart and Winston, 1973, pp. 197-211. [Reprinted in *Another Time.* Toronto. Press Porcépic, 1977.]
Melnyk, George. "Kroetsch: Leaving a Comfortable Exile", *Quill & Quire*, XLII (1976), 19-20.
New, W.H. "The Studhorse Quests", in *Articulating West.* Toronto: new press, 1972, pp. 179-86.
Nicolaisen, W.F.H. "Ordering the Chaos: Name Strategies in Robert Kroetsch's Novels", *Essays on Canadian Writing*, No. 11 (1978), pp. 55-65.
Ross, Morton L. "Robert Kroetsch and His Novels", in *Writers of the Prairies*, ed. Donald G. Stephens. Vancouver: University of British Columbia Press, 1973, pp. 101-114.
Smith, R. Fenwick. Review of *Gone Indian, Malahat Review*, No. 29 (1974), pp. 133-136.
Sullivan, Rosemary. "The Fascinating Place Between: The Fiction of Robert Kroetsch", *Mosaic*, XI, 3 (1978), 165-176.
Thomas, [D.] Peter. "Keeping Mum: Kroetsch's *Alberta*", *Journal of Canadian Fiction*, II, 2 (1973), 54-56.
_____. "Priapus in the Danse Macabre: The Novels of Robert Kroetsch", *Canadian Literature*, No. 61 (1974), pp. 54-64. [Reprinted in *The Canadian Novel in the Twentieth Century*, ed. George Woodcock. Toronto: McClelland and Stewart, 1975.]
Thomas, D.P. [eter]. "Robert Kroetsch and Silence", *Essays on Canadian Writing*, No. 17/18 (1980), pp. 33-53.
_____. "Robert Kroetsch, Rupert Brooke, The Voices of the Dead", *Studies in Canadian Literature*, I (1976), 124-129.

Bibliographies dealing with Kroetsch:

Lecker, Robert. "An Annotated Bibliography of Works by and about Robert Kroetsch", *Essays on Canadian Writing*. No. 7/8 (1977), pp. 74-96.

A Note on the Contributor

Russell Brown is an Associate Professor at Scarborough College (University of Toronto) where he teaches courses in Canadian fiction and creative writing. He has written on Canadian authors for *Essays on Canadian Writing, Modern Fiction Studies, Canadian Literature, Journal of Commonwealth Literature, Mosaic,* and other journals. He is presently editing a new anthology of Canadian literature for Oxford University Press and is the co-author of *Kicking Loose,* a book on the trickster figure in Canadian fiction to be published by ECW Press.

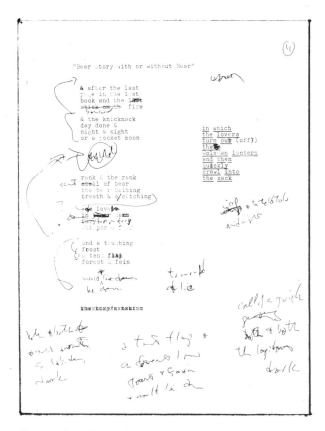

Original and final draft of "Bear Story with or without Bear".